AF395511

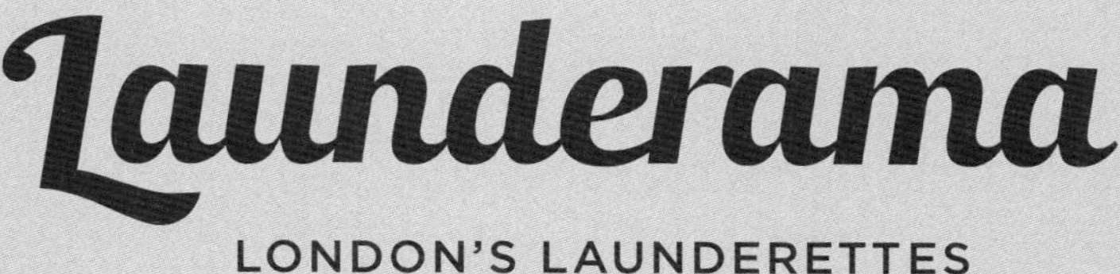
Launderama
LONDON'S LAUNDERETTES

JOSHUA BLACKBURN

Launderama

LONDON'S LAUNDERETTES

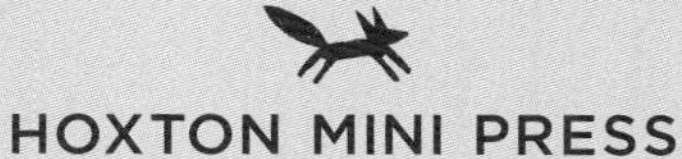

HOXTON MINI PRESS

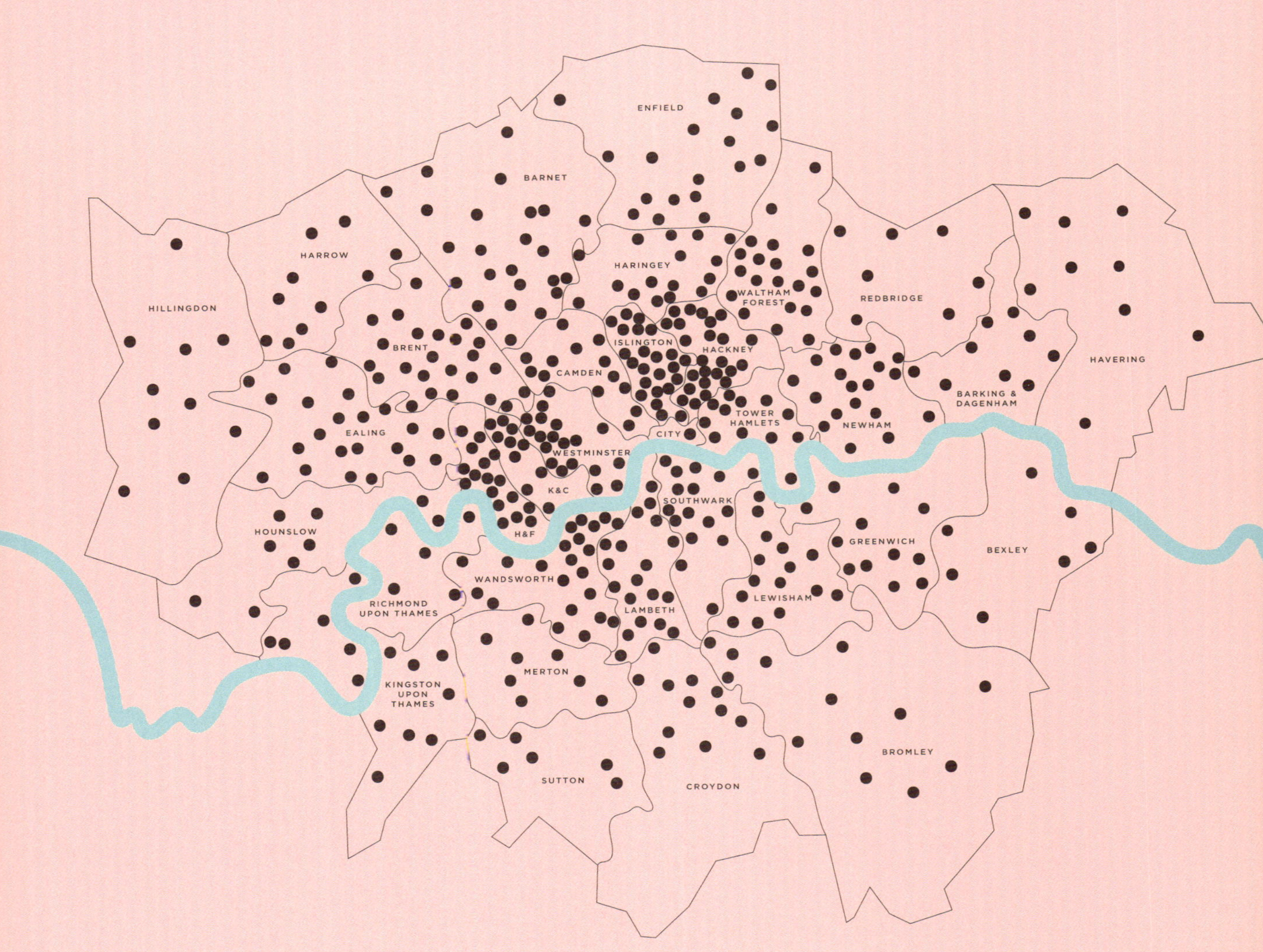

HILLINGDON
HARROW
ENFIELD
BARNET
HARINGEY
WALTHAM
FOREST
REDBRIDGE
HAVERING
BRENT
ISLINGTON
HACKNEY
CAMDEN
TOWER
HAMLETS
NEWHAM
BARKING &
DAGENHAM
EALING
CITY
WESTMINSTER
K&C
SOUTHWARK
GREENWICH
BEXLEY
HOUNSLOW
H&F
WANDSWORTH
LEWISHAM
RICHMOND
UPON THAMES
LAMBETH
MERTON
KINGSTON
UPON
THAMES
BROMLEY
SUTTON
CROYDON

Introduction

What is it about launderettes? I've been asked this question a lot over the last two years. Launderette owners in particular were baffled by why I wanted to photograph their place of work. 'Really?' they would ask, 'But why?' My problem was not that I didn't have a reason but that I had too many.

I started photographing launderettes in December 2017. My first was Central Wash on Queensway in west London – coincidentally, the first coin-operated launderette in the UK, opened in 1949. I was drawn like a moth to the flood of neon spilling onto the street at night and stood in the road taking pictures. It wasn't long before I began disappearing at strange times to visit local laundromats. The sign outside Posh Wash 2 on Fernhead Road was irresistible; the bank of machines at the launderette on Kilburn High Road delightfully symmetrical; and the shrine to soap powders at the Queen's Park Launderette spoke to me. But I kept it to myself. I loved launderettes, but suspected it was an obsession peculiar to me.

Soon, however, I started travelling further afield. My son played football in Wembley every Sunday. I'd drop him, then visit an ever-expanding list of nearby launderettes. It wasn't just their compelling geometry or marble-effect wall covering I admired, I loved everything about them. The smell of clean clothes tumbling in dryers; the sound of washers rinsing and spinning; the bright pastel colours particular to launderettes... it was a surfeit of sensation, reassuring and familiar.

At a purely aesthetic level, these launderettes were endlessly seductive. Those American machines from the 60s and 70s are like catnip to photographers, with their colourful enamel and analogue industrial design. A Speed Queen dryer could make my day, while the Nordwash machines in Colliers Wood, all burgundy and brushed steel, made me skip.

But this fascination with launderettes was about more than retro fetishism. My plan – because I had one now – was to visit every launderette in the Greater London Postcode District. To this end, I had a map, a spreadsheet and 462 names. When time allowed, I'd get in the car and visit launderettes. From Pinner to Penge, Catford to the Isle of Dogs, I was becoming an explorer in my own city.

What started as a portrait of London's launderettes was becoming a portrait of London itself, with each launderette bearing the imprint of the community it served and the customers who visited it. 'Launderettes are like station waiting rooms', I was told by the owner of a launderette in Wimbledon. Another said theirs was more of a self-help group. More than one launderette had photos of customers who had passed away, missed by those left behind. Some launderettes were empty, others alive with cackling laughter. Those were my favourites.

Over 300 languages are spoken in London. It's what makes the city so remarkable. And launderette owners are a microcosm of this beautiful, rich diversity. I spoke to owners from Guyana, Turkey, Iran, Poland, South Korea, Zambia, Greece and more. I'd ask them all how business was. Some were thriving, many were not. Running a launderette is hard, never-ending work. Open all hours, forever cleaning machines, doing service washes and dealing with broken dryers. More than once I was asked whether I'd like to buy the business.

Some days, my mood became a reflection of the launderettes I'd visited. The warmth of Wow Launderette in Croydon, where the manager was having her hair cut in the back room, brightened me up. The owner of Clean Zone in Colney Hatch radiated positive energy, chatting as she balled up socks. But I also saw the frustration and exhaustion of others who were watching their businesses barely survive. I really wanted their businesses to do well. They deserved to. But the outlook for many is uncertain.

The story of London's launderettes is a story of a changing urban landscape. In the last 30 years, over three quarters of the city's launderettes have closed. Gentrification, rising rents and changing household habits have all played their part. I was seeing this change happening in real time as

I travelled the city. I'd see launderettes boarded up or find ones already converted into a coffee shop or artisan baker. Launderettes I'd visited at the start of my project had closed down 18 months later.

The steady decline of this high-street fixture is especially sad given the unique relationship launderettes have with the local community. They are a space where people come together, noisier than libraries and more inclusive than pubs. For some customers, launderettes might be the only social contact they have all week. That said, I avoid getting overly romantic about launderettes. Many people are happy to dump their clothes or wait for their wash in silence. And many I visited were echoingly empty. But visit the launderettes on Yeading Lane, Bethnal Green Road or Beulah Road, to name but a few, and one finds the community launderette cheerfully alive.

Yet while launderettes struggle in the real world, one place they're flourishing is in our cultural imagination. In the imaginary world conjured by fashion and advertising, launderettes are almost revered. Anyone over 30 will remember the iconic Levi's commercial from 1985, but in the last few years brands like Prada, Hermès and Boohoo have all run campaigns featuring launderettes, turning their awkward charm into something potently nostalgic.

As a photographer, I'll admit to having been enchanted by this sense of nostalgia too. In an increasingly homogenous world – fast, convenient and digital – the launderette is resolutely analogue, both in spirit and practice. It is out of time and out of place – literally and emotionally – simultaneously creating the reason for their appeal and the cause of their decline. But nostalgia possesses an inherent tension. As I saw time and again, the appeal of a launderette's physical space often contrasted with its emptiness. They have become a living remains of a London that's passing.

My problem with nostalgia is that it has no future, and I dearly hope that launderettes do. London needs them.

So what is it about launderettes? Where do I begin?

Joshua Blackburn
London, 2019

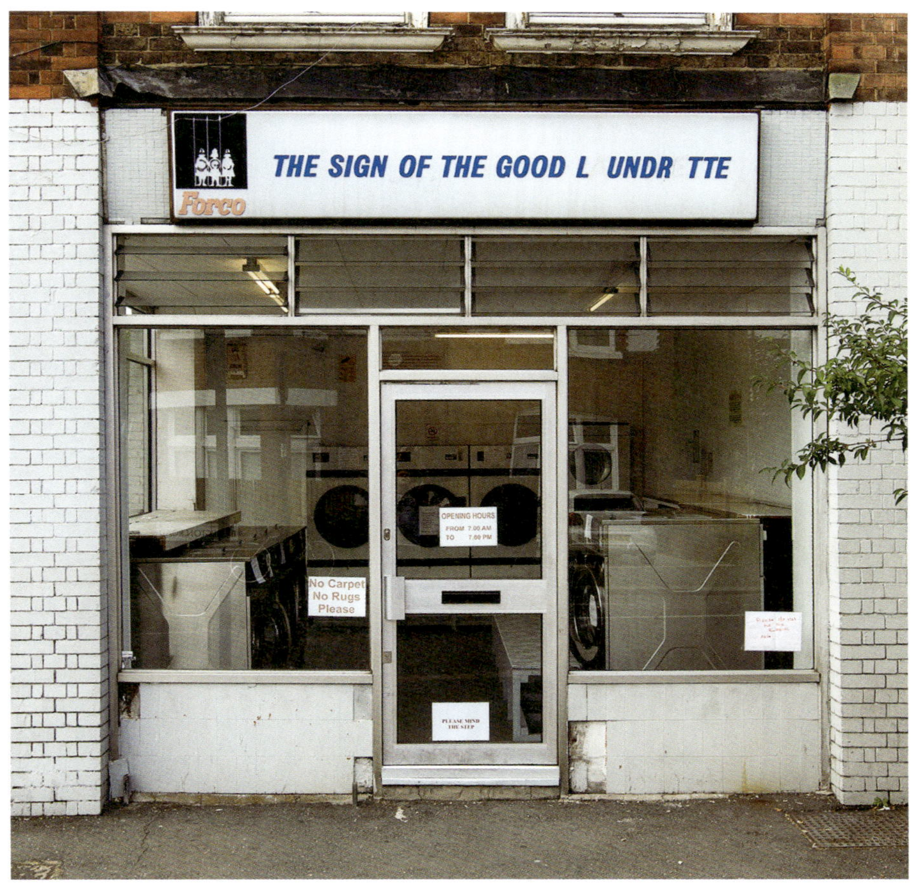
Forco
THE SIGN OF THE GOOD L UNDR TTE
No Carpet
No Rugs
Please
OPENING HOURS
FROM 7.00 AM
TO 7.00 PM
PLEASE MIND
THE STEP

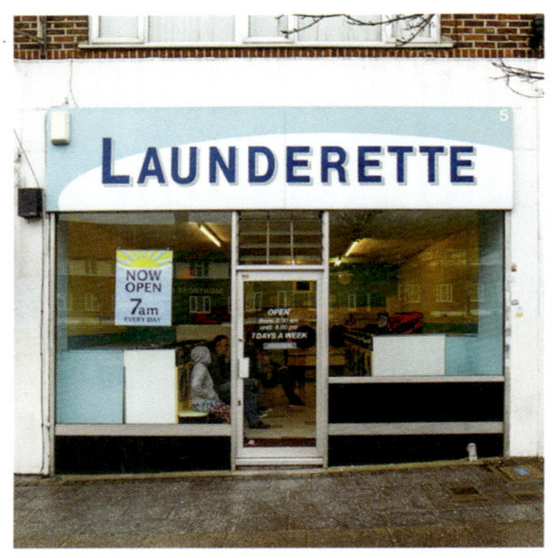
LAUNDERETTE
NOW OPEN
7am EVERY DAY
OPEN
7 DAYS A WEEK

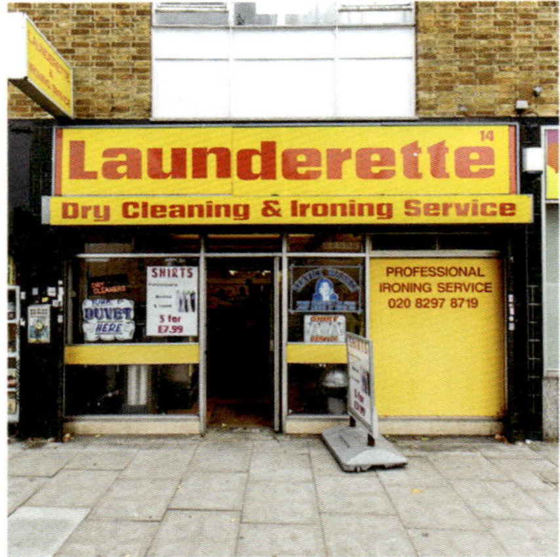
Launderette
Dry Cleaning & Ironing Service
SHIRTS
PROFESSIONAL
IRONING SERVICE
020 8297 8719

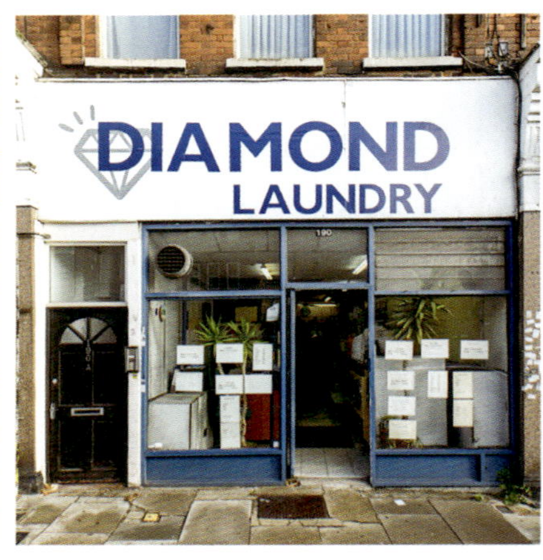
DIAMOND
LAUNDRY

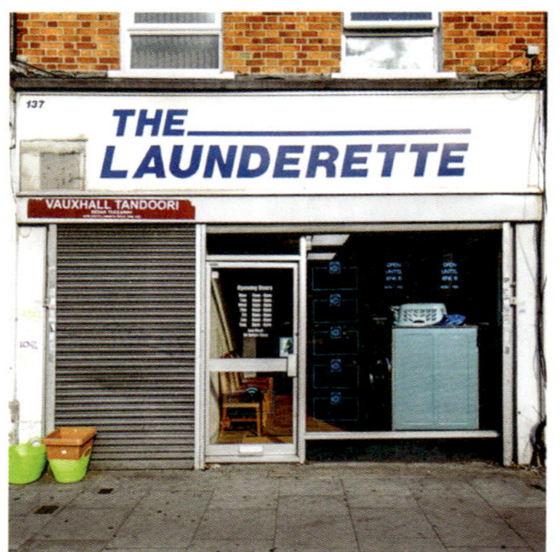
THE
LAUNDERETTE
VAUXHALL TANDOORI

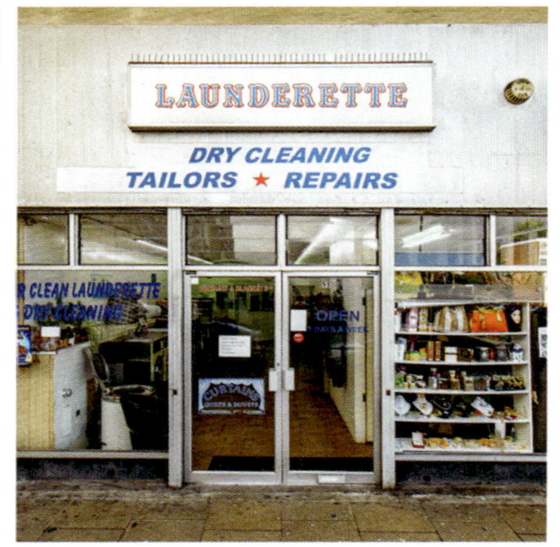
LAUNDERETTE
DRY CLEANING
TAILORS ★ REPAIRS
OPEN

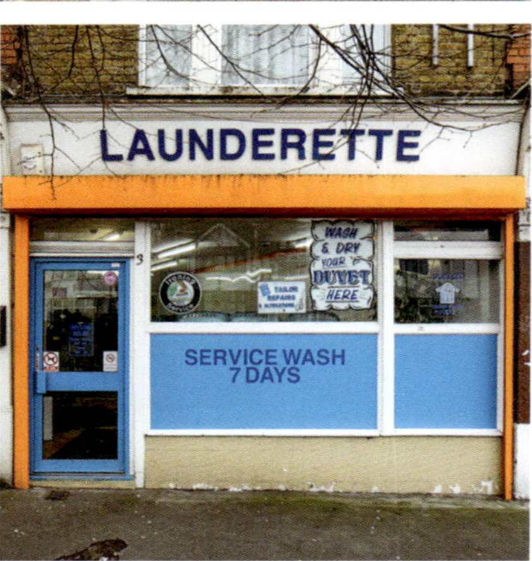
LAUNDERETTE
WASH & DRY YOUR DUVET HERE
SERVICE WASH
7 DAYS

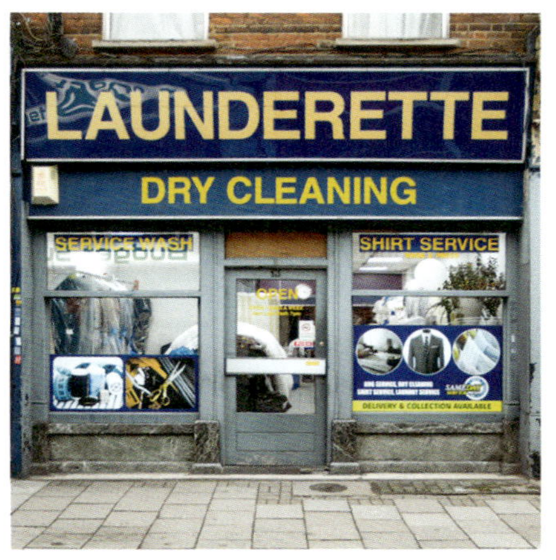

LAUNDERETTE
DRY CLEANING
SERVICE WASH
SHIRT SERVICE
OPEN
DELIVERY & COLLECTION AVAILABLE

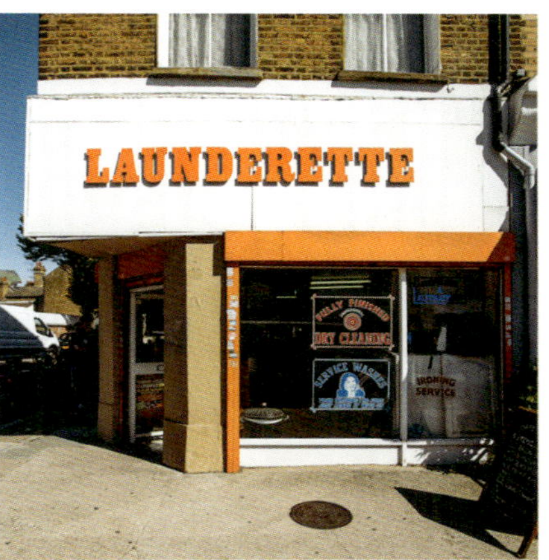

LAUNDERETTE
DRY CLEANING
SERVICE WASHES
IRONING SERVICE

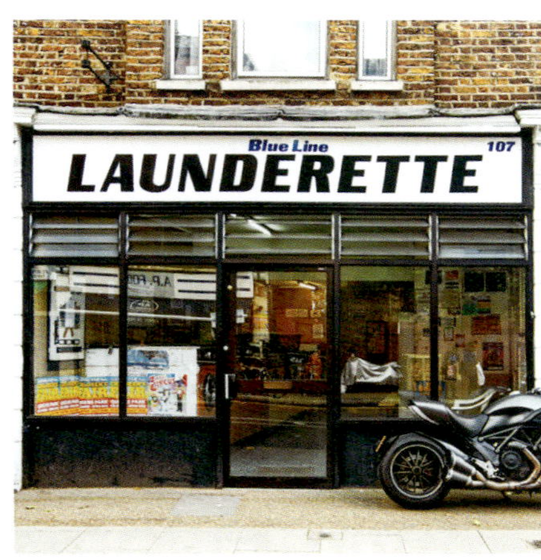

Blue Line
LAUNDERETTE
107

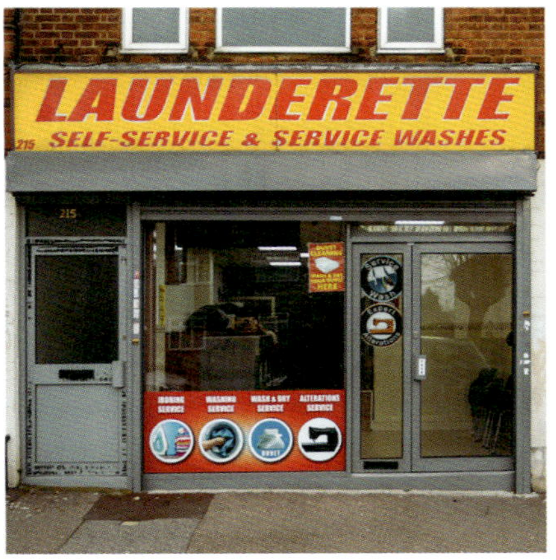

LAUNDERETTE
SELF-SERVICE & SERVICE WASHES
215
IRONING SERVICE
WASHING SERVICE
WASH & DRY SERVICE
ALTERATIONS SERVICE

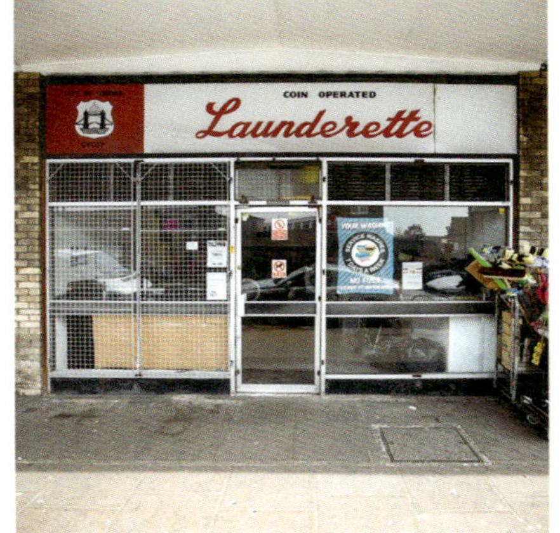

COIN OPERATED
Launderette

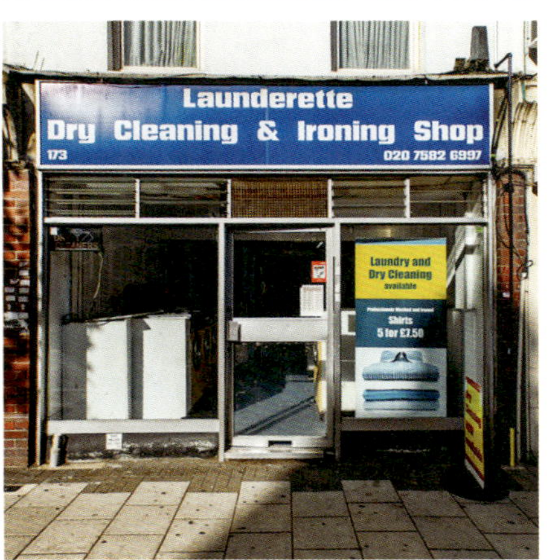

Launderette
Dry Cleaning & Ironing Shop
173
020 7582 6997
Laundry and Dry Cleaning available
Shirts 5 for £7.50

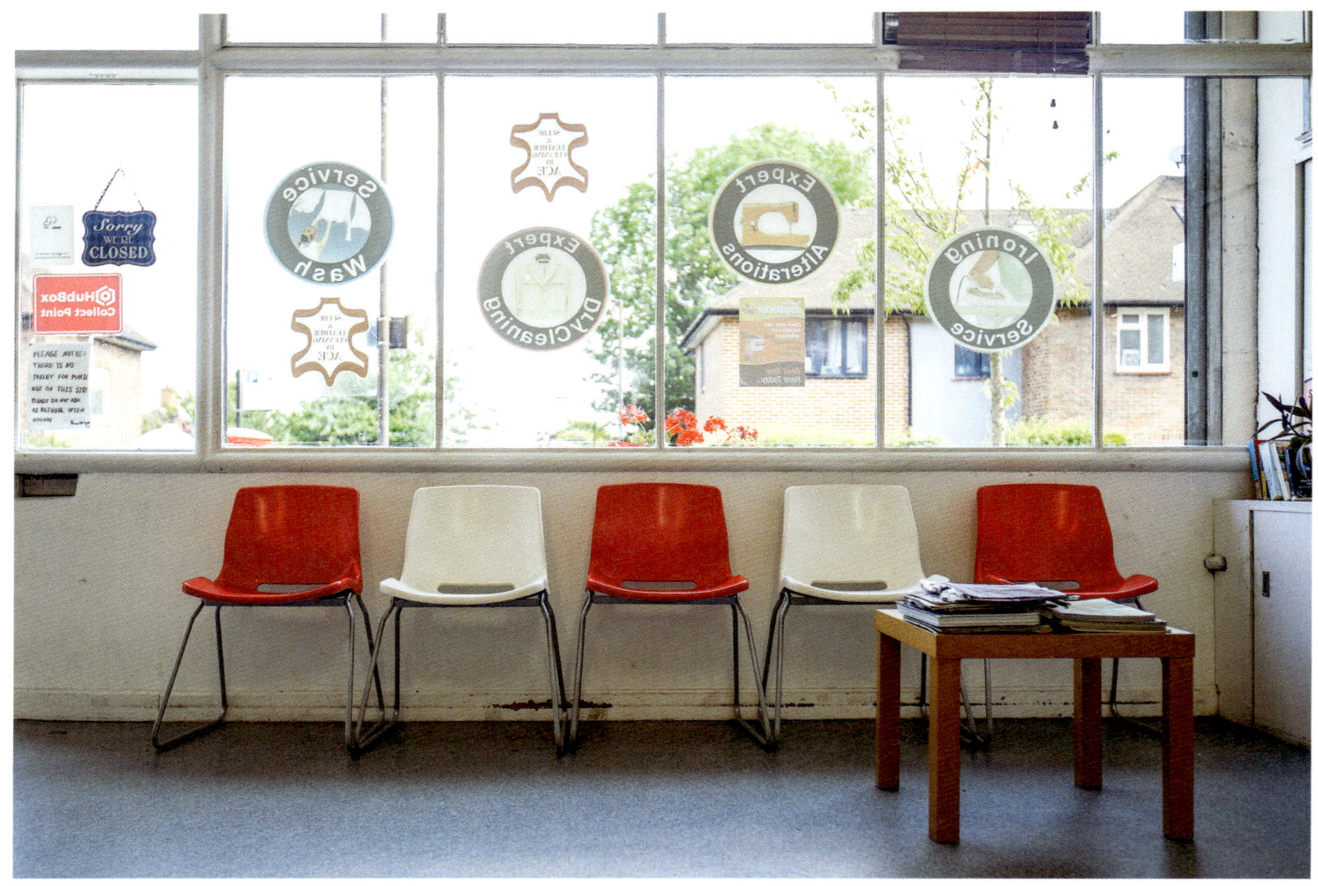
Sorry WE'RE CLOSED
HubBox Collect Point
Service Wash
Expert Dry Cleaning
Expert Alterations
Ironing Service

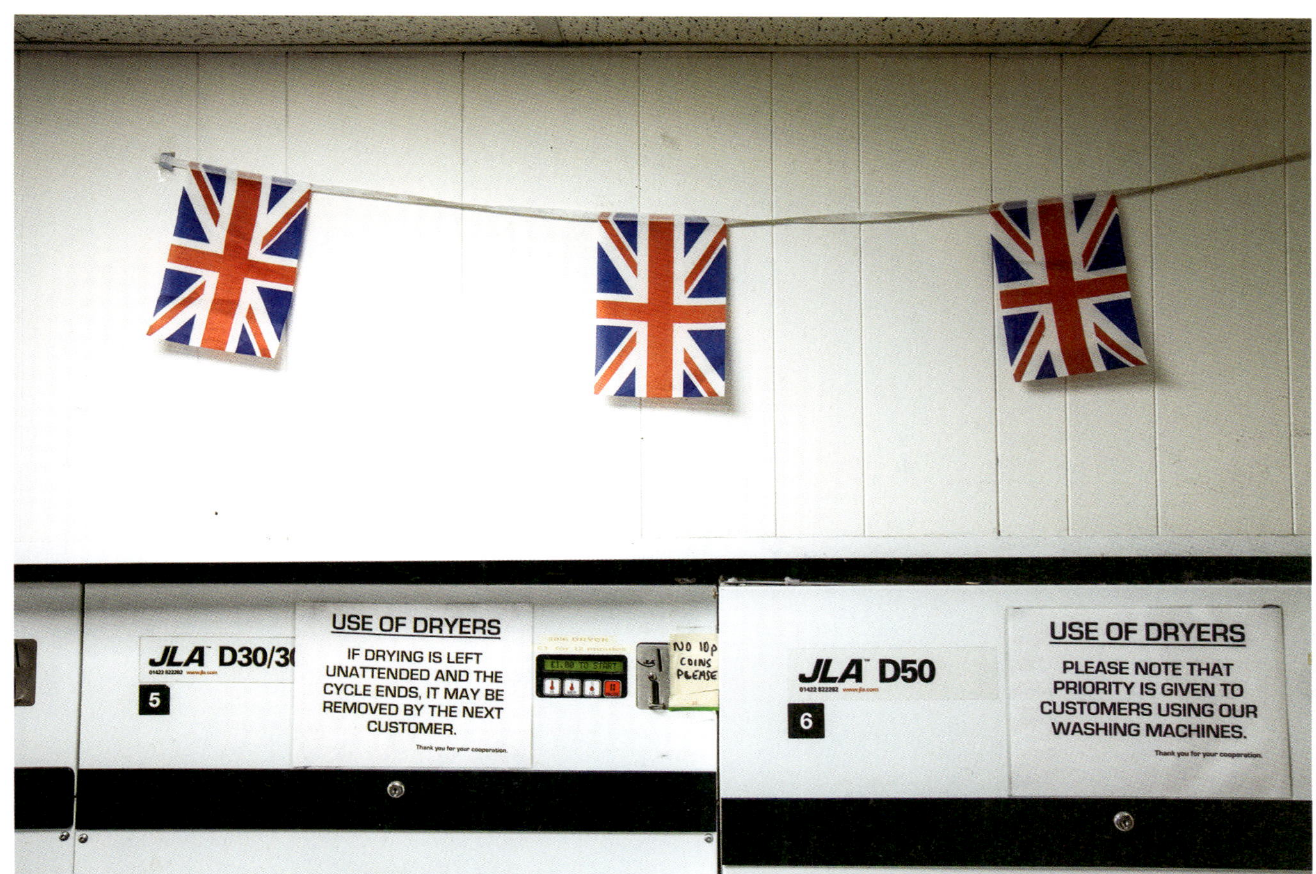
JLA D30/30
5
USE OF DRYERS
IF DRYING IS LEFT UNATTENDED AND THE CYCLE ENDS, IT MAY BE REMOVED BY THE NEXT CUSTOMER.
Thank you for your cooperation.
£1.00 TO START
NO 10p COINS PLEASE
JLA D50
6
USE OF DRYERS
PLEASE NOTE THAT PRIORITY IS GIVEN TO CUSTOMERS USING OUR WASHING MACHINES.
Thank you for your cooperation.

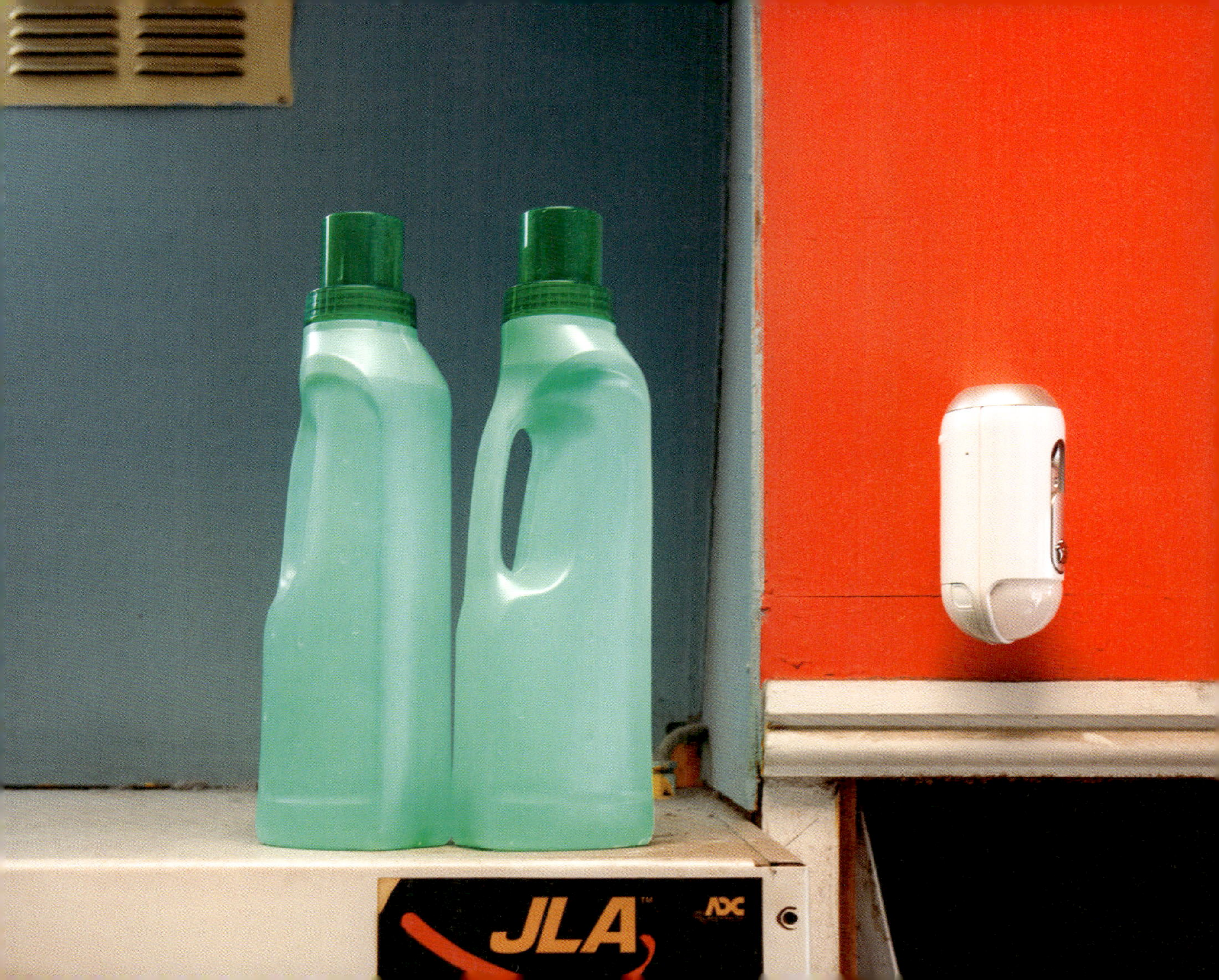

JLA
AJC

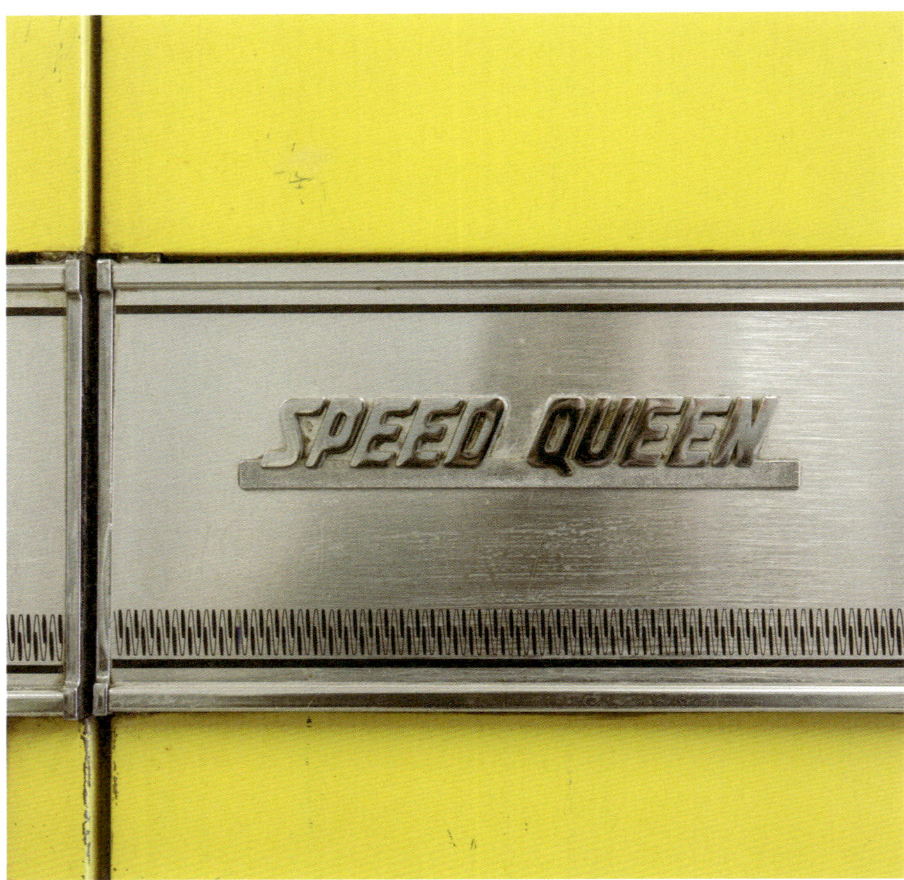
SPEED QUEEN

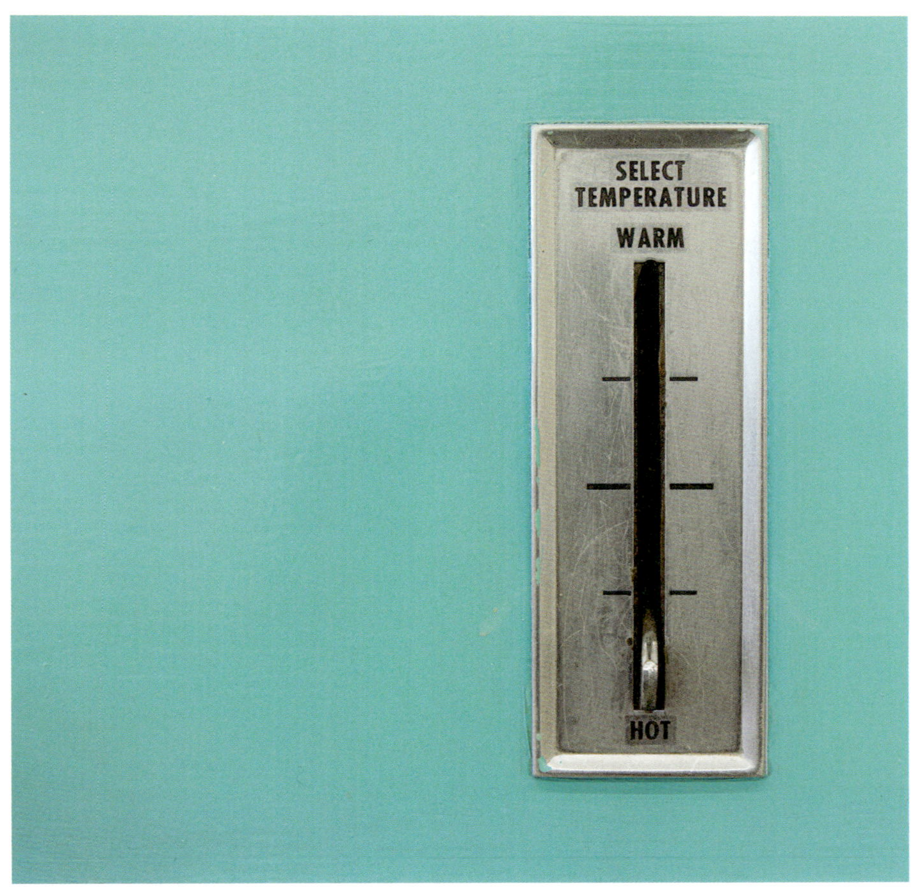

SELECT
TEMPERATURE
WARM
HOT

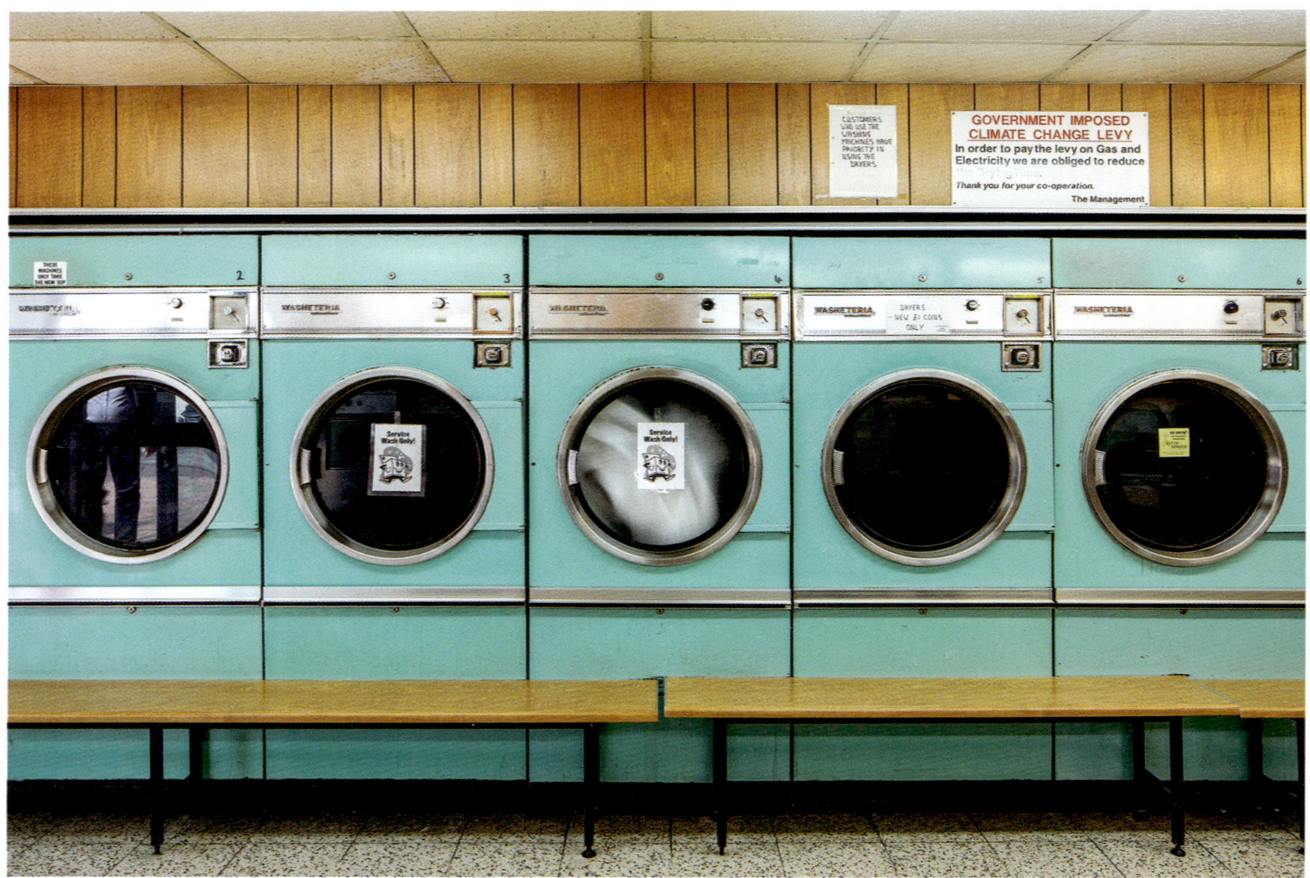

CUSTOMERS WHO USE THE WASHING MACHINES HAVE PRIORITY IN USING THE DRYERS
GOVERNMENT IMPOSED CLIMATE CHANGE LEVY
In order to pay the levy on Gas and Electricity we are obliged to reduce the Drying Time.
Thank you for your co-operation.
The Management
THESE MACHINES ONLY TAKE THE NEW 50P
WASHETERIA
DRYERS — NEW £1 COINS ONLY
Service Wash Only!
2
3
4
5
6

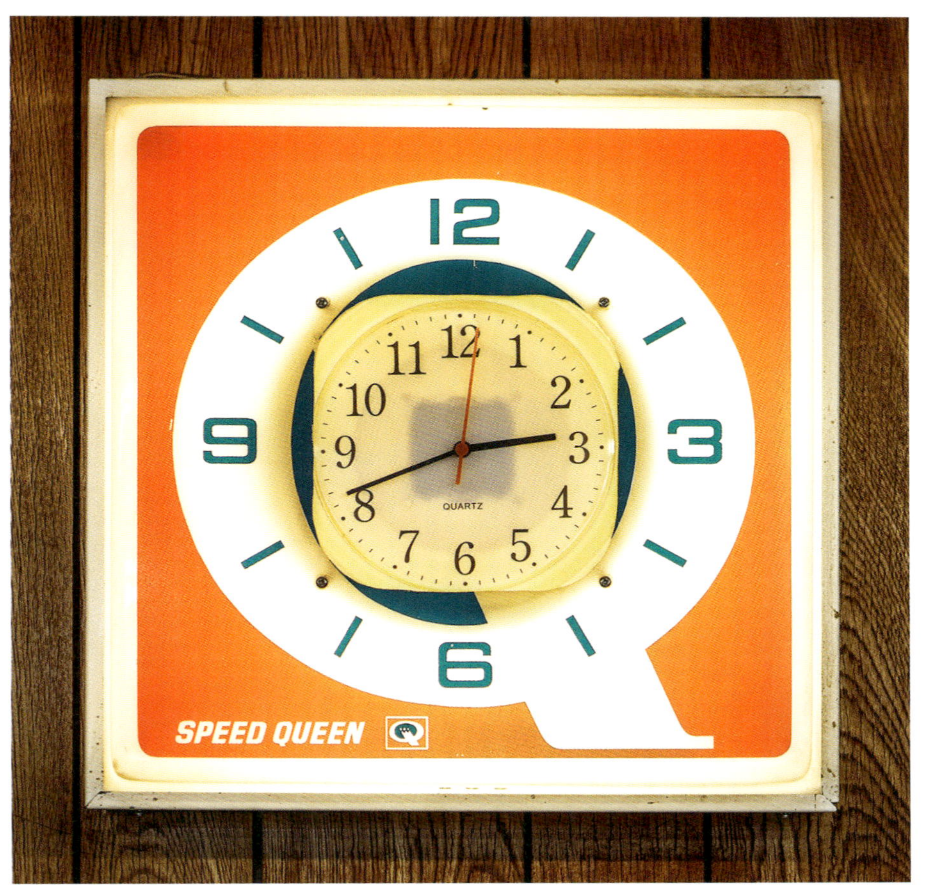
12
11 12 1
10 2
9 3
8 4
7 6 5
QUARTZ
9
3
6
SPEED QUEEN

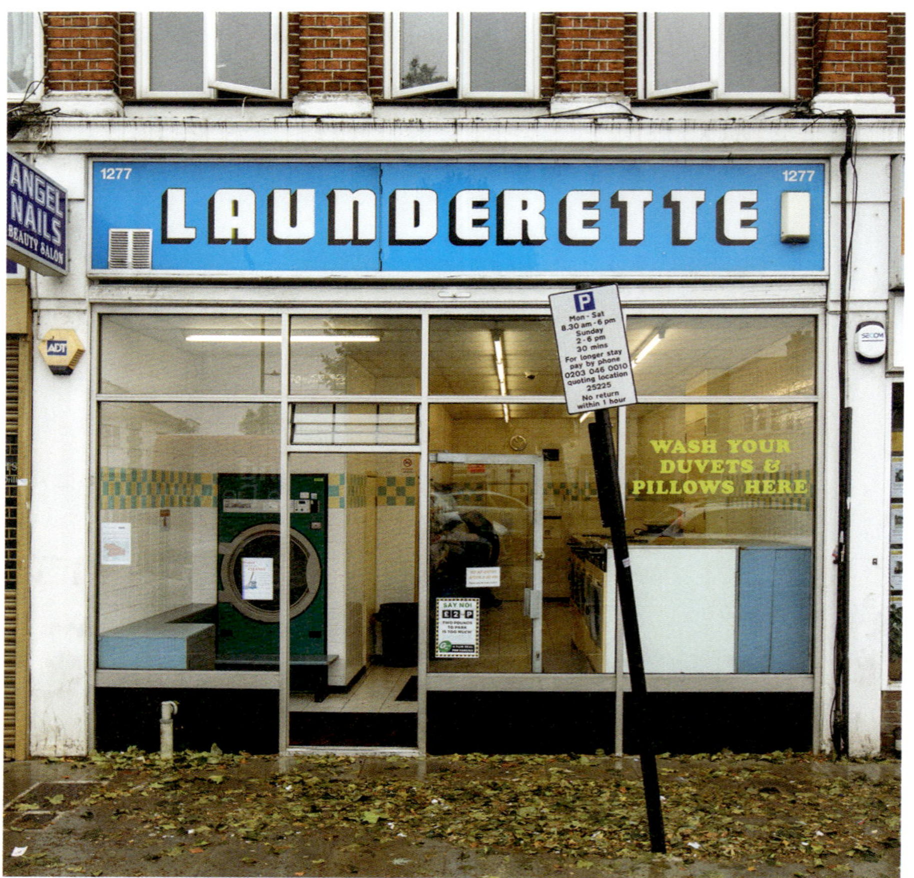

ANGEL NAILS
BEAUTY SALON
1277
LAUNDERETTE
1277
P
Mon - Sat
8.30 am - 6 pm
Sunday
2 - 6 pm
30 mins
For longer stay
pay by phone
0203 046 0010
quoting location
25225
No return
within 1 hour
WASH YOUR
DUVETS &
PILLOWS HERE

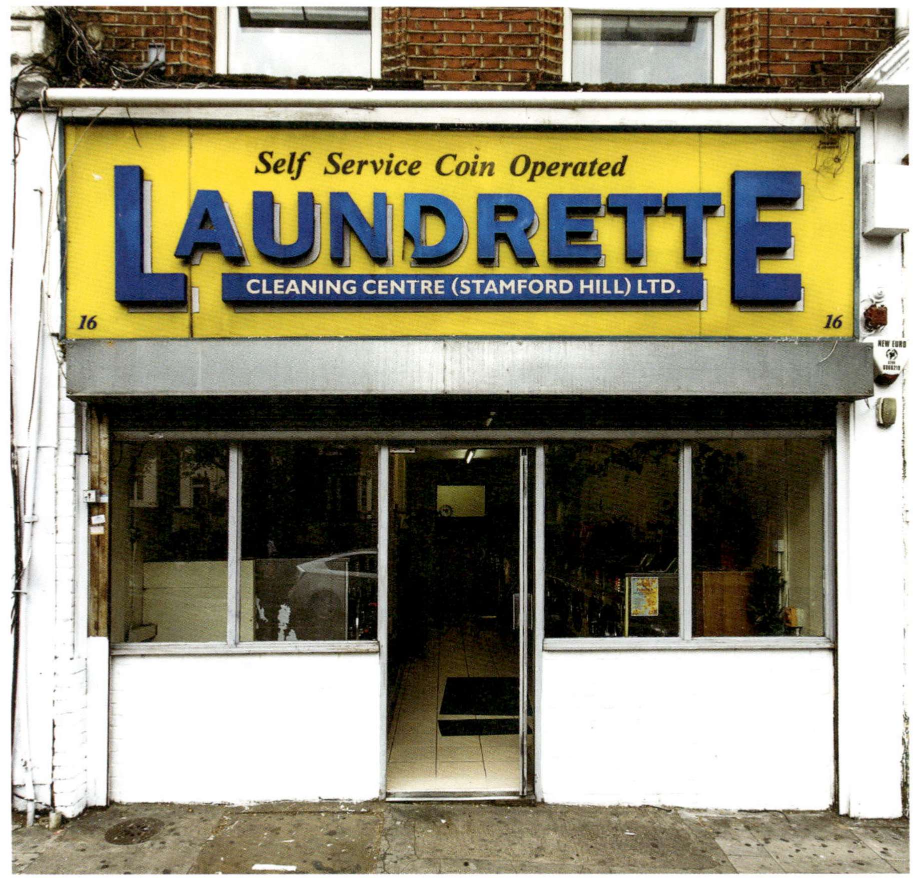

Self Service Coin Operated
LAUNDRETTE
CLEANING CENTRE (STAMFORD HILL) LTD.
16
16

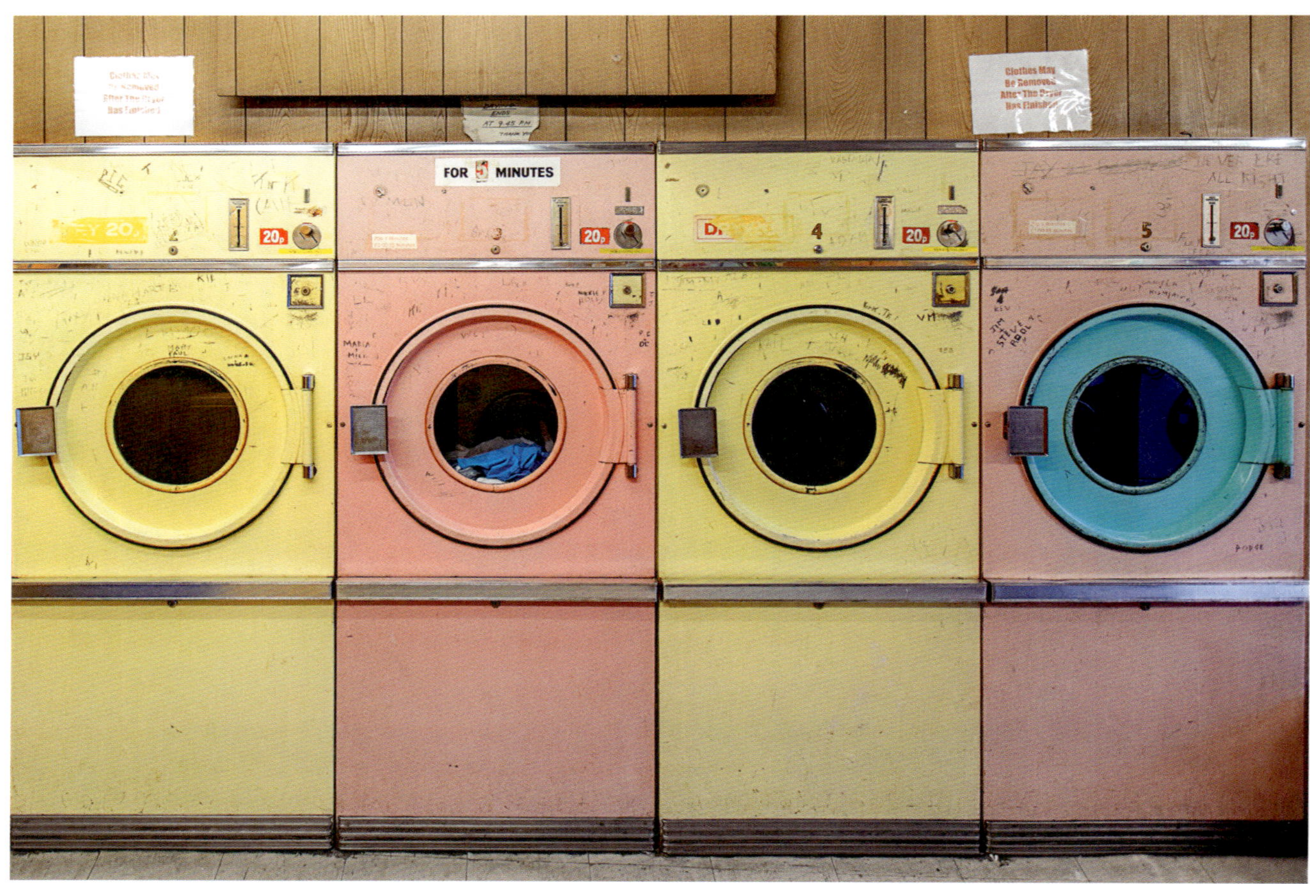

Clothes May
Be Removed
After The Dryer
Has Finished
FOR 5 MINUTES
20p
20p
20p
20p
4
5
Clothes May
Be Removed
After The Dryer
Has Finished

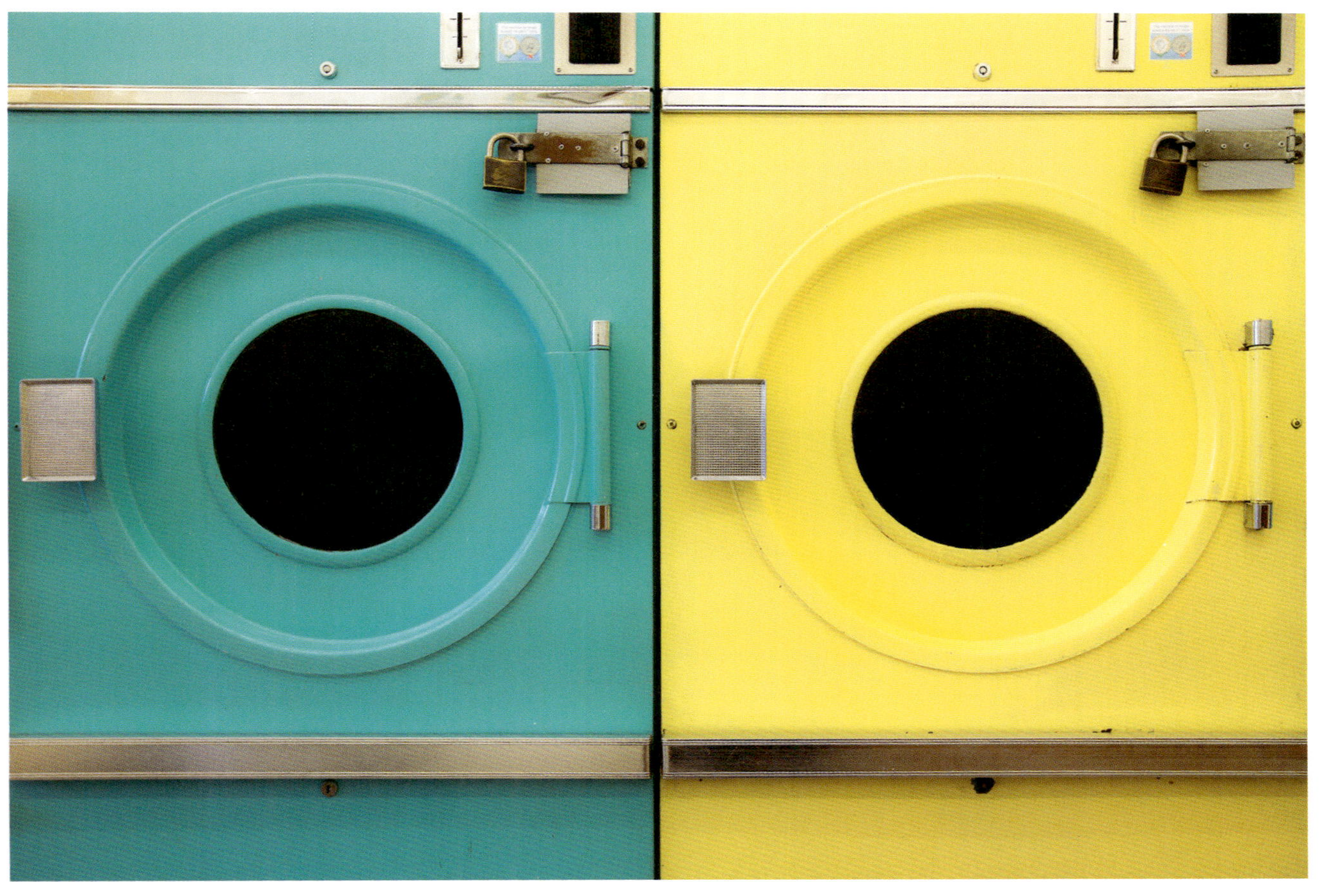

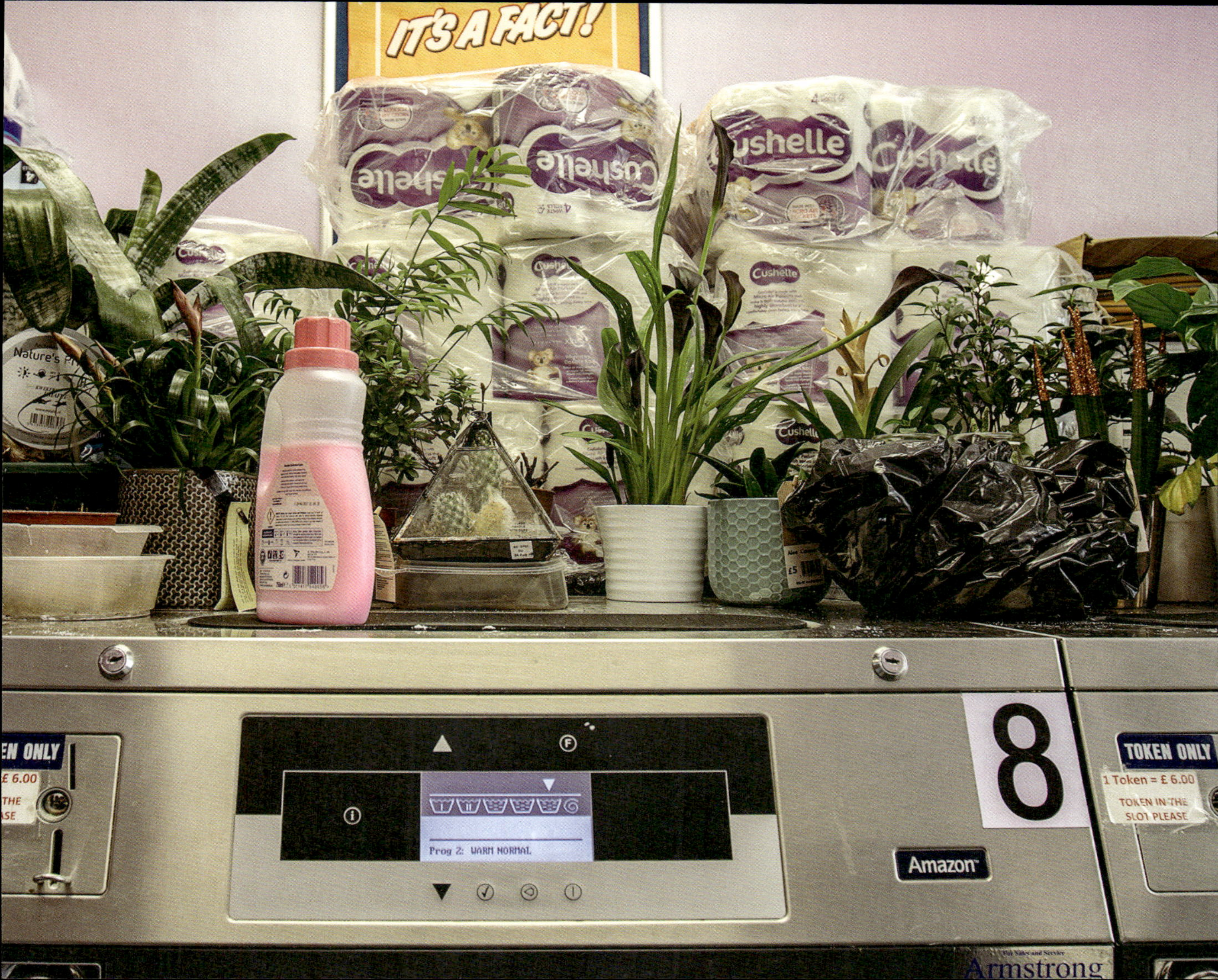
IT'S A FACT!
Cushelle
Cushelle
Cushelle
Cushelle
Nature's
8
TOKEN ONLY
1 Token = £ 6.00
TOKEN IN THE
SLOT PLEASE
EN ONLY
E 6.00
THE
Prog 2: WARM NORMAL.
Amazon
Armstrong

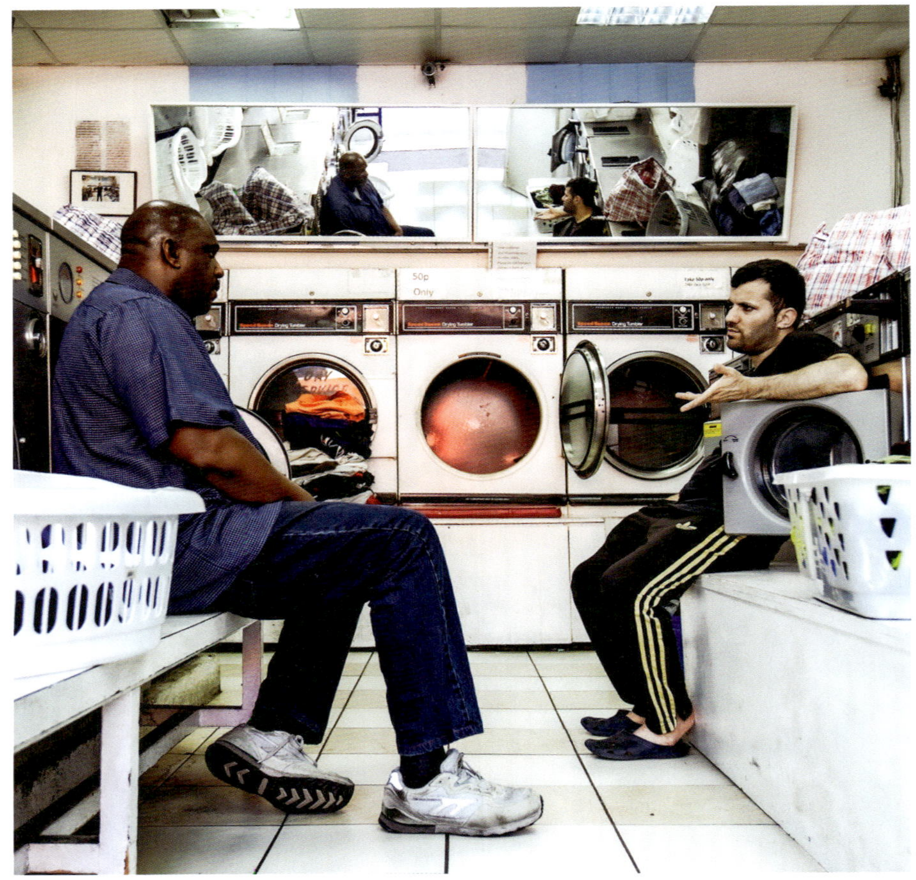

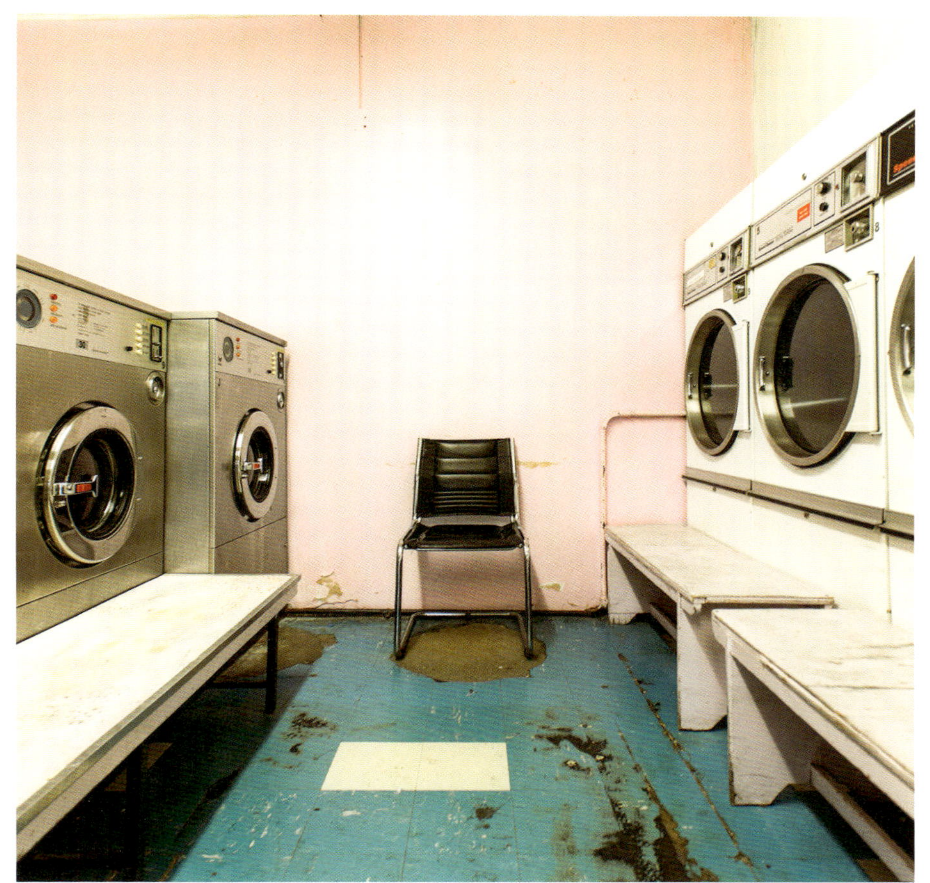

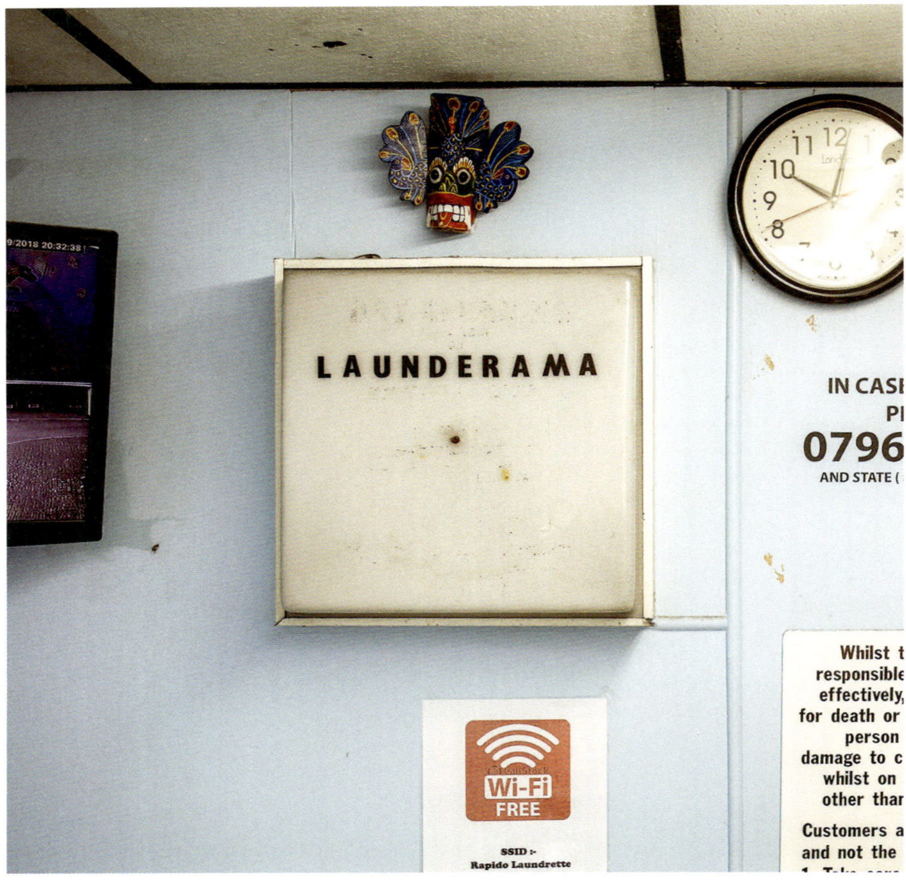
LAUNDERAMA
Wi-Fi FREE
SSID :-
Rapido Laundrette
IN CASE
PI
0796
AND STATE (
Whilst t
responsible
effectively,
for death or
person
damage to c
whilst on
other than
Customers a
and not the

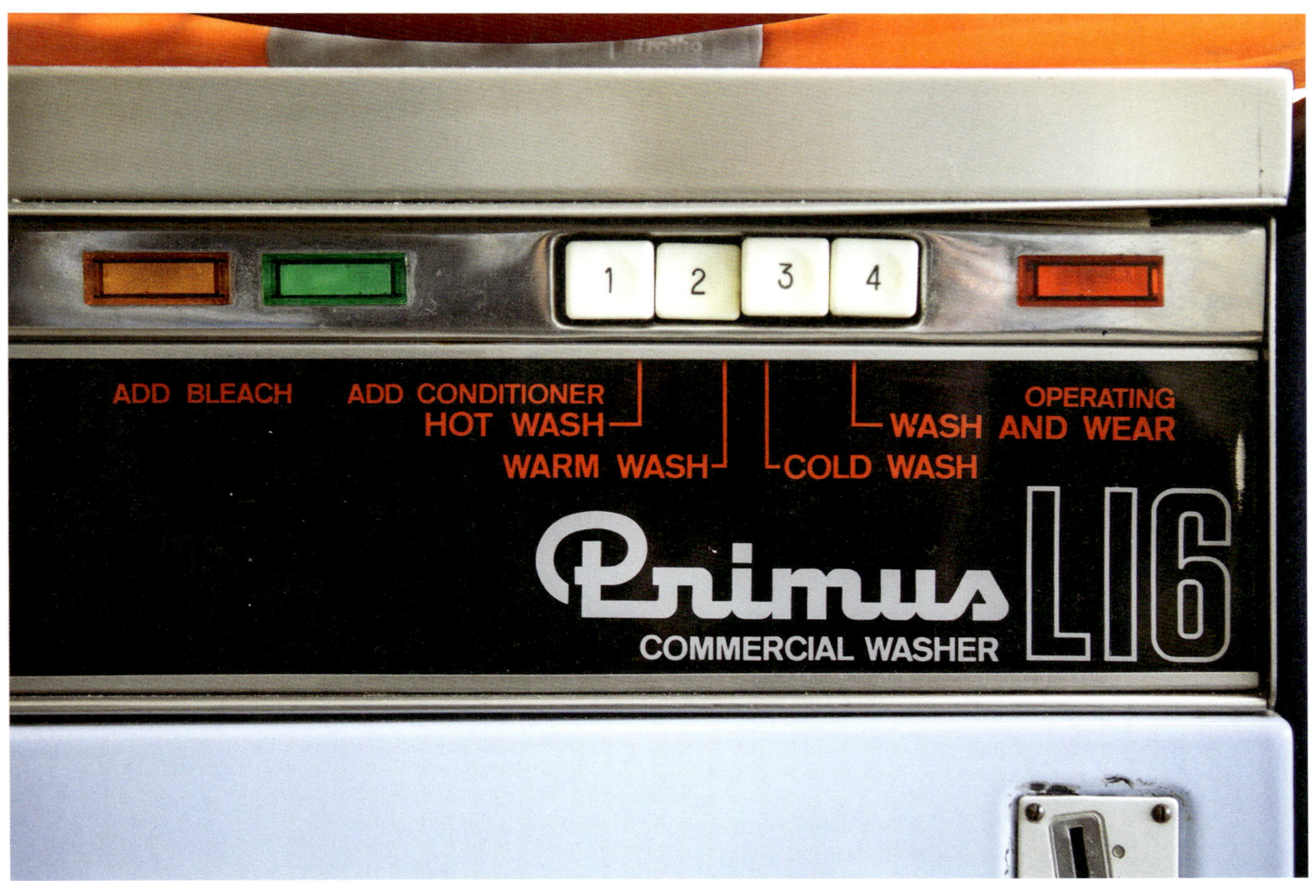
1 2 3 4
ADD BLEACH
ADD CONDITIONER
HOT WASH
WARM WASH
COLD WASH
WASH AND WEAR
OPERATING
Primus
COMMERCIAL WASHER
L16

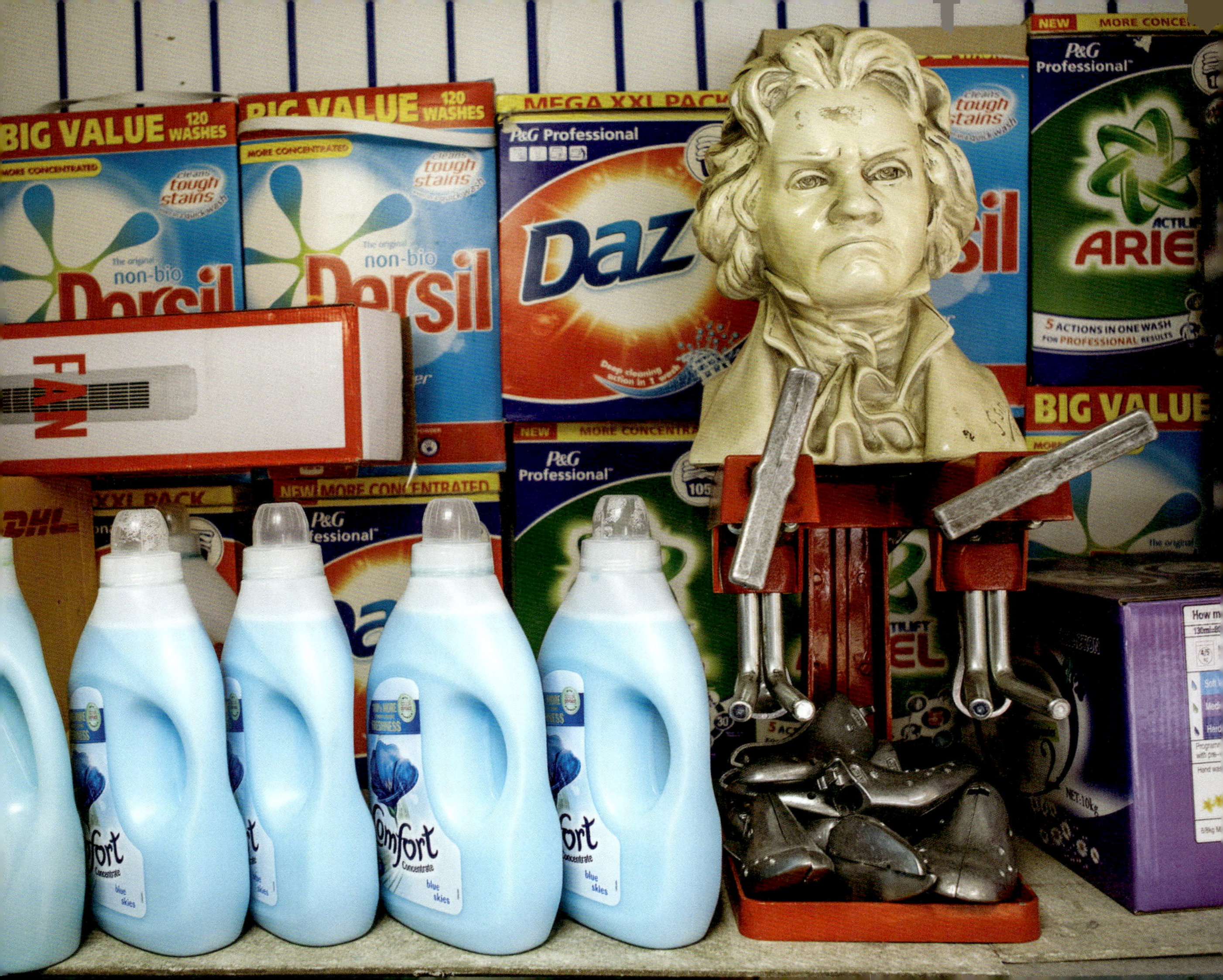

BIG VALUE 120 WASHES
MORE CONCENTRATED
cleans tough stains
The original non-bio Persil
BIG VALUE 120 WASHES
MORE CONCENTRATED
cleans tough stains
The original non-bio Persil
MEGA XXL PACK
P&G Professional
Daz
Deep cleaning action in 1 wash
cleans tough stains
Persil
NEW MORE CONCE
P&G Professional
ARIEL
ACTILIFT
5 ACTIONS IN ONE WASH
FOR PROFESSIONAL RESULTS
FAN
DHL
XXL PACK
NEW MORE CONCENTRATED
P&G Professional
P&G Professional
BIG VALUE
MORE
105
Daz
ACTILIFT
EL
the original
Comfort
Concentrate
blue skies
Comfort
Concentrate
blue skies
Comfort
Concentrate
blue skies
How m
NET:10kg

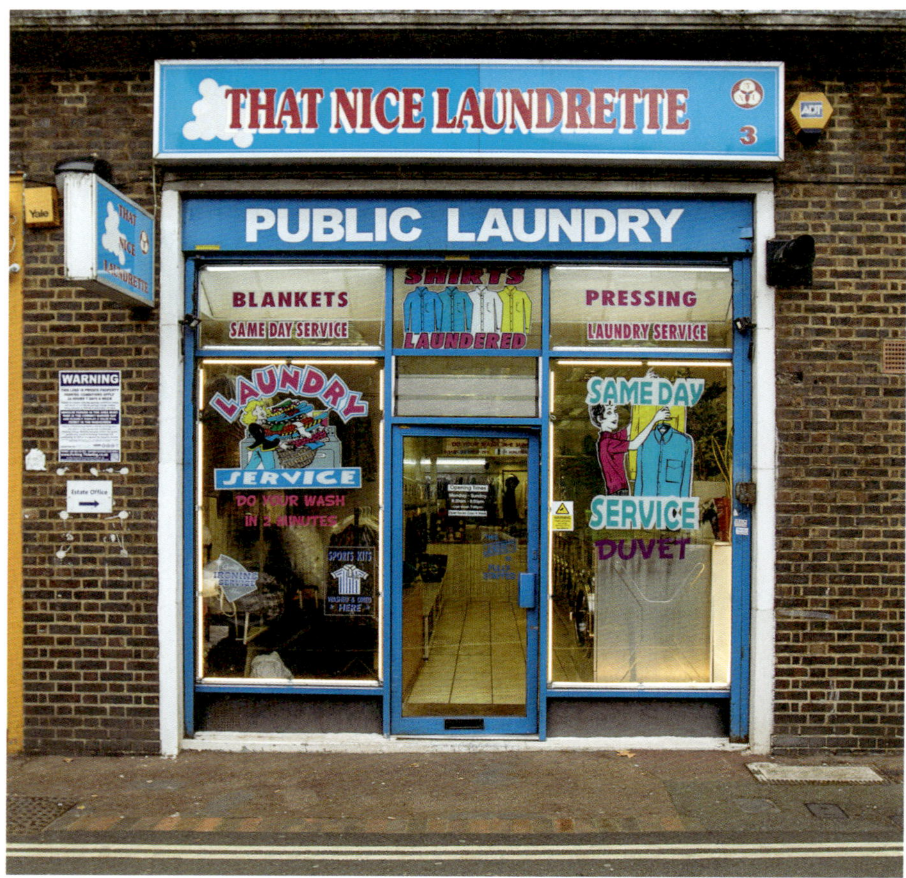

THAT NICE LAUNDRETTE
3
ADT
Yale
THAT NICE LAUNDRETTE
WARNING
Estate Office
PUBLIC LAUNDRY
BLANKETS
SAME DAY SERVICE
SHIRTS
LAUNDERED
PRESSING
LAUNDRY SERVICE
LAUNDRY
SERVICE
DO YOUR WASH
IN 2 MINUTES
SAME DAY
SERVICE
DUVET
SPORTS KITS
IRONING
Opening Times

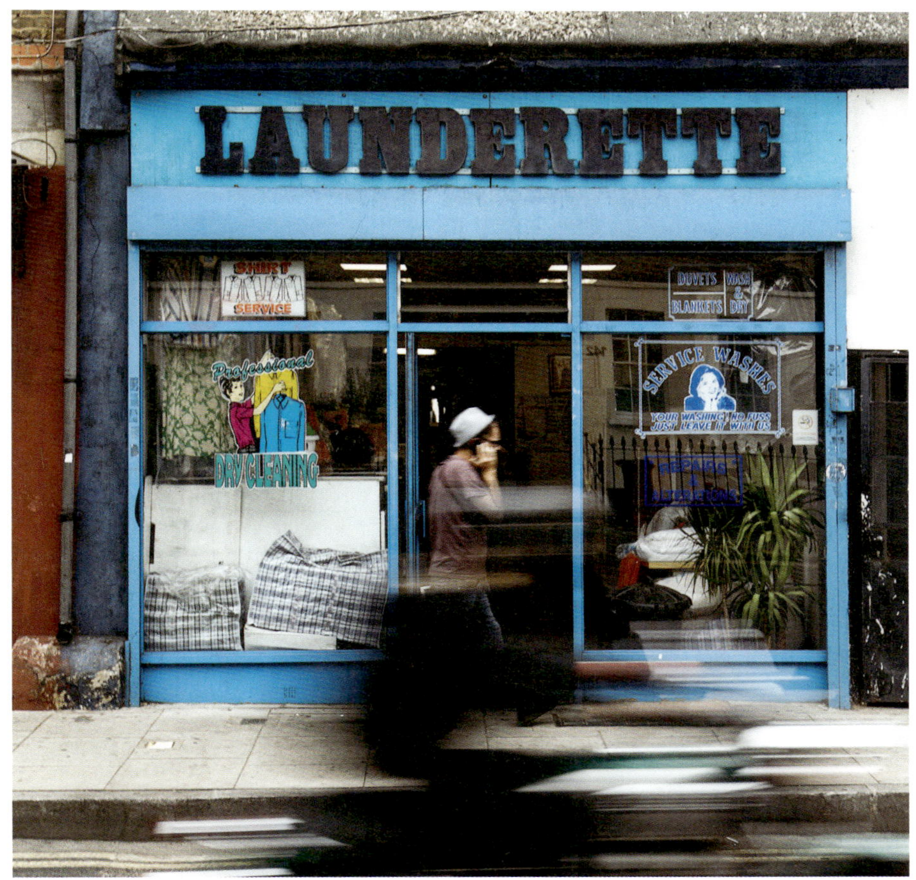

LAUNDERETTE
SHIRT SERVICE
DUVETS BLANKETS WASH & DRY
Professional DRY CLEANING
SERVICE WASHES
YOUR WASHING NO FUSS JUST LEAVE IT WITH US
REPAIRS & ALTERATIONS

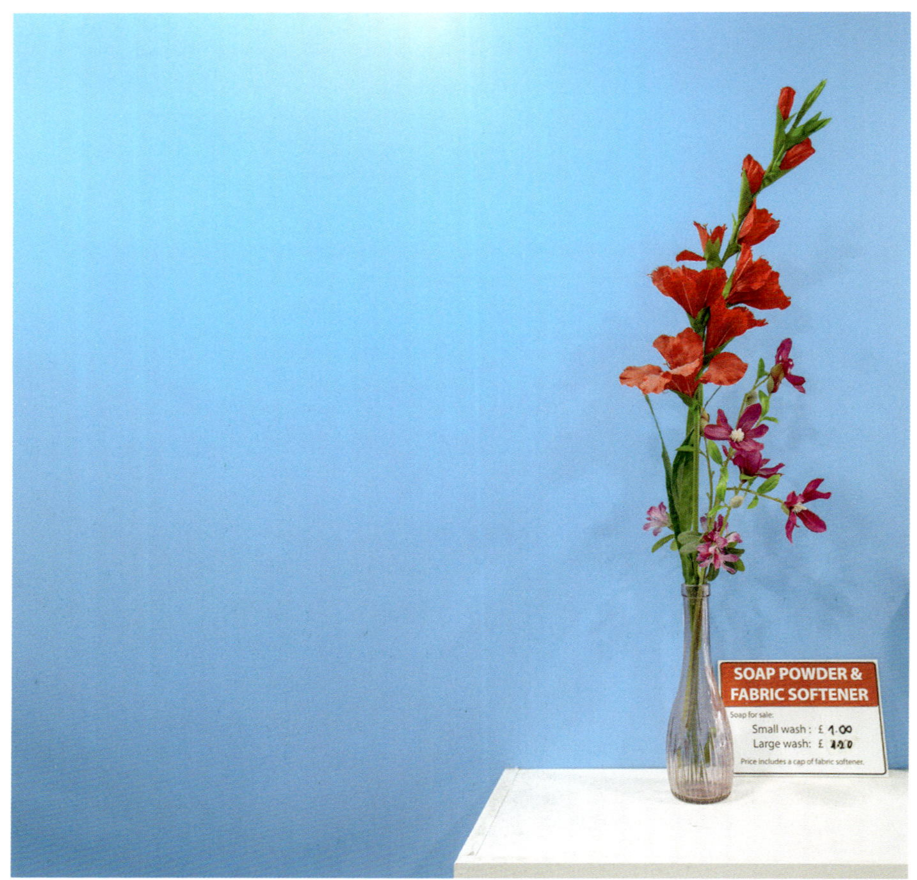

SOAP POWDER &
FABRIC SOFTENER
Soap for sale:
Small wash : £ 1.00
Large wash: £ 1.20
Price includes a cap of fabric softener.

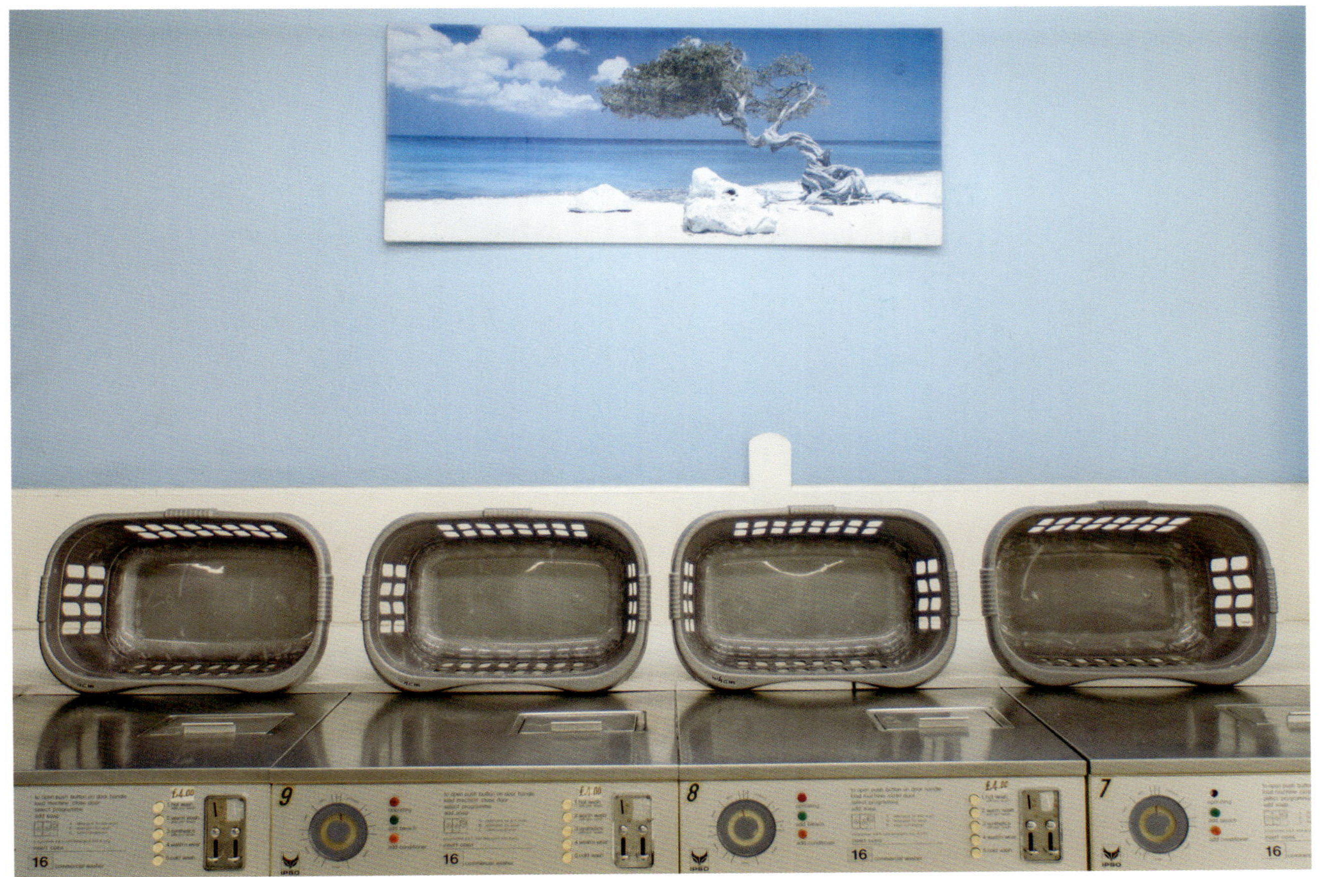

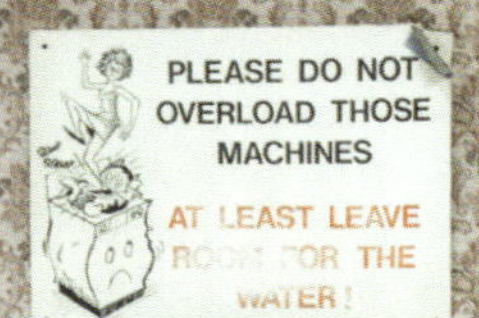

PLEASE DO NOT OVERLOAD THOSE MACHINES
AT LEAST LEAVE ROOM FOR THE WATER !

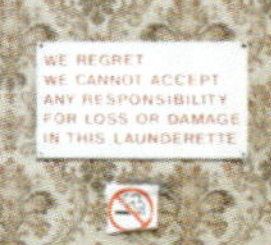

WE REGRET
WE CANNOT ACCEPT
ANY RESPONSIBILITY
FOR LOSS OR DAMAGE
IN THIS LAUNDERETTE

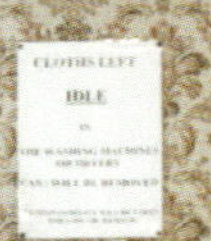

CLOTHS LEFT
IDLE
IN
THE WASHING MACHINES
OR DRYERS
WILL WILL BE REMOVED

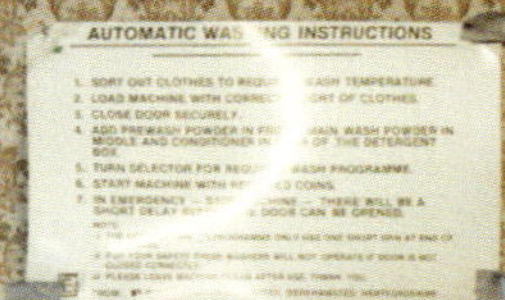

AUTOMATIC WASHING INSTRUCTIONS
1. SORT OUT CLOTHES TO REQUIRED WASH TEMPERATURE
2. LOAD MACHINE WITH CORRECT SORT OF CLOTHES
3. CLOSE DOOR SECURELY.
4. ADD PREWASH POWDER IN FIRST, MAIN WASH POWDER IN MIDDLE AND CONDITIONER IN END OF THE DETERGENT BOX
5. TURN SELECTOR FOR REQUIRED WASH PROGRAMME.
6. START MACHINE WITH REQUIRED COINS.
7. IN EMERGENCY — STOP MACHINE — THERE WILL BE A SHORT DELAY BEFORE DOOR CAN BE OPENED.

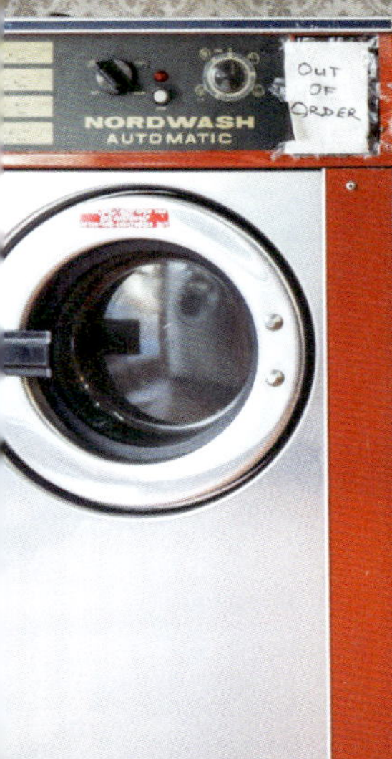

NORDWASH AUTOMATIC
OUT OF ORDER

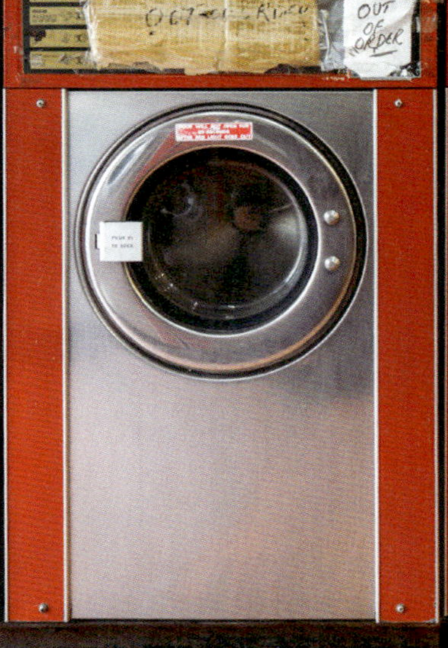

OUT OF ORDER

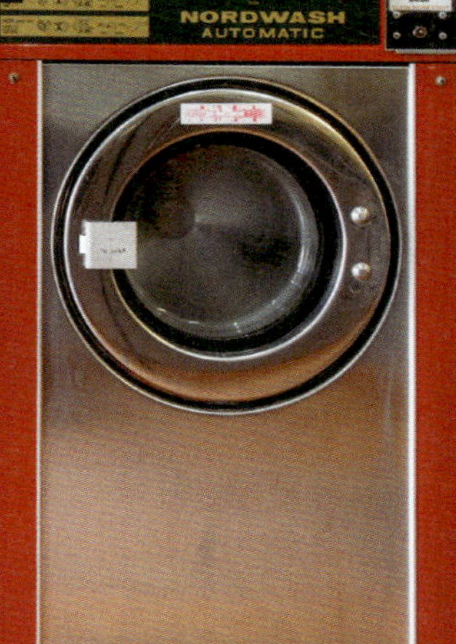

NORDWASH AUTOMATIC
8x50p

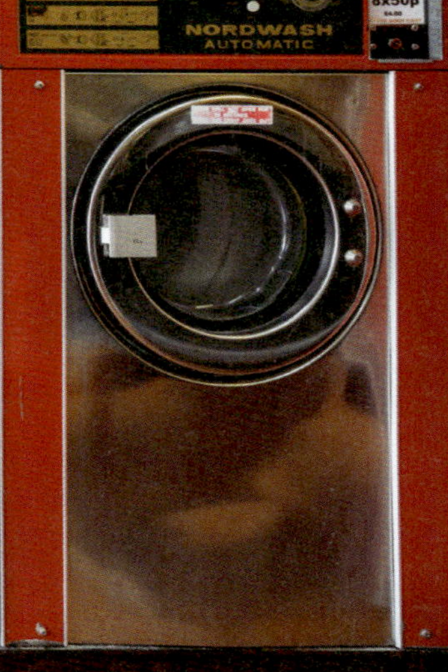

NORDWASH AUTOMATIC
8x50p

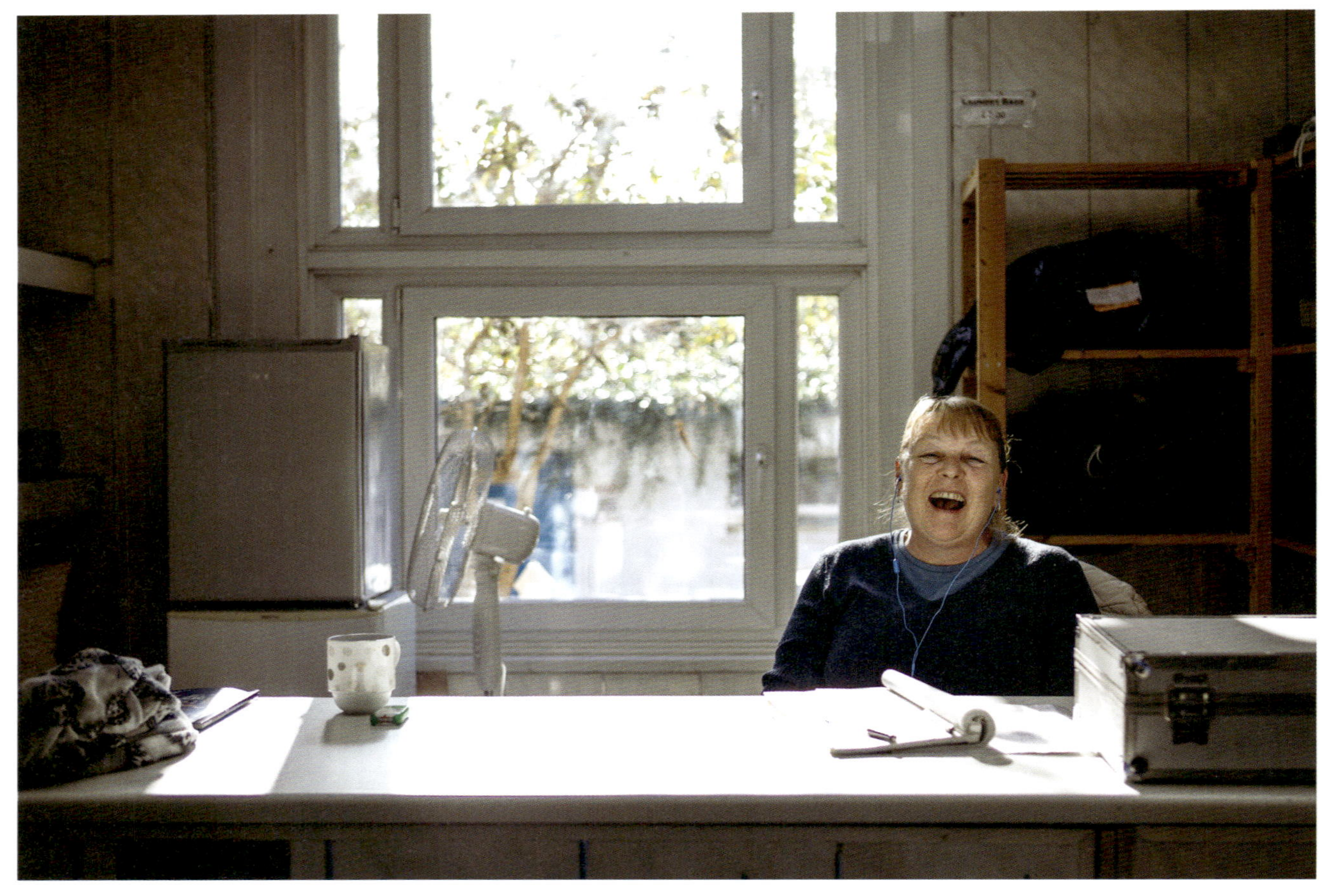

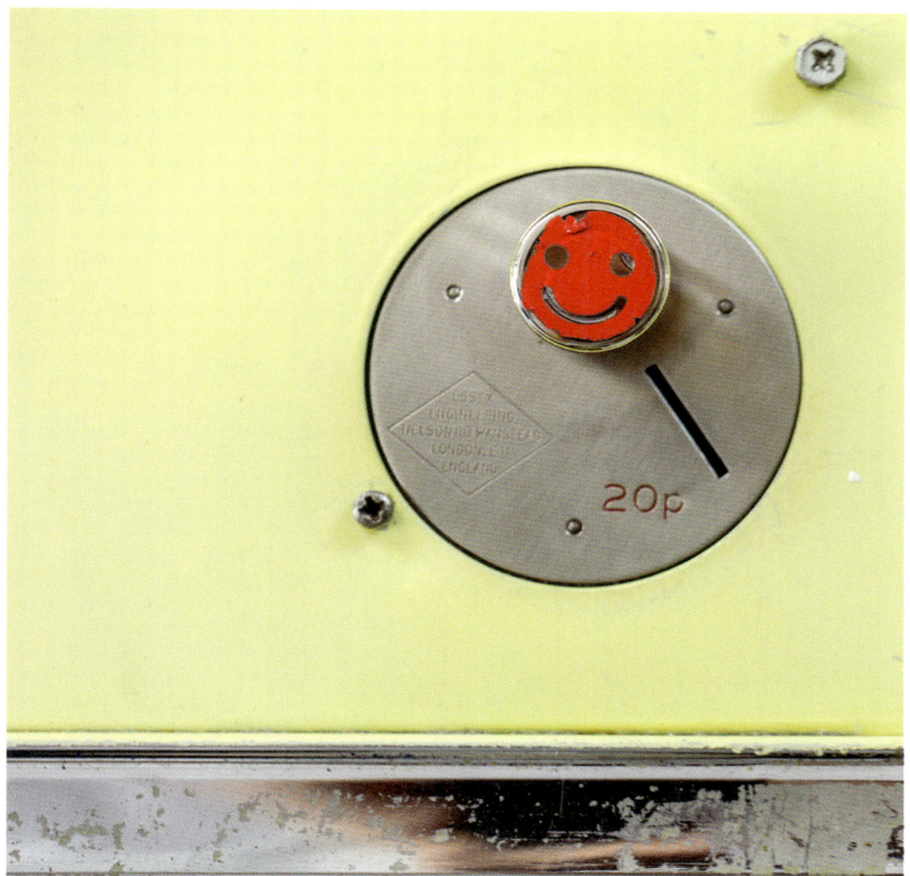
20p

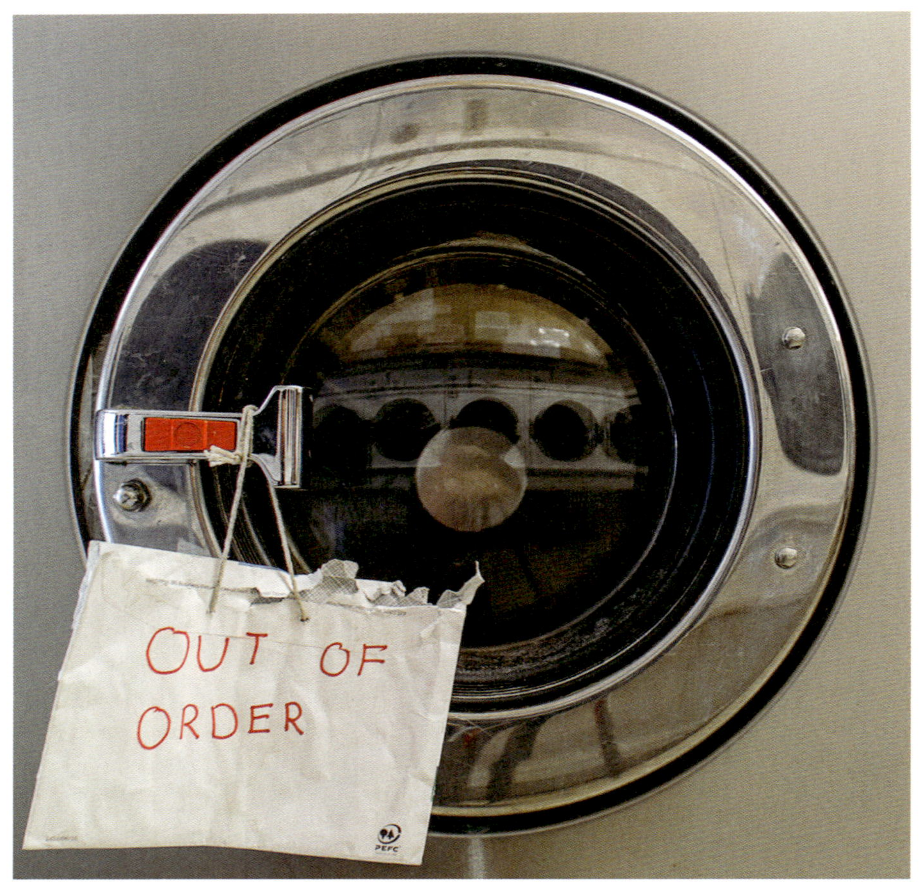
OUT OF
ORDER

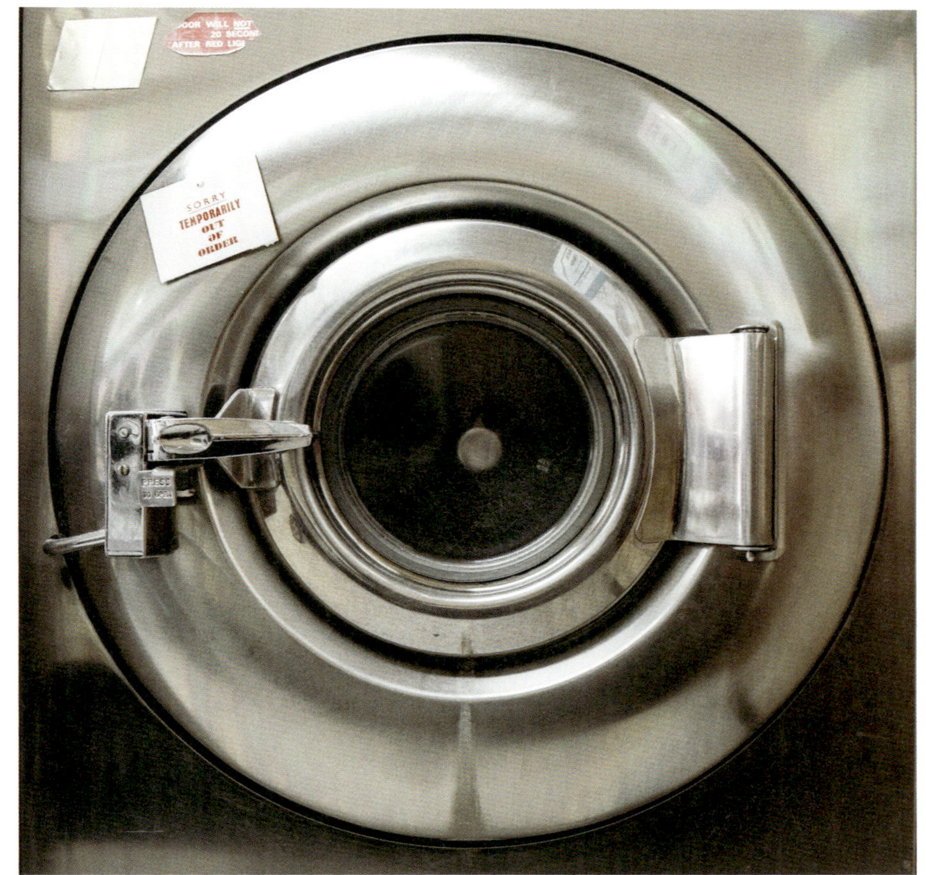
SORRY
TEMPORARILY
OUT
OF
ORDER

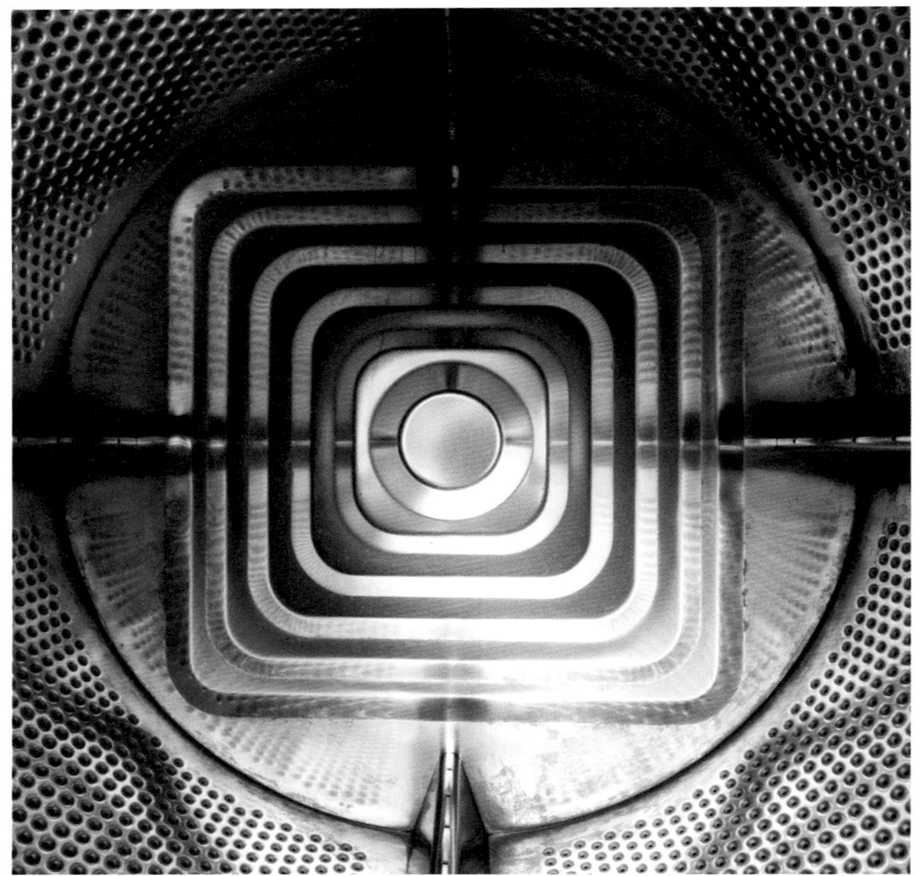

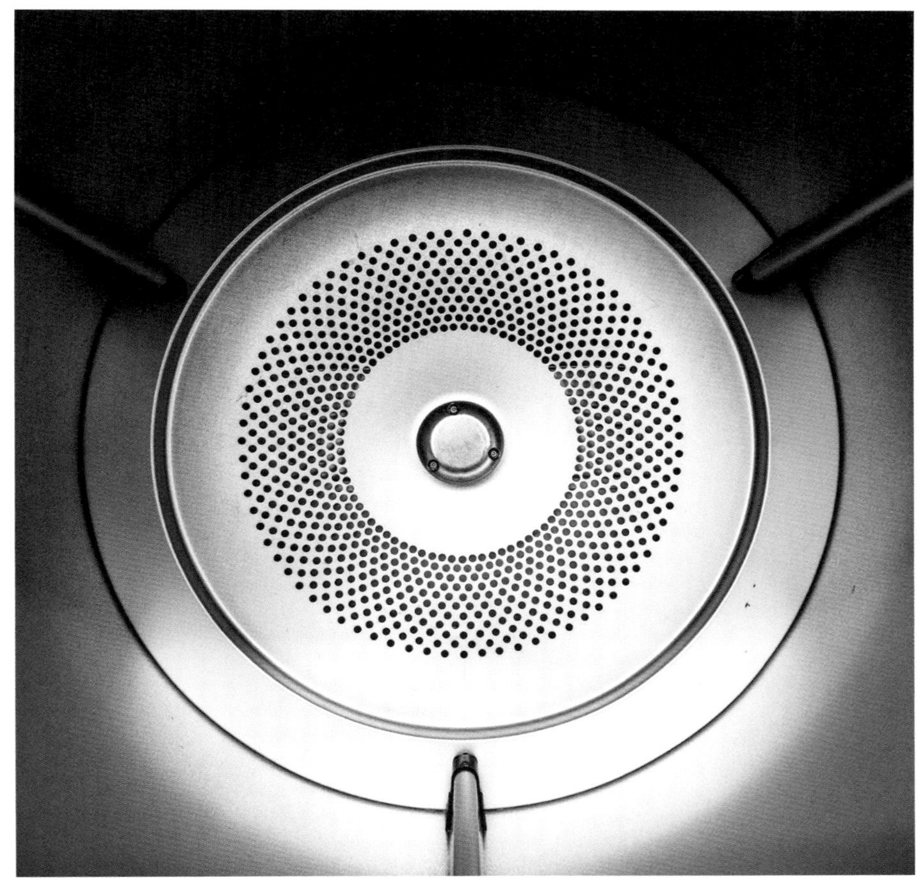

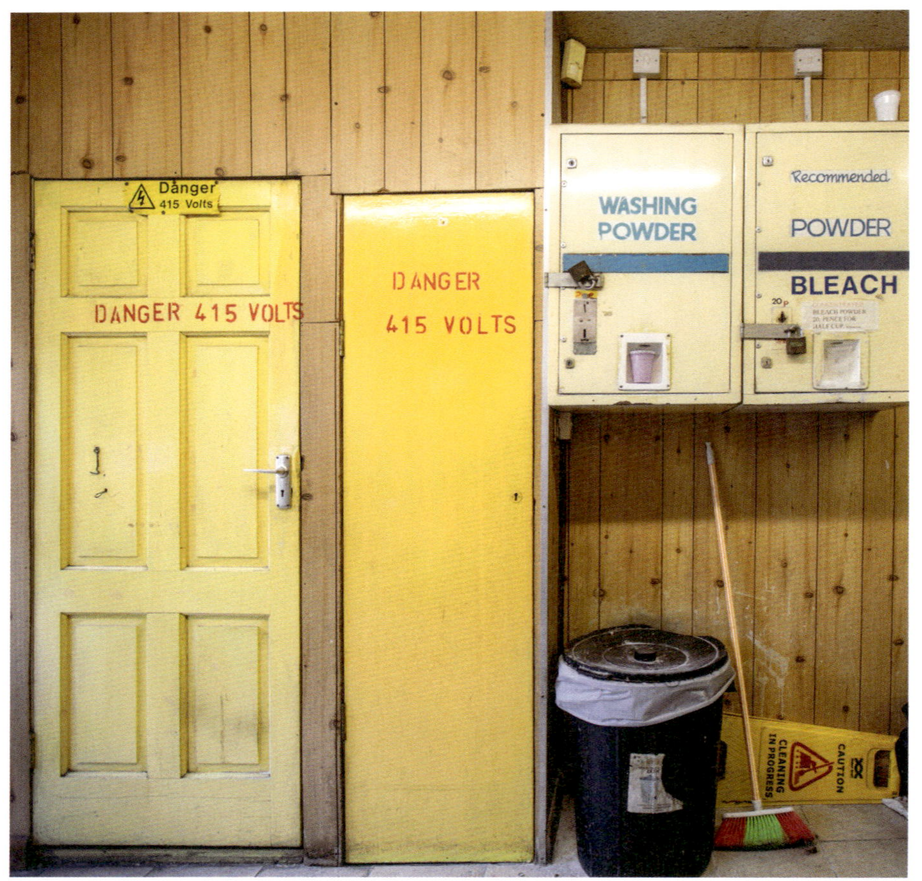
Danger
415 Volts
DANGER 415 VOLTS
DANGER
415 VOLTS
WASHING
POWDER
Recommended
POWDER
BLEACH
20 p
CLEANING IN PROGRESS
CAUTION

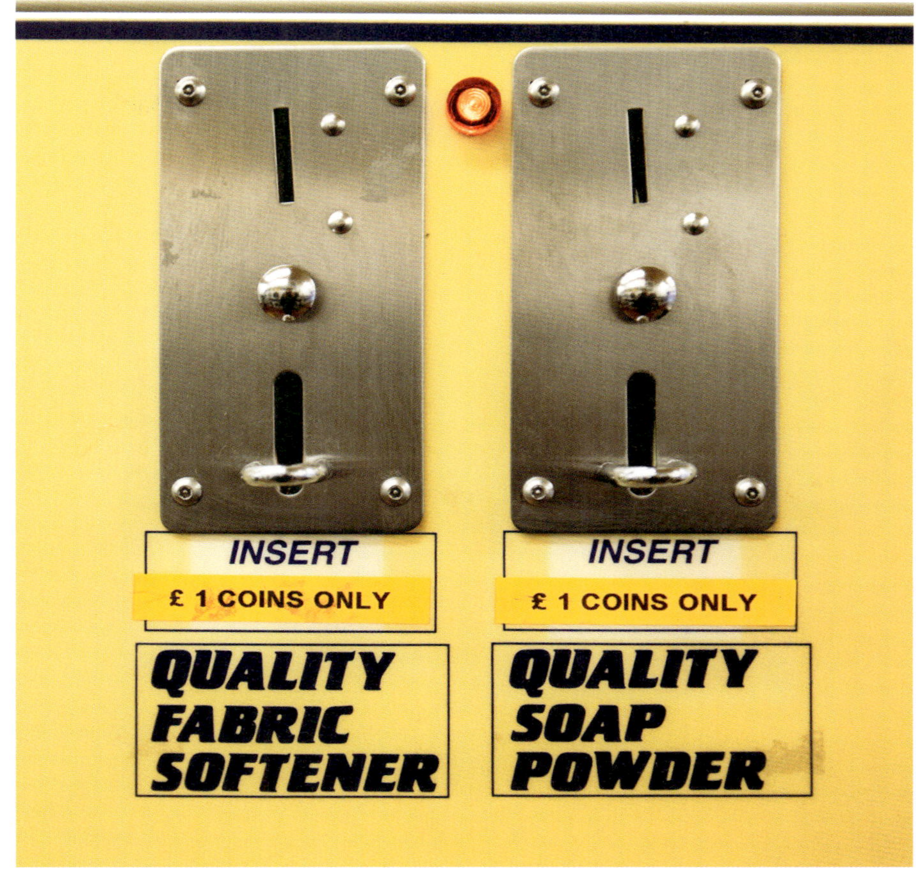

INSERT
£ 1 COINS ONLY
QUALITY FABRIC SOFTENER
INSERT
£ 1 COINS ONLY
QUALITY SOAP POWDER

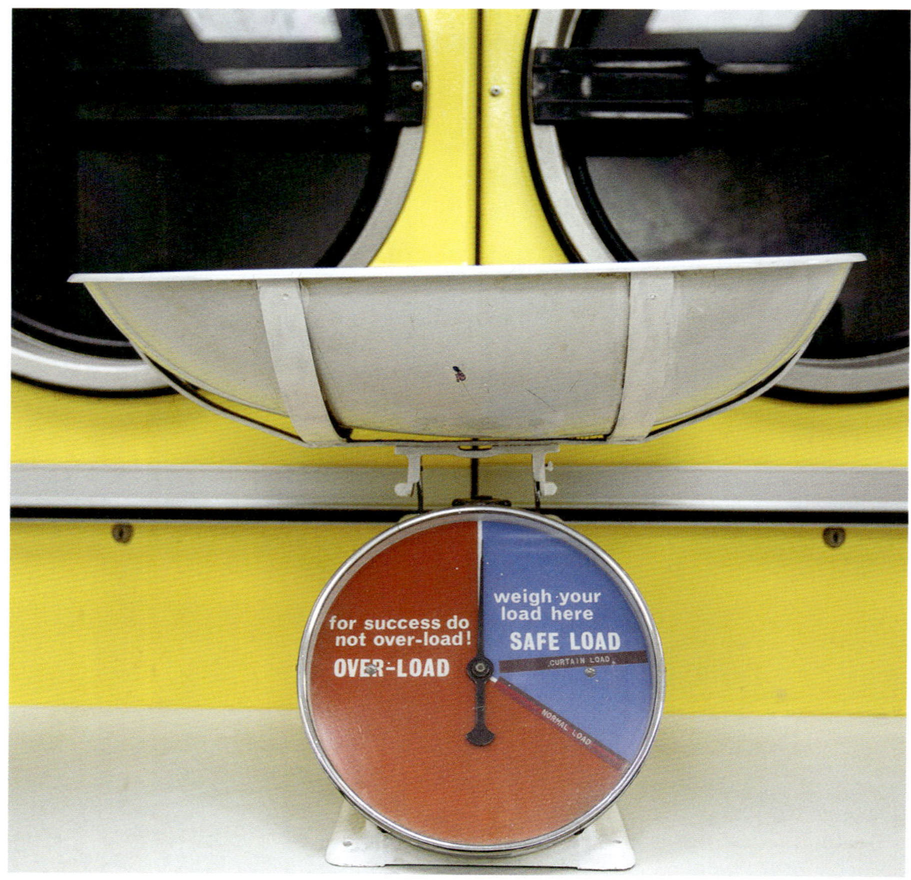
weigh your
load here
SAFE LOAD
for success do
not over-load!
OVER-LOAD
CURTAIN LOAD
NORMAL LOAD

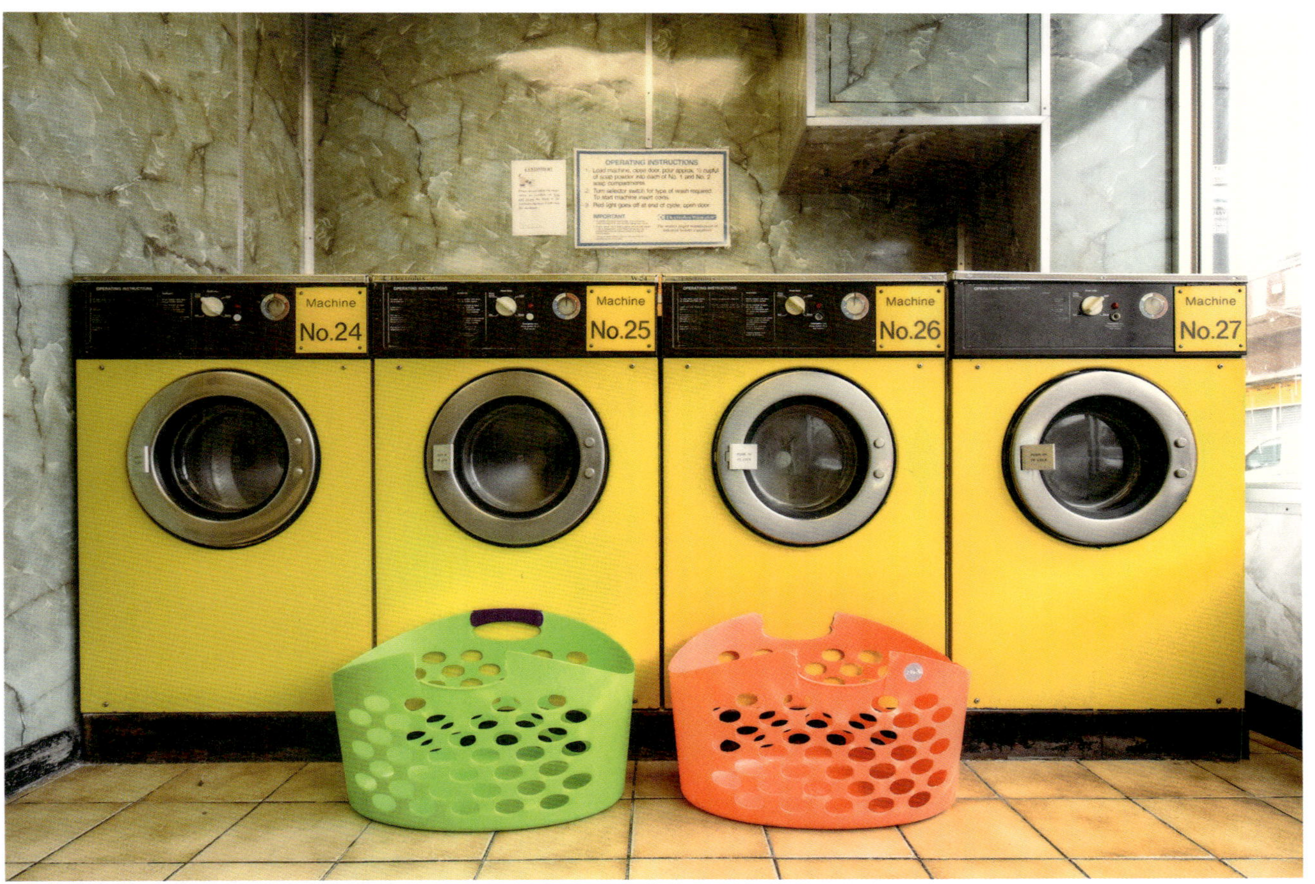
OPERATING INSTRUCTIONS
Machine No.24
Machine No.25
Machine No.26
Machine No.27

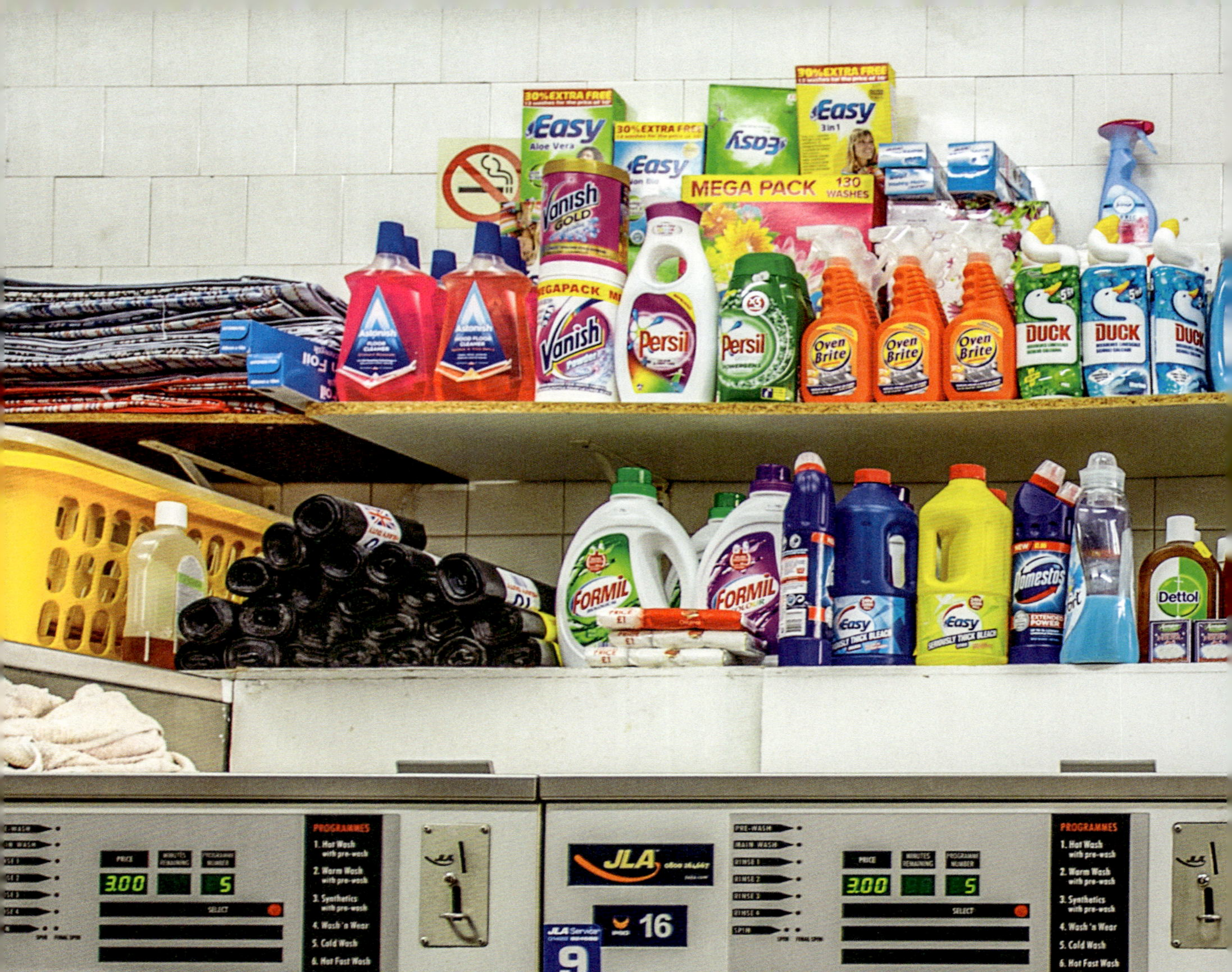
30% EXTRA FREE
Easy
Aloe Vera
30% EXTRA FREE
Easy
Easy
ASDA
Easy
3 in 1
90% EXTRA FREE
Vanish
GOLD
MEGA PACK
130 WASHES
MEGAPACK
Vanish
Persil
Persil
Oven Brite
Oven Brite
Oven Brite
DUCK
DUCK
DUCK
Astonish
FLOOR CLEANER
Astonish
WOOD FLOOR CLEANER
Foil
Formil
Formil
COLOUR
£1
£1
£1
Easy
THICK BLEACH
Easy
SERIOUSLY THICK BLEACH
NEW
Domestos
EXTENDED POWER
Dettol
PROGRAMMES
1. Hot Wash with pre-wash
2. Warm Wash with pre-wash
3. Synthetics with pre-wash
4. Wash 'n Wear
5. Cold Wash
6. Hot Fast Wash
PRICE
MINUTES REMAINING
PROGRAMME NUMBER
3.00
5
SELECT
PRE-WASH
MAIN WASH
RINSE 1
RINSE 2
RINSE 3
RINSE 4
SPIN
FINAL SPIN
JLA
0800 264667
JLA Service
16
9
PRICE
MINUTES REMAINING
PROGRAMME NUMBER
3.00
5
SELECT
PROGRAMMES
1. Hot Wash with pre-wash
2. Warm Wash with pre-wash
3. Synthetics with pre-wash
4. Wash 'n Wear
5. Cold Wash
6. Hot Fast Wash

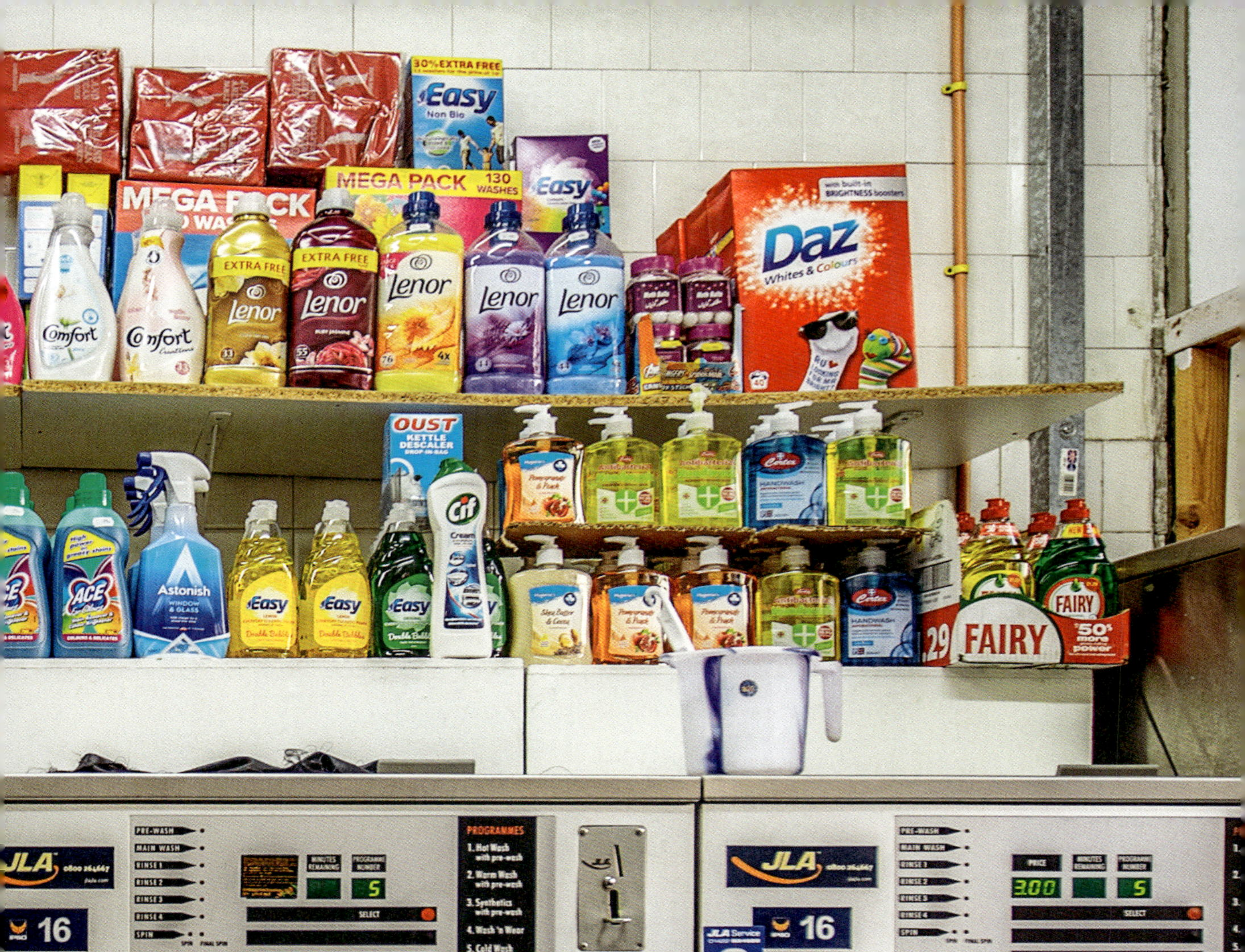
30% EXTRA FREE
Easy
Non Bio
MEGA PACK
MEGA PACK 130 WASHES
Easy
Comfort
Comfort
EXTRA FREE
EXTRA FREE
Lenor
Lenor
Lenor
Lenor
Daz
Whites & Colours
with built-in BRIGHTNESS boosters
OUST
KETTLE DESCALER
DROP-IN-BAG
Cif
Cream
ACE
Astonish
WINDOW & GLASS
Easy
Lemon
Double Bubble
Easy
Lemon
Double Bubble
Easy
Double Bubble
Cortex
HANDWASH
Shea Butter & Cocoa
Pomegranate & Peach
Pomegranate & Peach
Cortex
HANDWASH
FAIRY
NEW
FAIRY
50% more power
29
JLA
0800 264667
jla.com
PRE-WASH
MAIN WASH
RINSE 1
RINSE 2
RINSE 3
RINSE 4
SPIN
FINAL SPIN
MINUTES REMAINING
PROGRAMME NUMBER
5
SELECT
PROGRAMMES
1. Hot Wash with pre-wash
2. Warm Wash with pre-wash
3. Synthetics with pre-wash
4. Wash 'n Wear
5. Cold Wash
6. Hot Fast Wash
16
JLA
0800 264667
jla.com
PRE-WASH
MAIN WASH
RINSE 1
RINSE 2
RINSE 3
RINSE 4
SPIN
FINAL SPIN
PRICE
3.00
MINUTES REMAINING
PROGRAMME NUMBER
5
SELECT
JLA Service
8
16

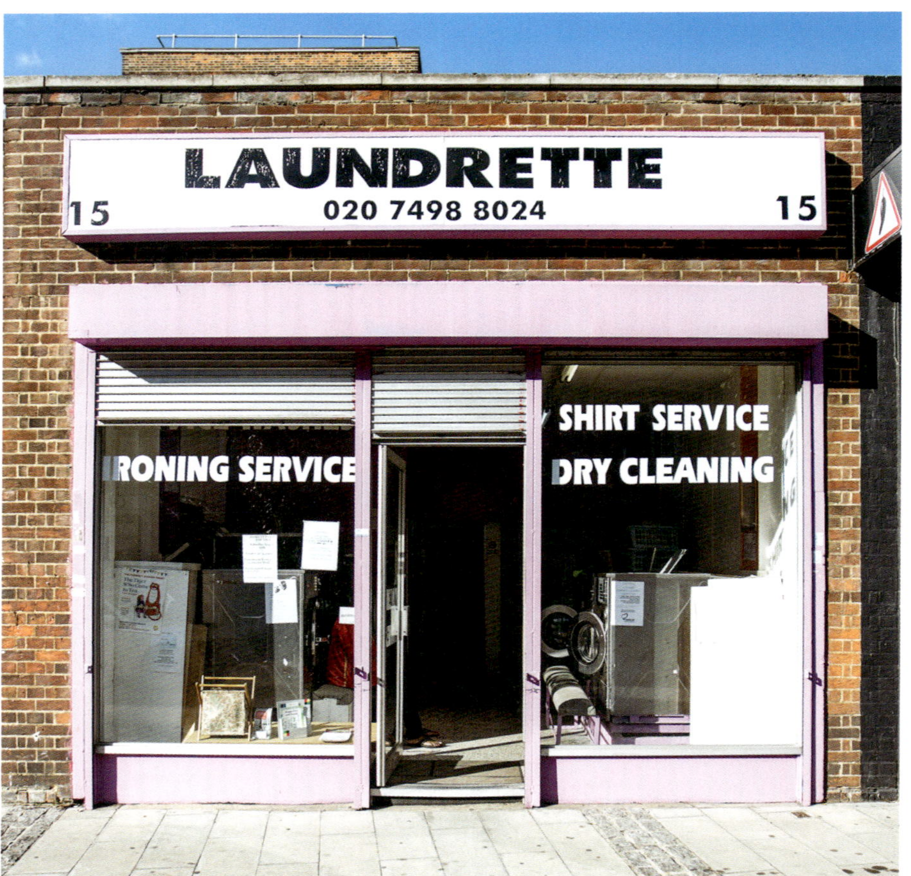
LAUNDRETTE
020 7498 8024
15
15
IRONING SERVICE
SHIRT SERVICE
DRY CLEANING

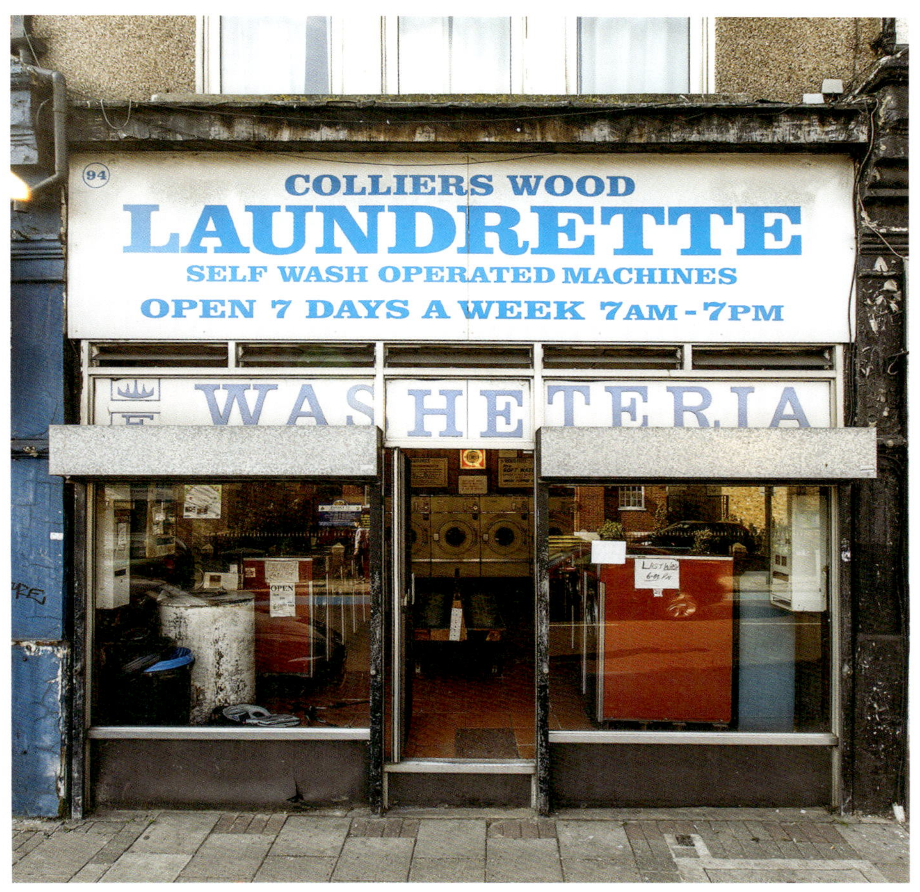
94
COLLIERS WOOD
LAUNDRETTE
SELF WASH OPERATED MACHINES
OPEN 7 DAYS A WEEK 7AM - 7PM
WASHETERIA

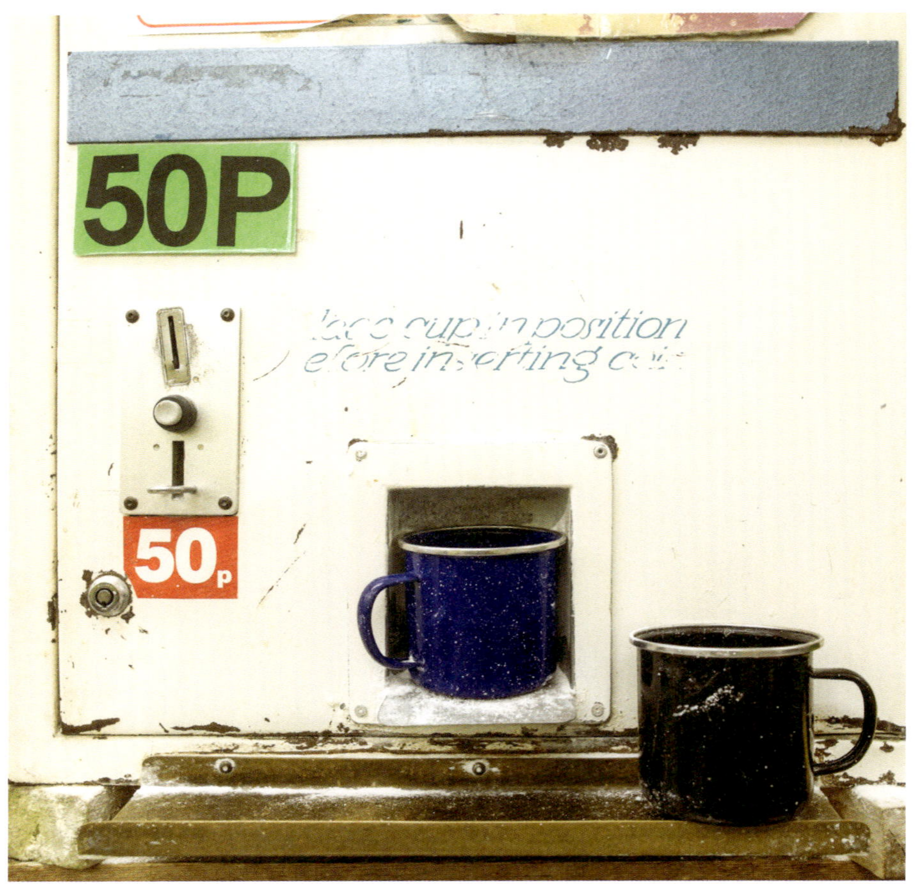

50P
lace cup in position
efore inserting coin
50p

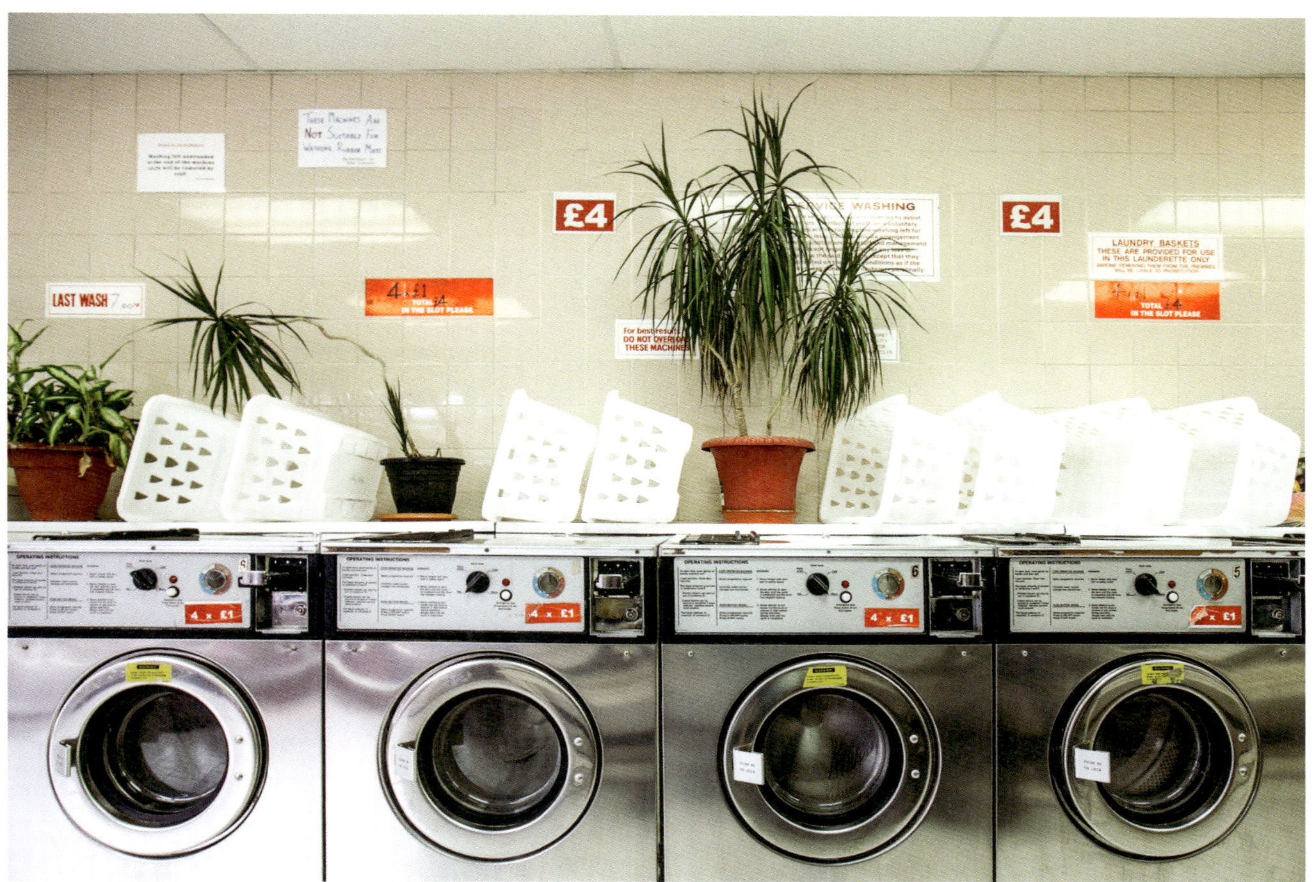
THESE MACHINES ARE
NOT SUITABLE FOR
WASHING RUBBER MATS
£4
£4
SERVICE WASHING
LAST WASH 7.00PM
LAUNDRY BASKETS
THESE ARE PROVIDED FOR USE
IN THIS LAUNDERETTE ONLY
For best results
DO NOT OVERLOAD
THESE MACHINES
TOTAL £4
IN THE SLOT PLEASE
TOTAL £4
IN THE SLOT PLEASE
OPERATING INSTRUCTIONS
OPERATING INSTRUCTIONS
OPERATING INSTRUCTIONS
OPERATING INSTRUCTIONS
4 x £1
4 x £1
4 x £1
x £1

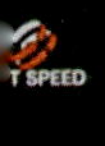

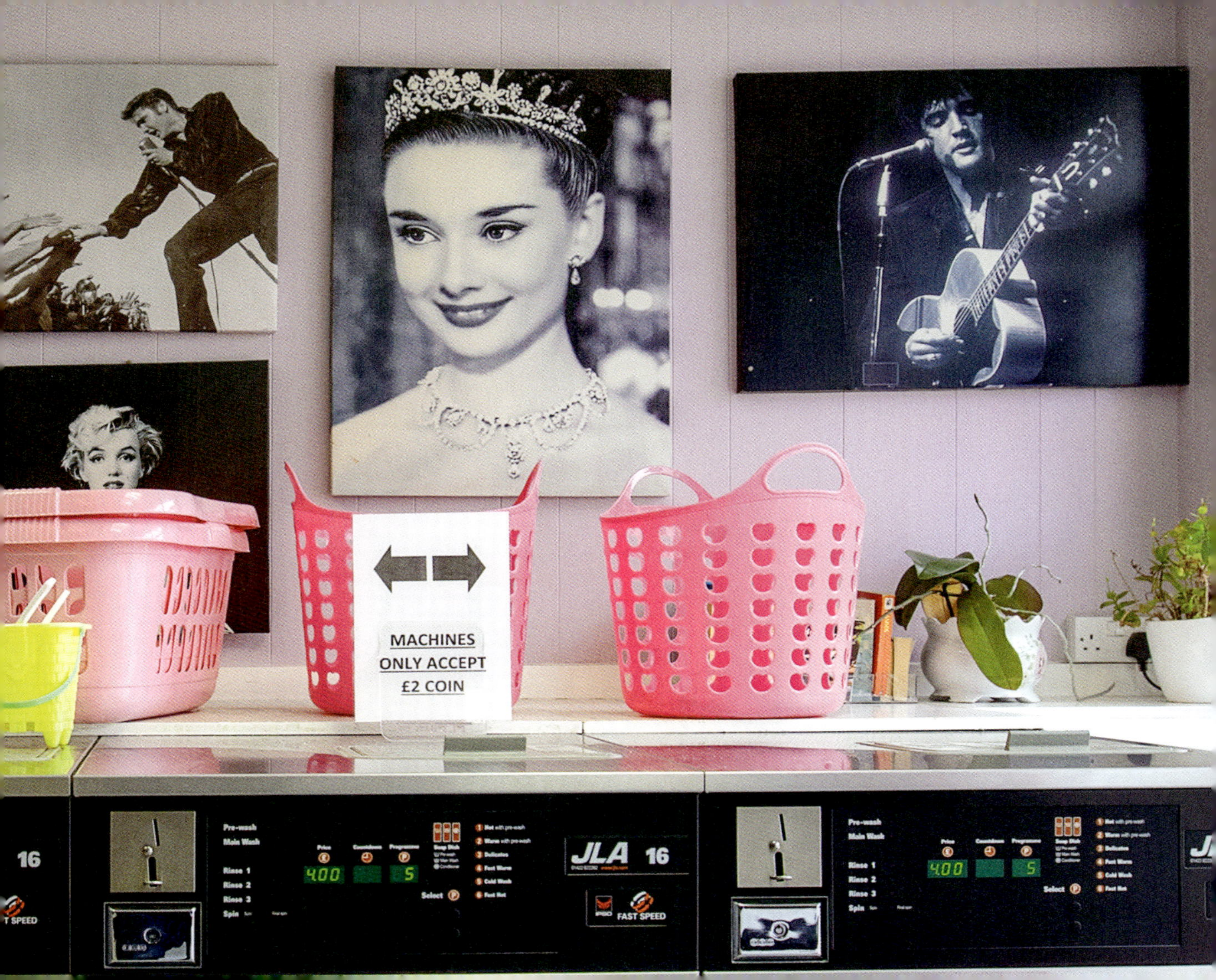

MACHINES
ONLY ACCEPT
£2 COIN
Pre-wash
Main Wash
Rinse 1
Rinse 2
Rinse 3
Spin
Price £
Countdown
Programme P
Soap Dish
Select P
1 Hot with pre-wash
2 Warm with pre-wash
3 Delicates
4 Fast Warm
5 Cold Wash
6 Fast Hot
JLA 16
FAST SPEED
4.00
5
16
T SPEED

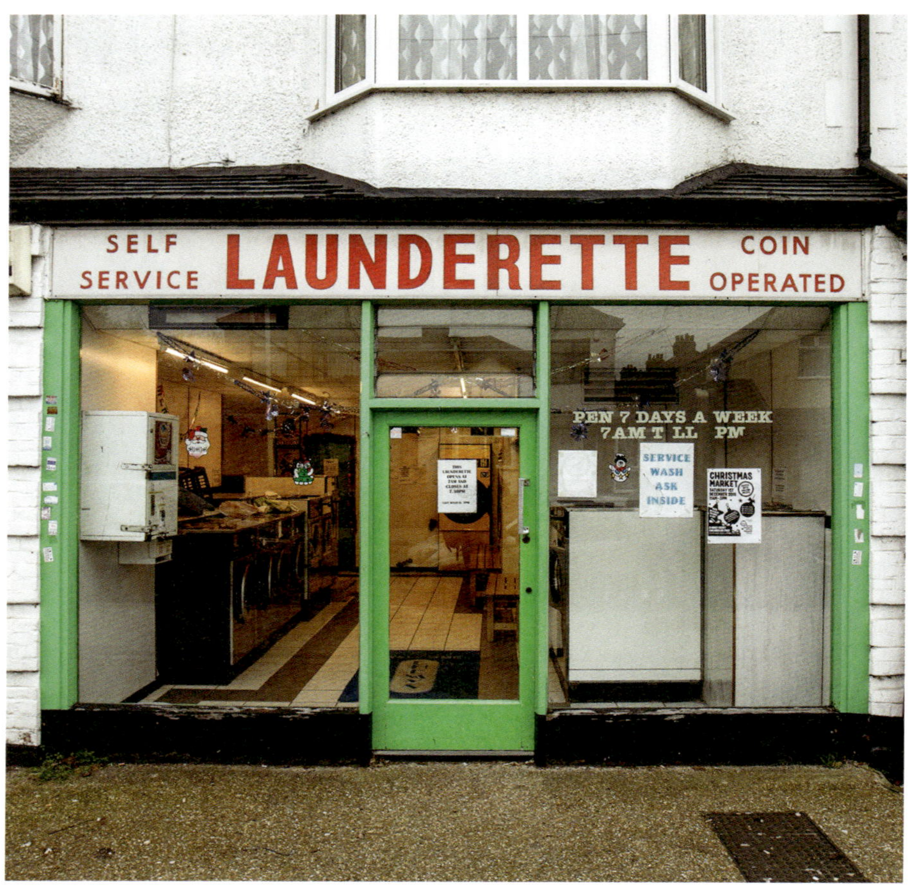

SELF SERVICE
LAUNDERETTE
COIN OPERATED
PEN 7 DAYS A WEEK
7AM T LL PM
SERVICE
WASH
ASK
INSIDE
CHRISTMAS
MARKET

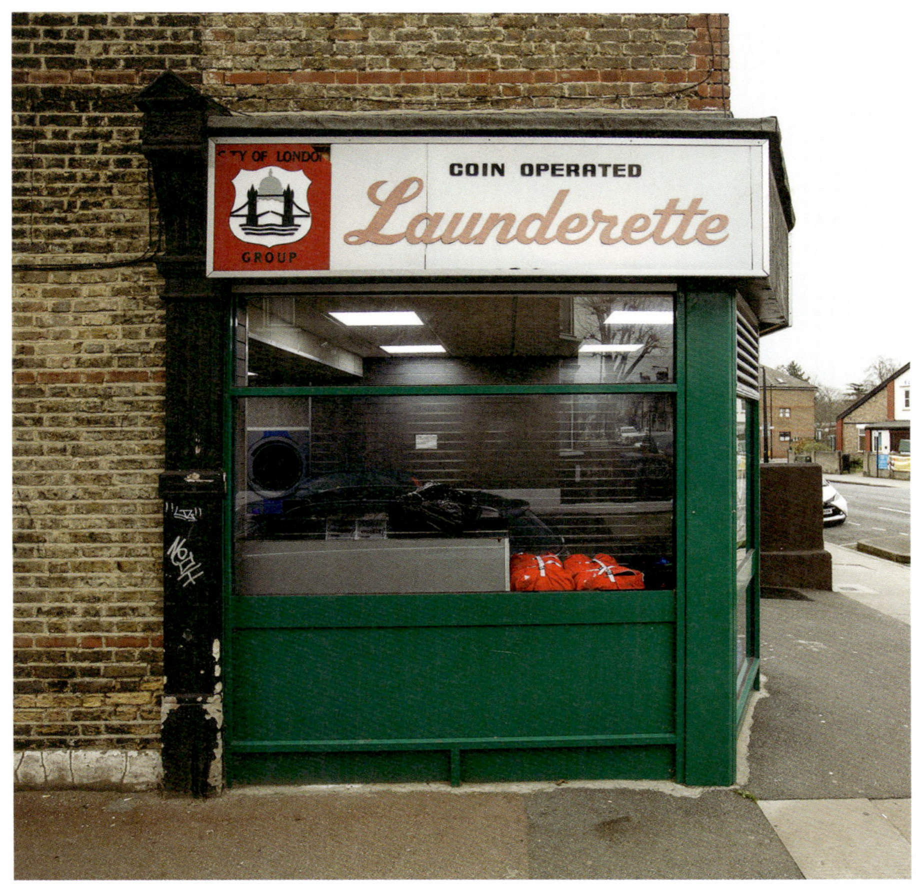
CITY OF LONDON
GROUP
COIN OPERATED
Launderette

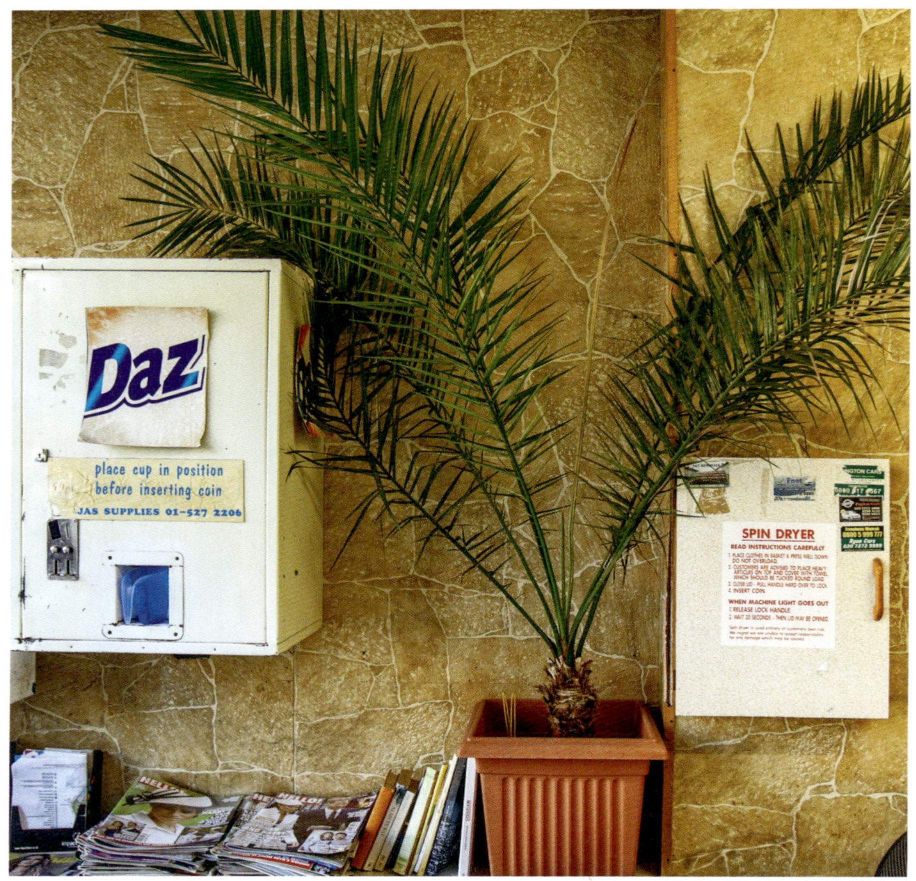
Daz
place cup in position
before inserting coin
JAS SUPPLIES 01-527 2206
SPIN DRYER
READ INSTRUCTIONS CAREFULLY
1. PLACE CLOTHES IN BASKET & PRESS WELL DOWN. DO NOT OVERLOAD.
2. CUSTOMERS ARE ADVISED TO PLACE HEAVY ARTICLES ON TOP AND COVER WITH TOWEL WHICH SHOULD BE TUCKED ROUND LOAD.
3. CLOSE LID - PULL HANDLE HARD OVER TO LOCK.
4. INSERT COIN.
WHEN MACHINE LIGHT GOES OUT
1. RELEASE LOCK HANDLE.
2. WAIT 20 SECONDS - THEN LID MAY BE OPENED.

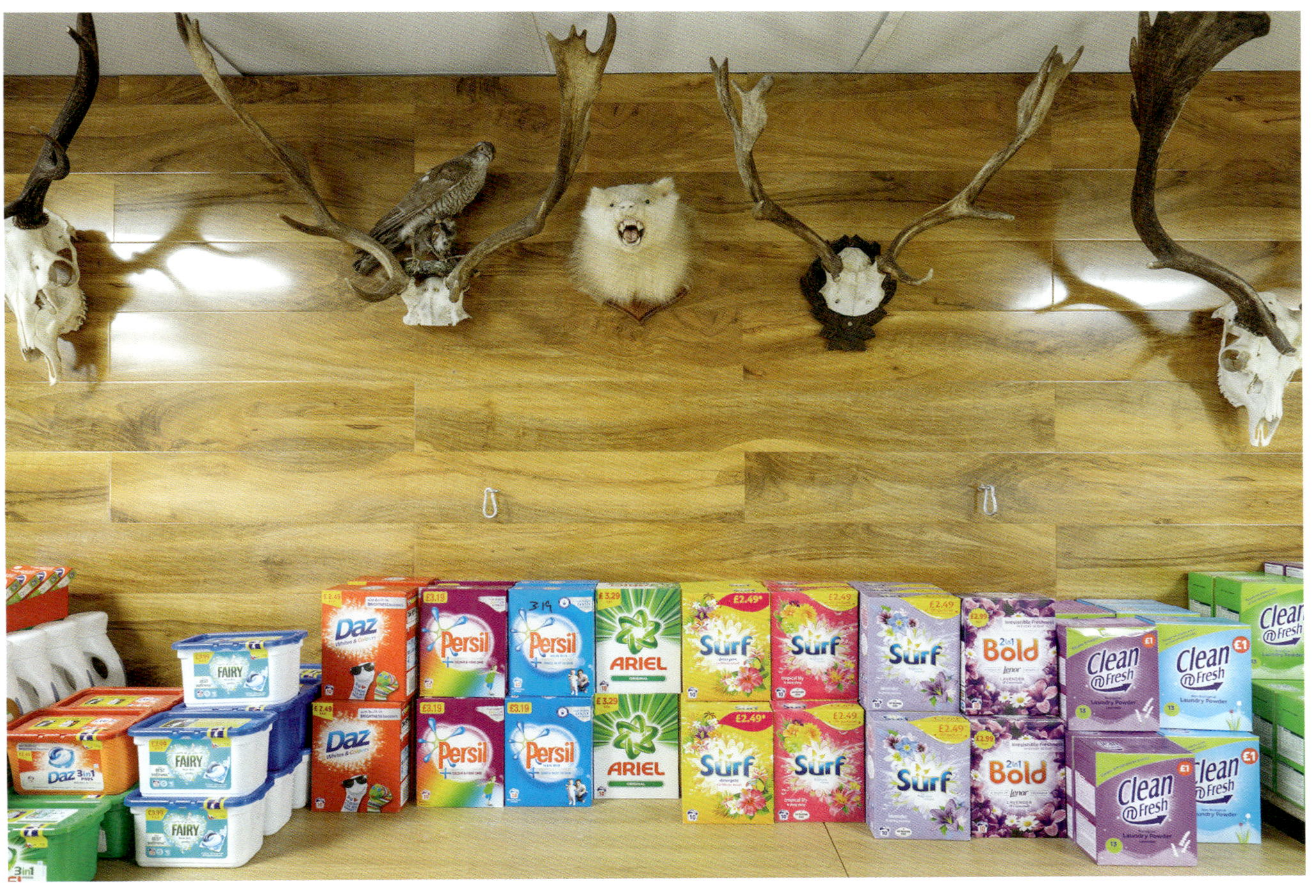

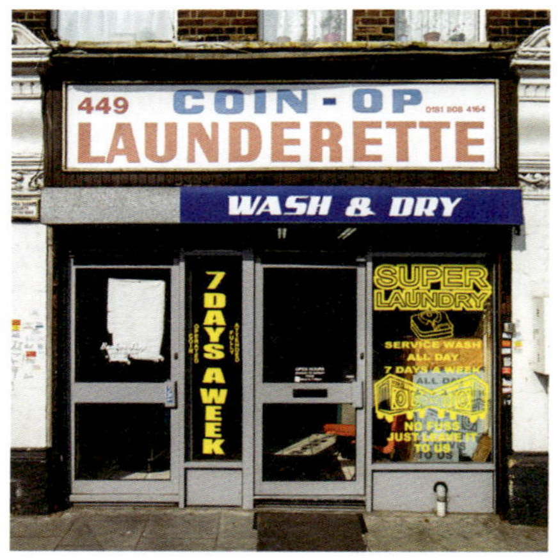

449
COIN - OP
0181 808 4164
LAUNDERETTE
WASH & DRY
7 DAYS A WEEK
SUPER LAUNDRY
SERVICE WASH ALL DAY 7 DAYS A WEEK ALL DAY
NO FUSS JUST LEAVE IT TO US

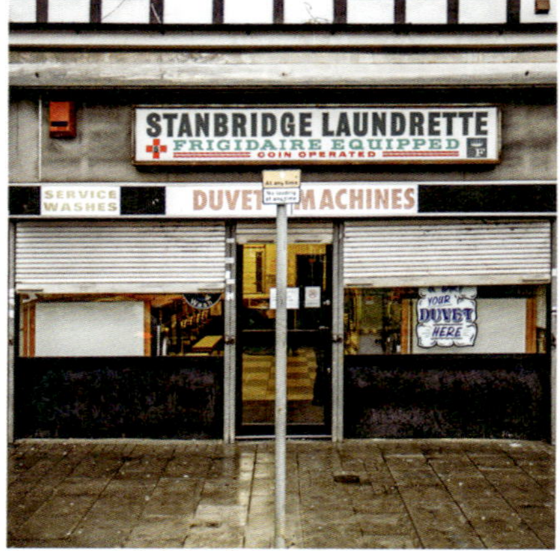

STANBRIDGE LAUNDRETTE
FRIGIDAIRE EQUIPPED
COIN OPERATED
SERVICE WASHES
DUVET MACHINES
YOUR DUVET HERE

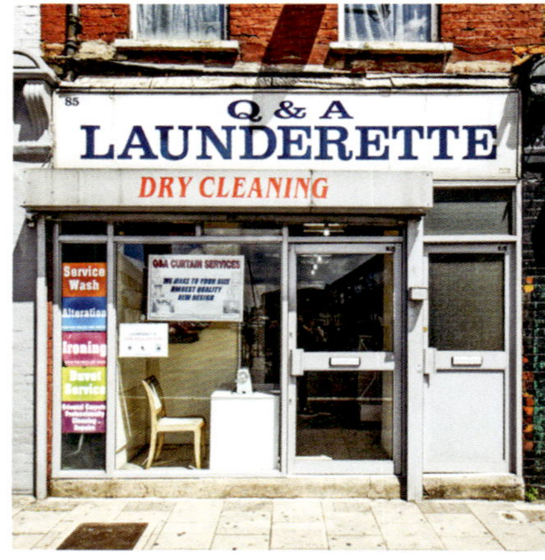

85
Q & A
LAUNDERETTE
DRY CLEANING
Service Wash
Alteration
Ironing
Duvet Service
Q&A CURTAIN SERVICES

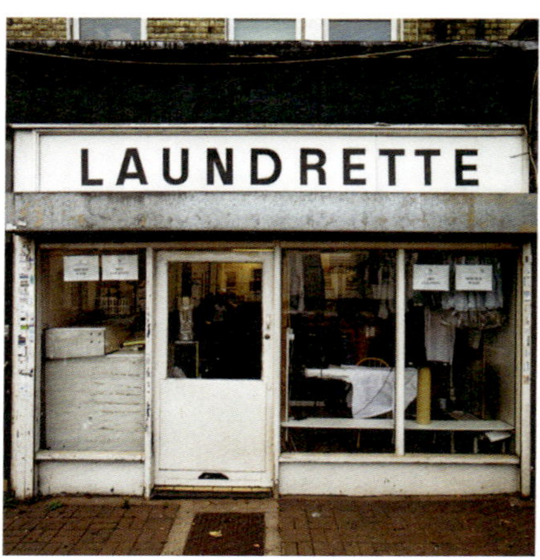

LAUNDRETTE

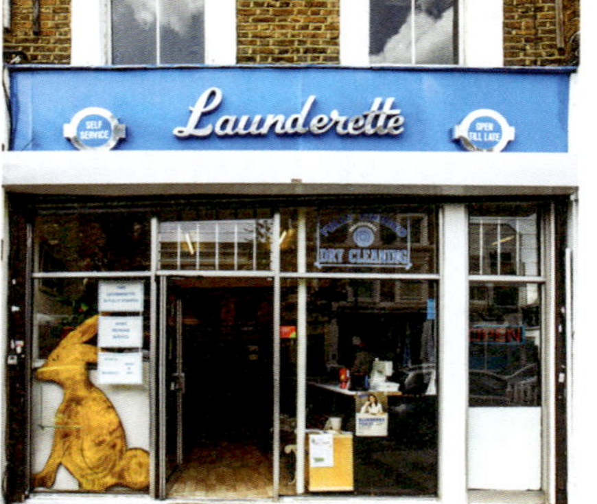

SELF SERVICE
Launderette
OPEN TILL LATE
DRY CLEANING

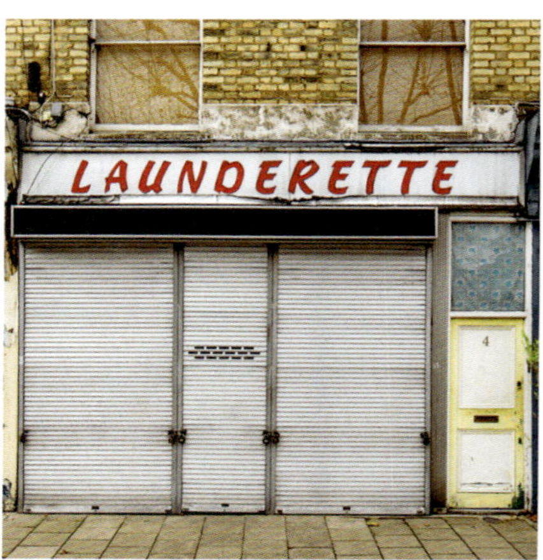

LAUNDERETTE
4

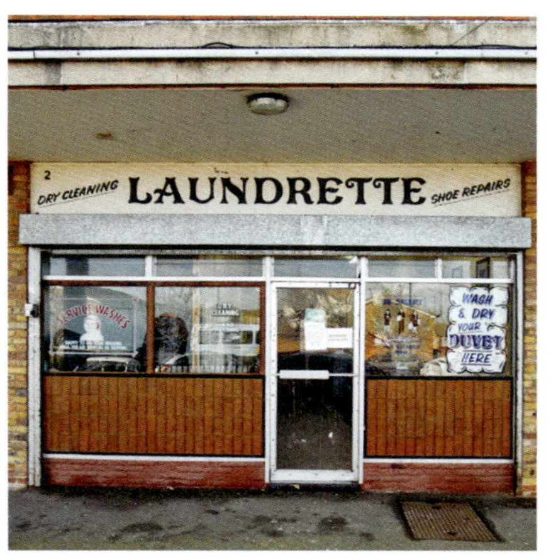
2
DRY CLEANING
LAUNDRETTE
SHOE REPAIRS
WASH & DRY YOUR DUVET HERE

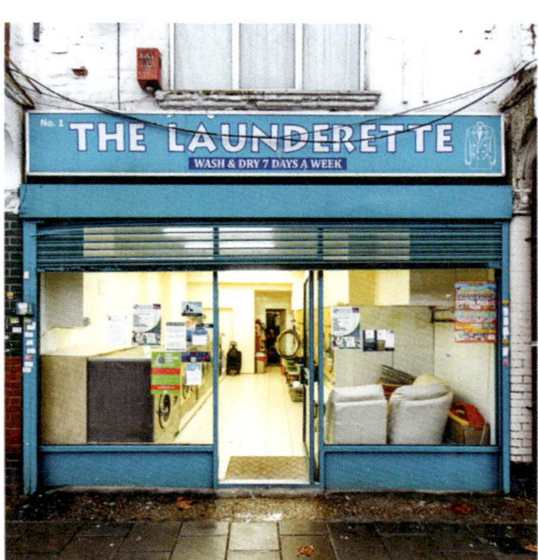
No. 1
THE LAUNDERETTE
WASH & DRY 7 DAYS A WEEK

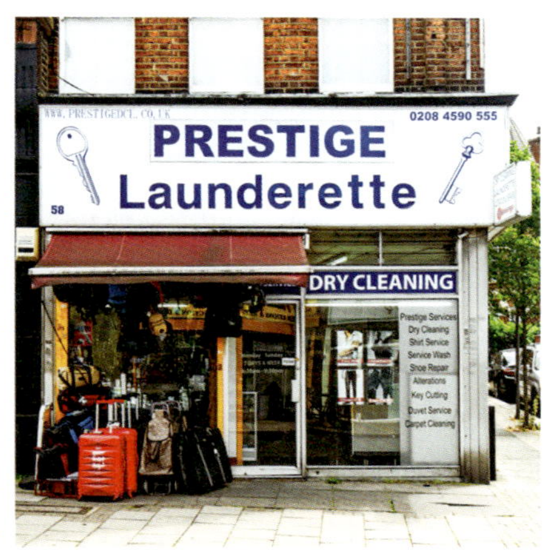
WWW.PRESTIGEDCL.CO.UK
0208 4590 555
PRESTIGE
Launderette
58
DRY CLEANING
Prestige Services
Dry Cleaning
Shirt Service
Service Wash
Shoe Repair
Alterations
Key Cutting
Duvet Service
Carpet Cleaning

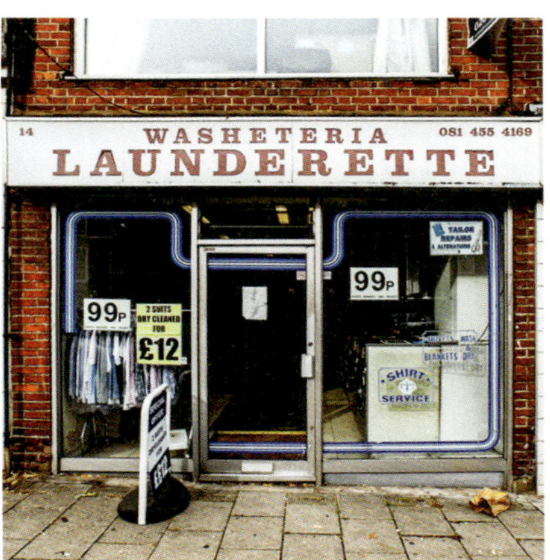
14
081 455 4169
WASHETERIA
LAUNDERETTE
TAILOR REPAIRS & ALTERATIONS
99p
99p
2 SUITS DRY CLEANED FOR £12
SHIRT SERVICE

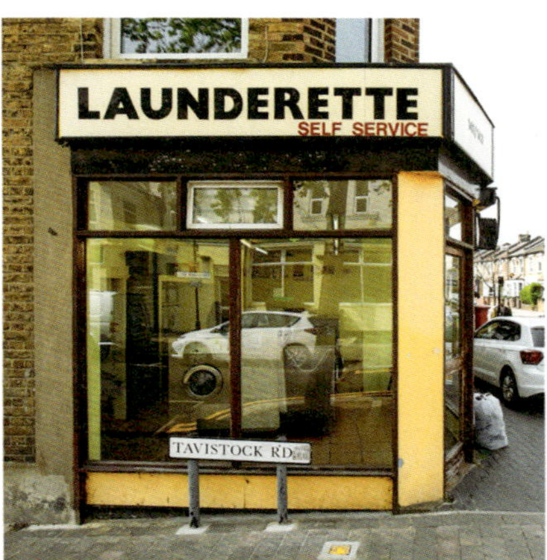
LAUNDERETTE
SELF SERVICE
TAVISTOCK RD

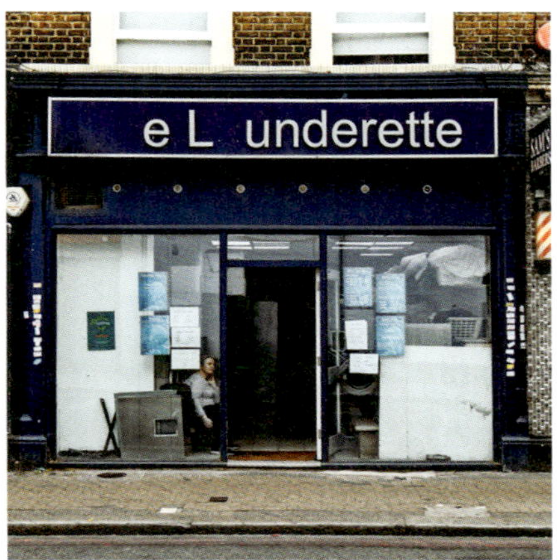
e L underette

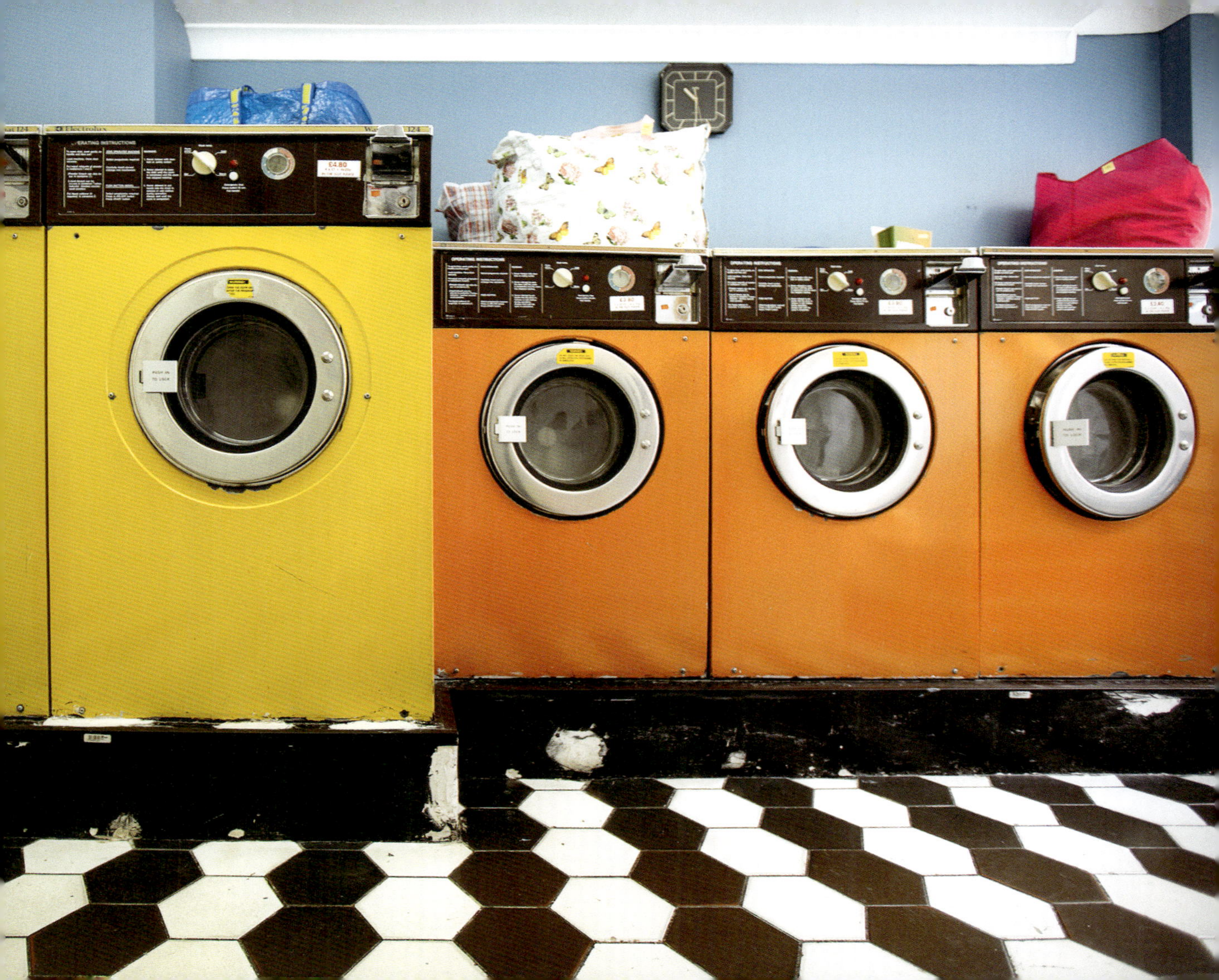

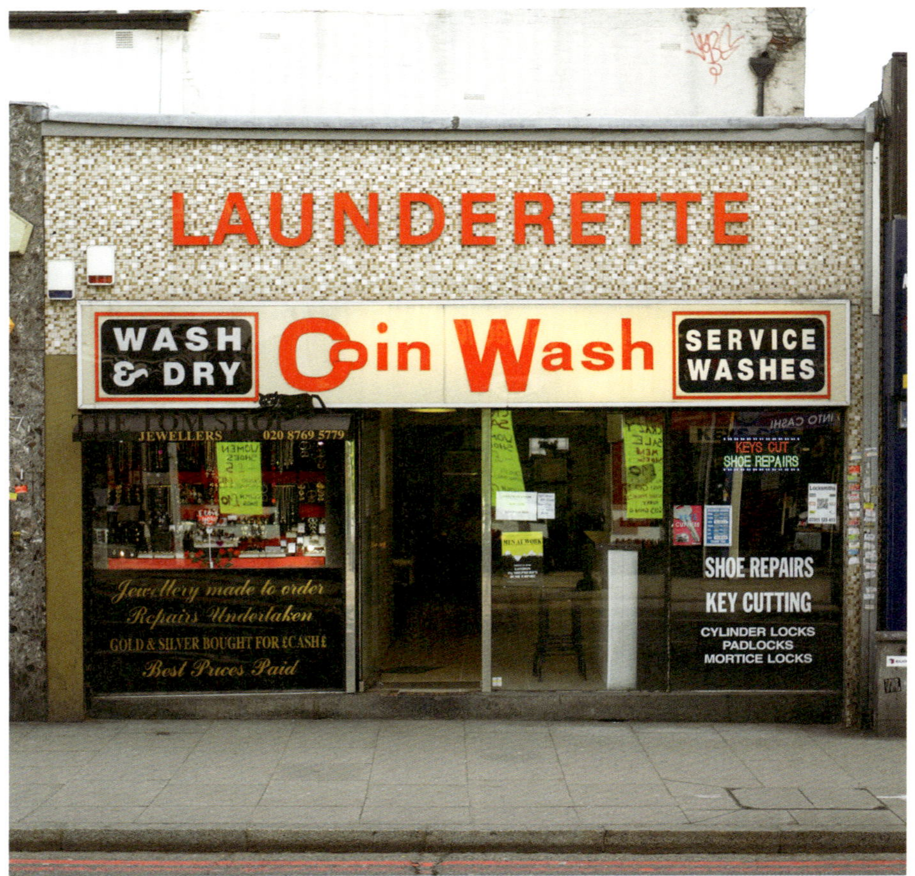

LAUNDERETTE
WASH & DRY
Coin Wash
SERVICE WASHES
JEWELLERS   020 8769 5779
Jewellery made to order
Repairs Undertaken
GOLD & SILVER BOUGHT FOR £CASH£
Best Prices Paid
KEYS CUT
SHOE REPAIRS
SHOE REPAIRS
KEY CUTTING
CYLINDER LOCKS
PADLOCKS
MORTICE LOCKS

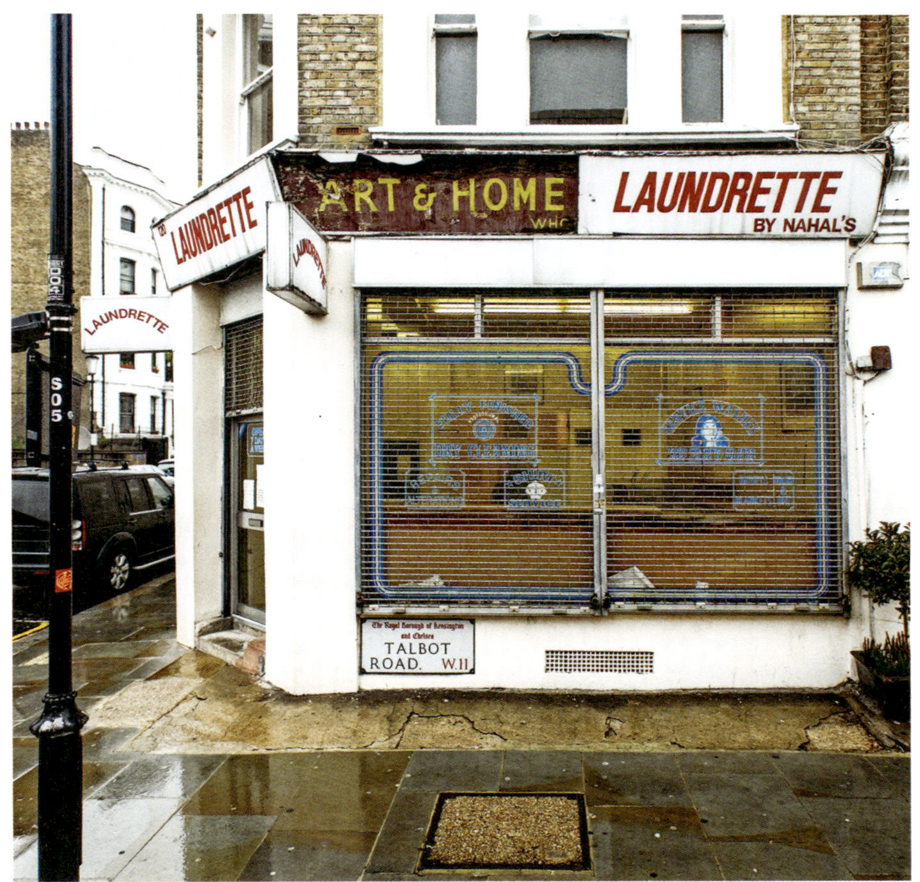
LAUNDRETTE
LAUNDRETTE
LAUNDRETTE
ART & HOME
LAUNDRETTE
BY NAHAL'S
DRY CLEANING
SERVICE
The Royal Borough of Kensington
and Chelsea
TALBOT
ROAD. W.11

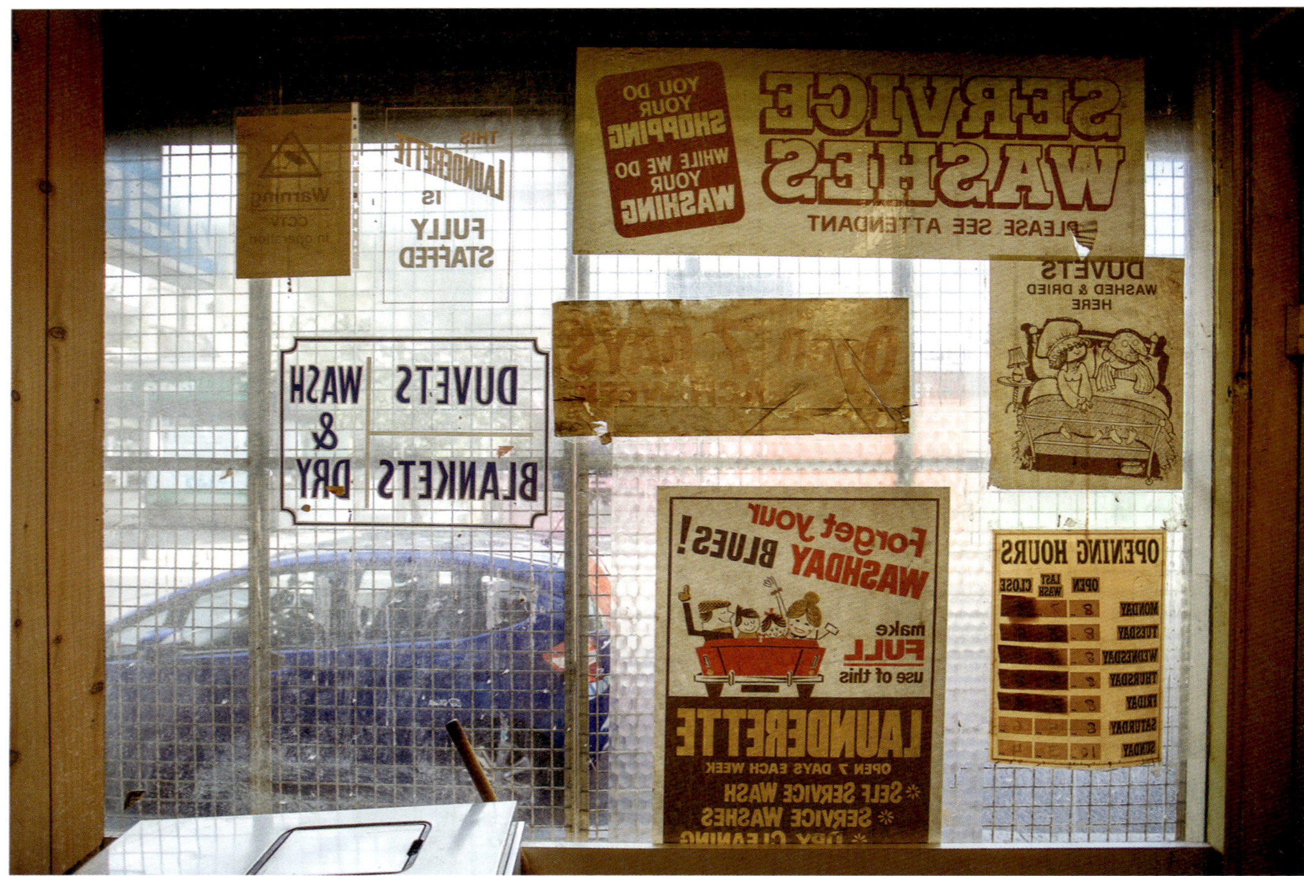
SERVICE WASHES
PLEASE SEE ATTENDANT
YOU DO YOUR SHOPPING
WHILE WE DO YOUR WASHING
THIS LAUNDERETTE IS FULLY STAFFED
Warning
CCTV in operation
DUVETS WASH & DRY BLANKETS
DUVETS WASHED & DRIED HERE
Forget your WASHDAY BLUES!
make FULL use of this
LAUNDERETTE
OPEN 7 DAYS EACH WEEK
* SELF SERVICE WASH
* SERVICE WASHES
* DRY CLEANING
OPENING HOURS
OPEN LAST WASH CLOSE
MONDAY
TUESDAY
WEDNESDAY
THURSDAY
FRIDAY
SATURDAY
SUNDAY

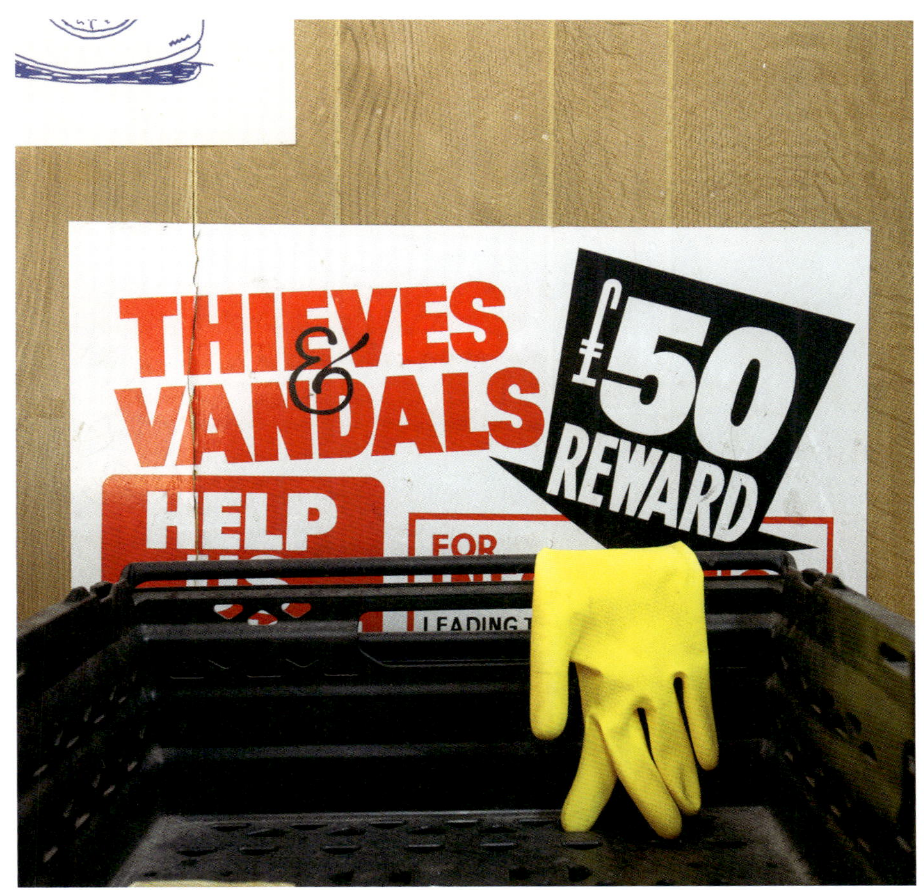
THIEVES & VANDALS
£50 REWARD
HELP
FOR
LEADING

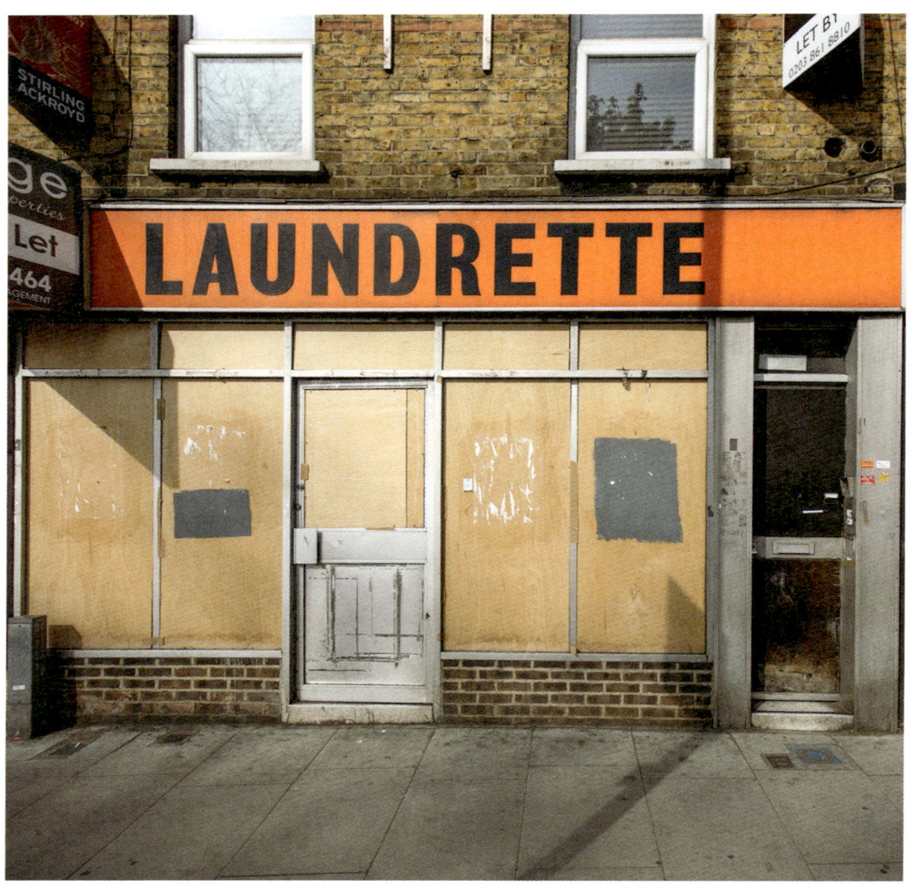
STIRLING
ACKROYD
perties
Let
464
AGEMENT
LAUNDRETTE
LET BY
0203 861 8810

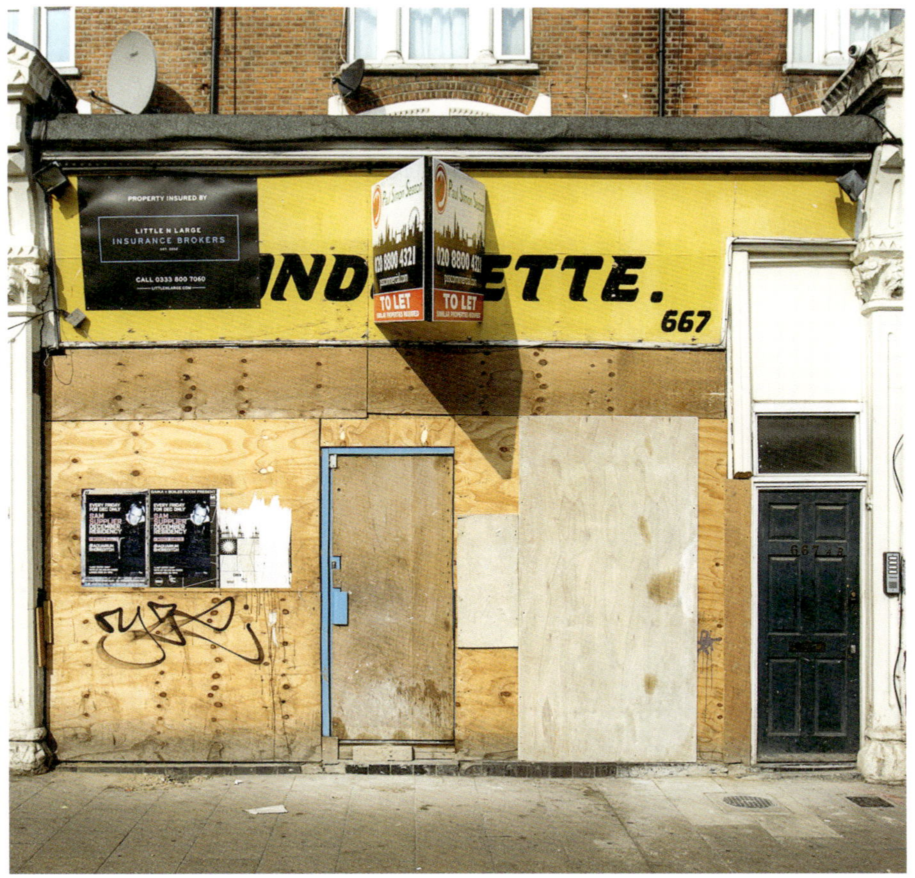
PROPERTY INSURED BY
LITTLE N LARGE
INSURANCE BROKERS
CALL 0333 800 7060
Paul Simon Sutton
020 8800 4321
Paul Simon Sutton
020 8800 4321
TO LET
TO LET
NDETTE.
667
667

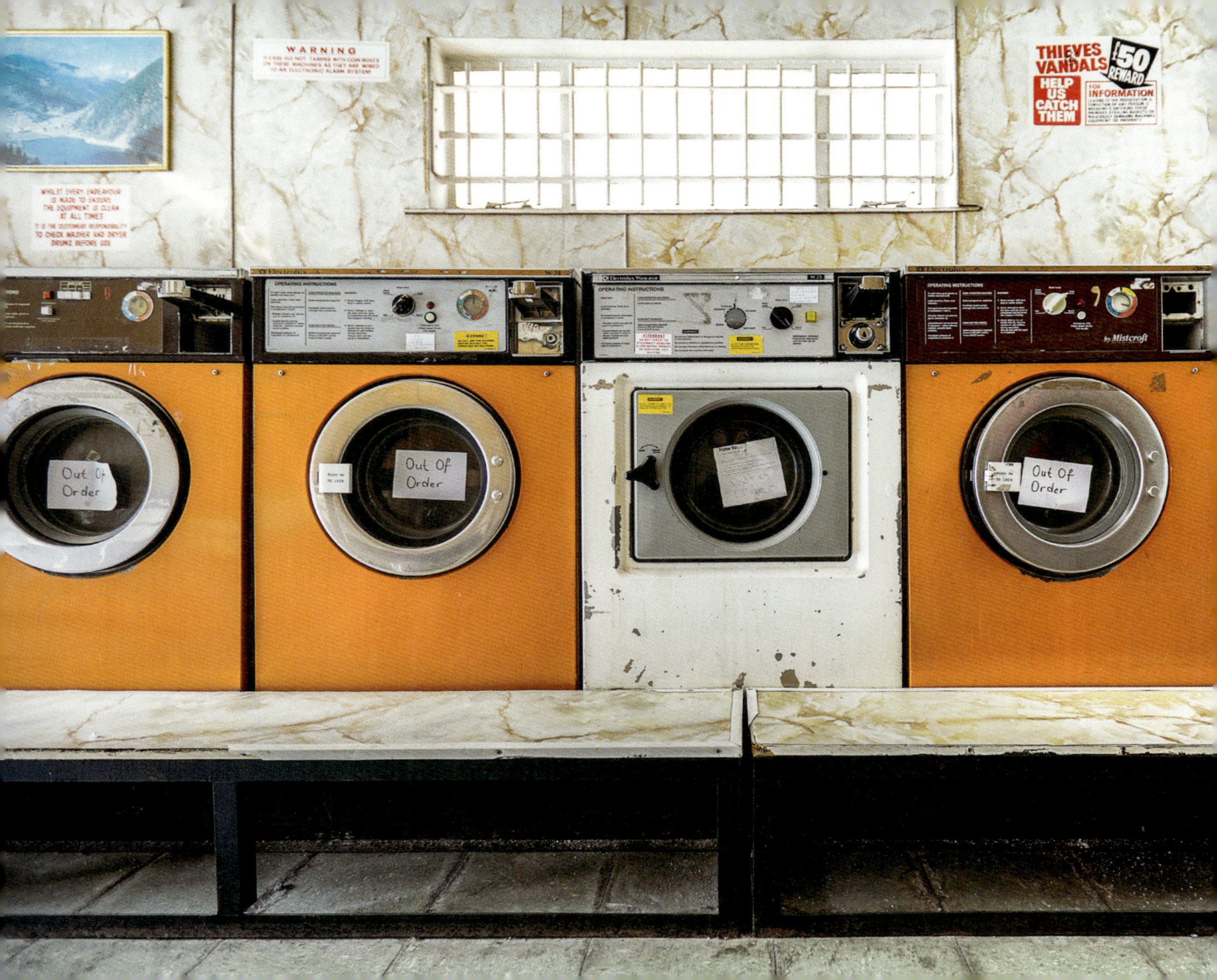

WARNING
THIEVES VANDALS £50 REWARD
HELP US CATCH THEM
Out Of Order
Out Of Order
Out Of Order
OPERATING INSTRUCTIONS
by Mistcroft
Electrolux

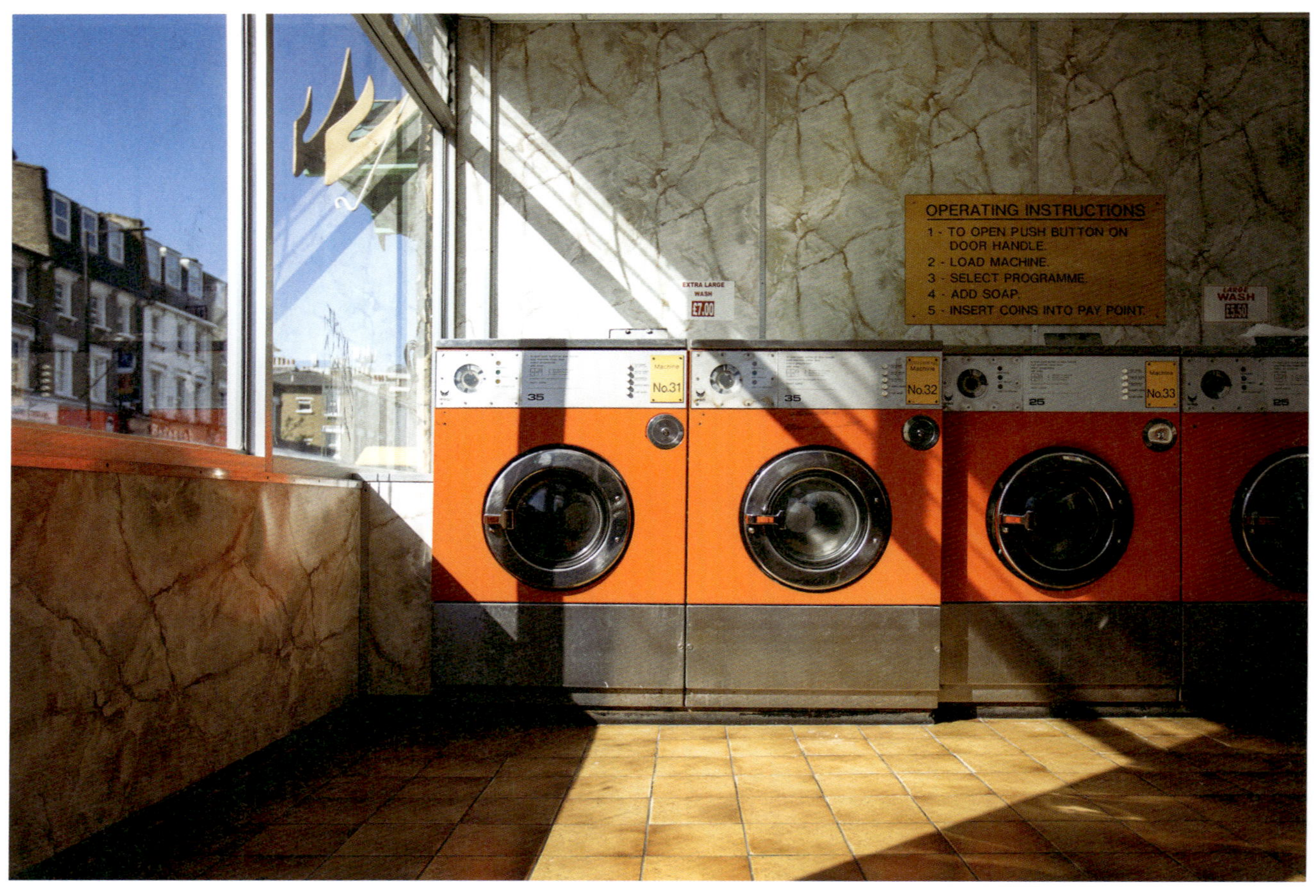
OPERATING INSTRUCTIONS
1 - TO OPEN PUSH BUTTON ON
    DOOR HANDLE.
2 - LOAD MACHINE.
3 - SELECT PROGRAMME.
4 - ADD SOAP.
5 - INSERT COINS INTO PAY POINT.
EXTRA LARGE WASH £7.00
LARGE WASH £3.50
Machine No.31
Machine No.32
Machine No.33
35
35
25
25

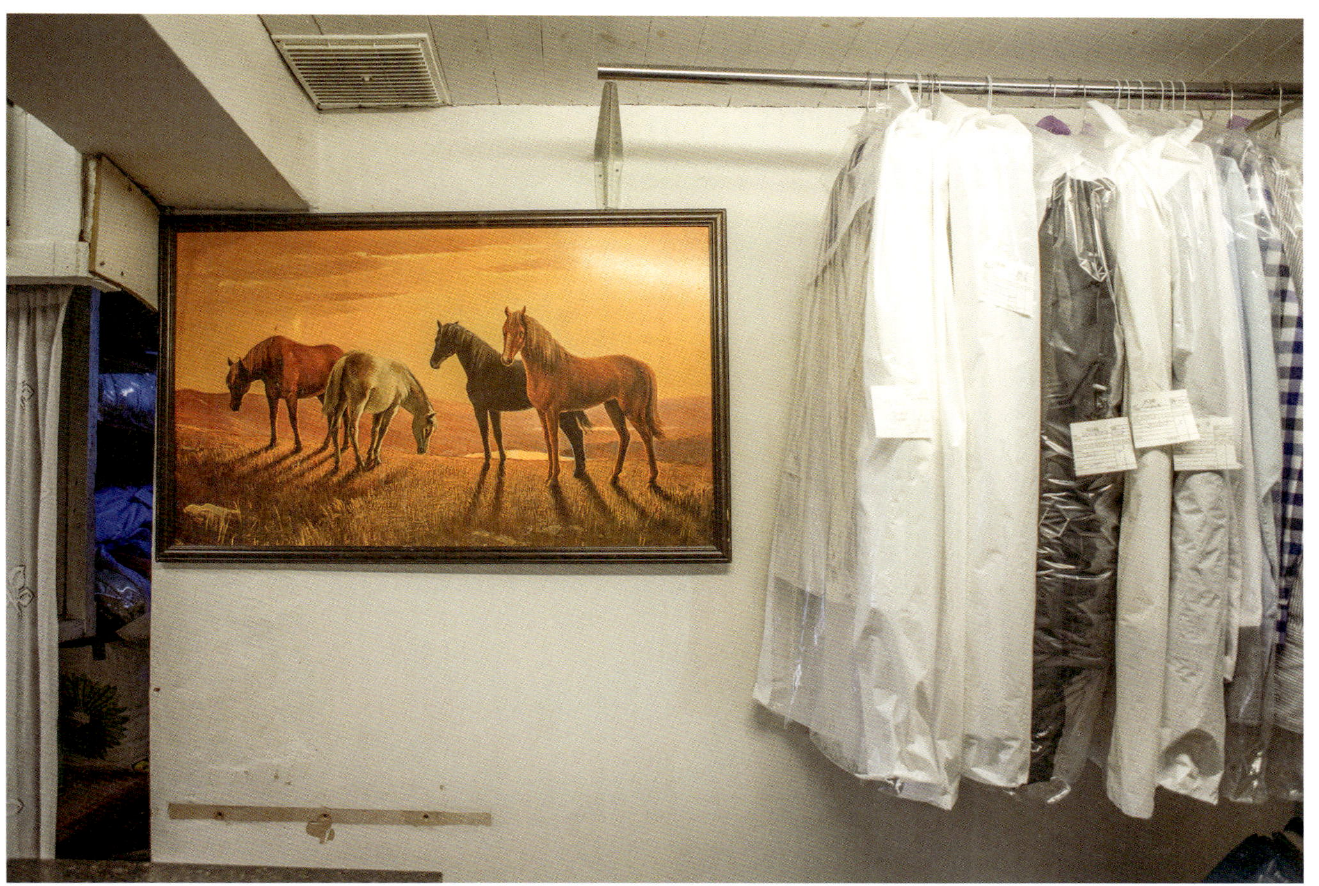

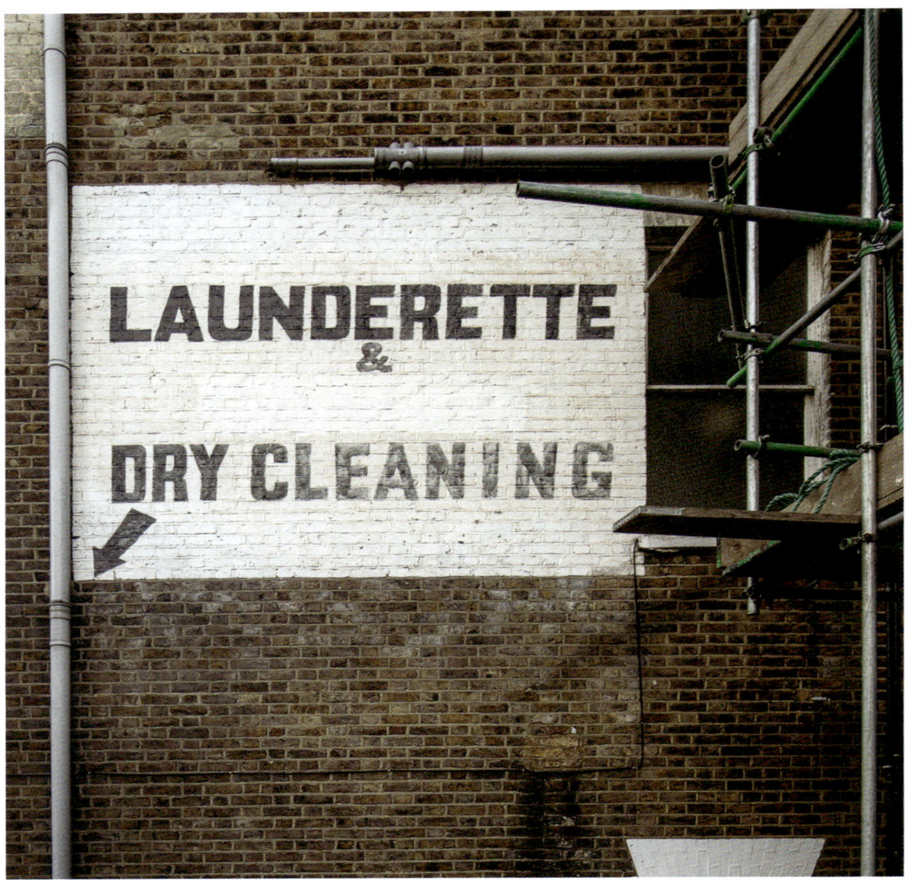

LAUNDERETTE
&
DRY CLEANING

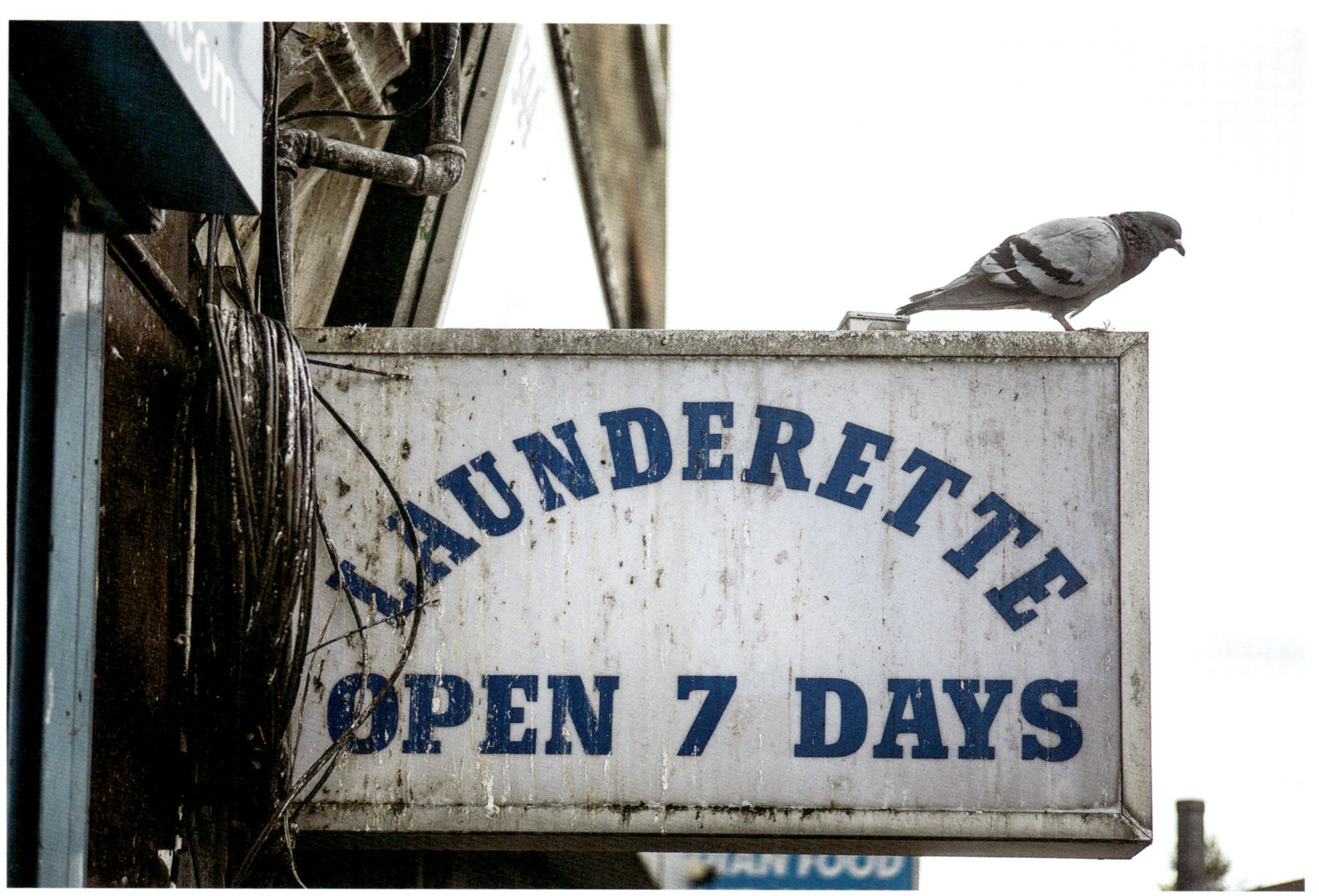

LAUNDERETTE
OPEN 7 DAYS

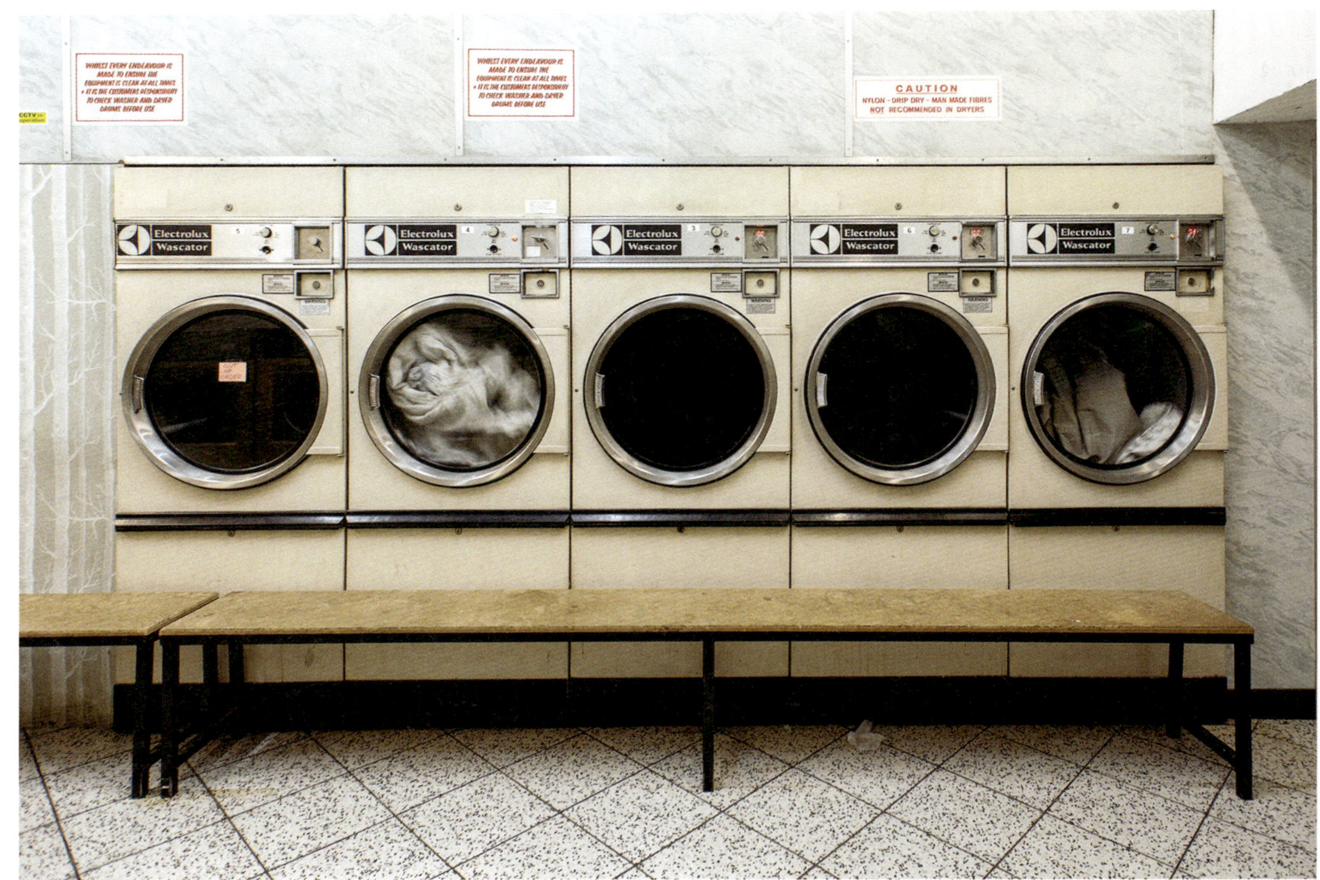

WHILST EVERY ENDEAVOUR IS MADE TO ENSURE THE EQUIPMENT IS CLEAN AT ALL TIMES • IT IS THE CUSTOMERS RESPONSIBILITY TO CHECK WASHER AND DRYER DRUMS BEFORE USE
WHILST EVERY ENDEAVOUR IS MADE TO ENSURE THE EQUIPMENT IS CLEAN AT ALL TIMES • IT IS THE CUSTOMERS RESPONSIBILITY TO CHECK WASHER AND DRYER DRUMS BEFORE USE
CAUTION
NYLON - DRIP DRY - MAN MADE FIBRES NOT RECOMMENDED IN DRYERS
Electrolux Wascator
Electrolux Wascator
Electrolux Wascator
Electrolux Wascator
Electrolux Wascator

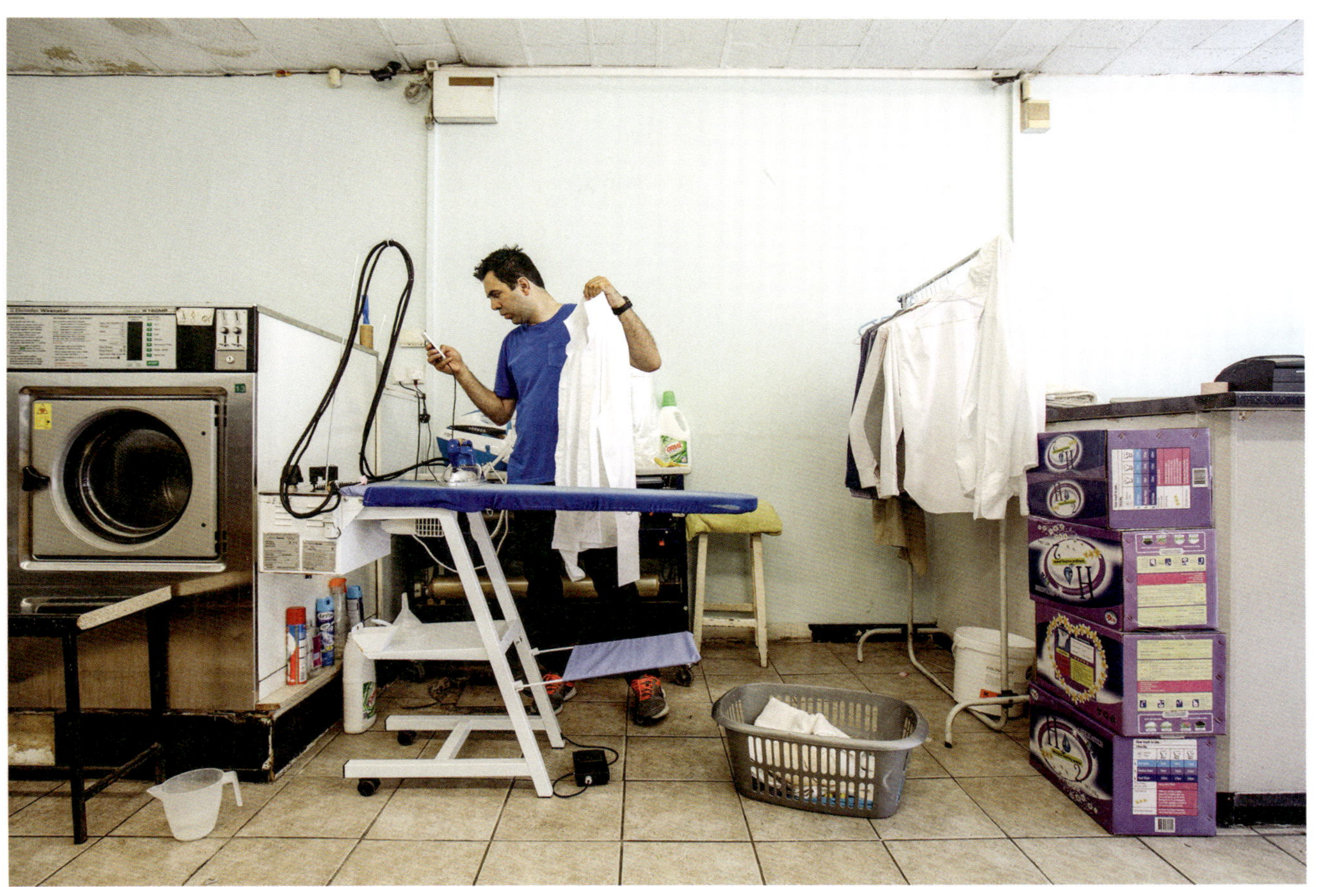

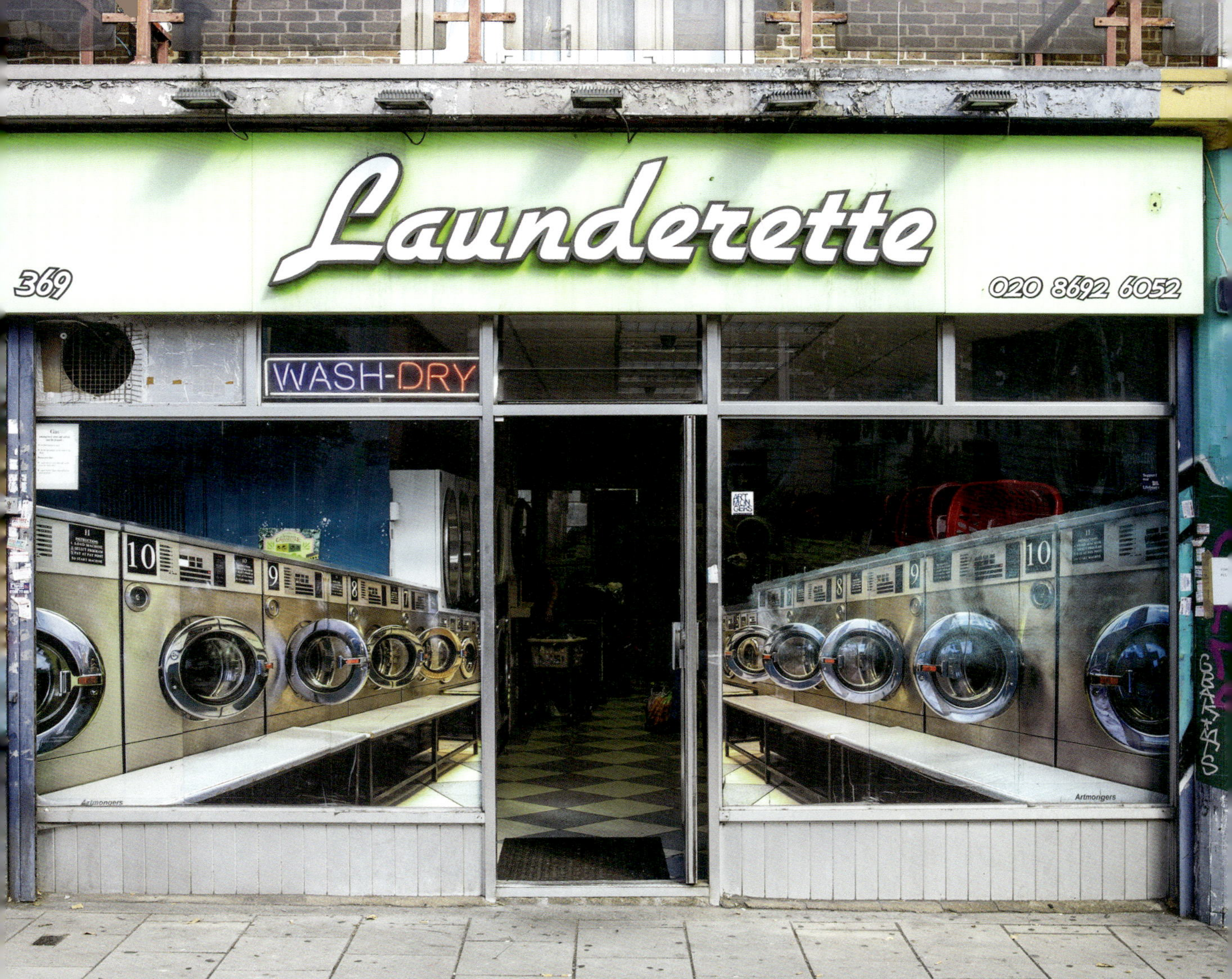

Launderette
369
020 8692 6052
WASH-DRY
10
9
8
10
9
8
Artmongers
Artmongers

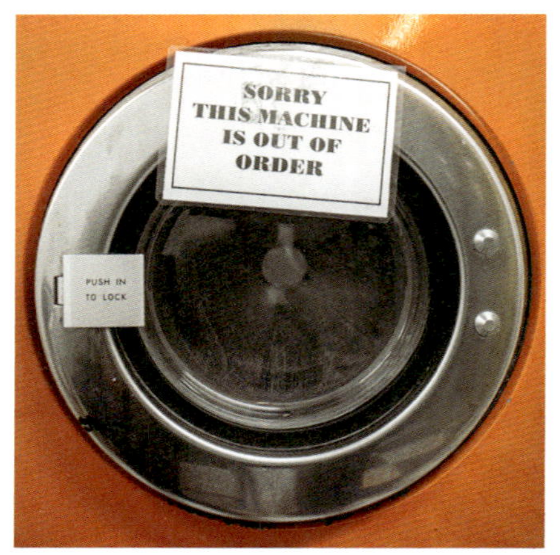
SORRY
THIS MACHINE
IS OUT OF
ORDER
PUSH IN
TO LOCK
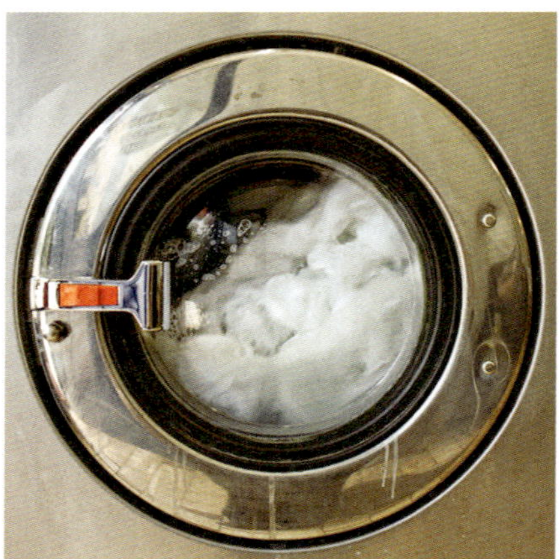
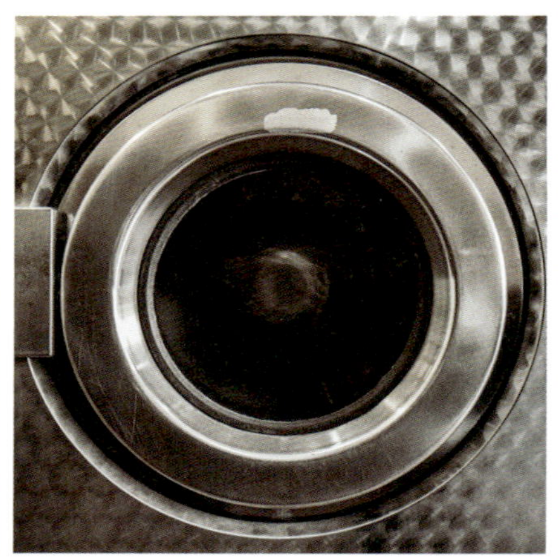
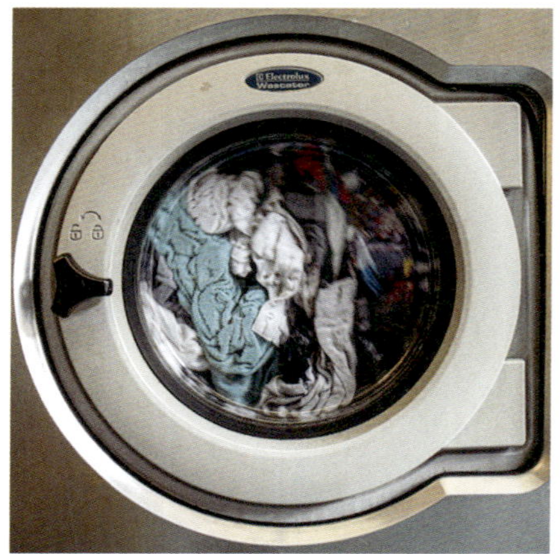
Electrolux
Wascator
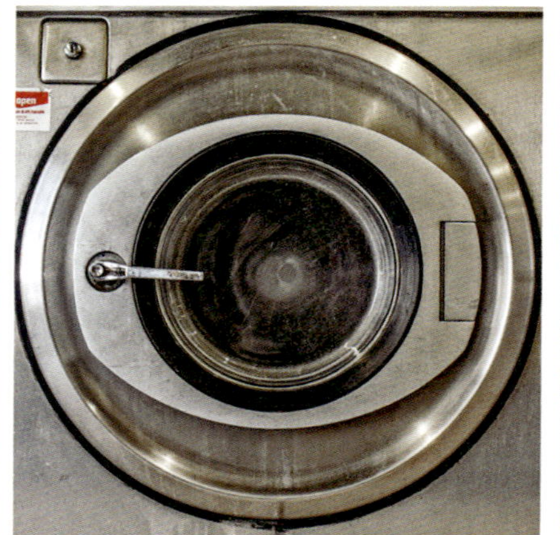
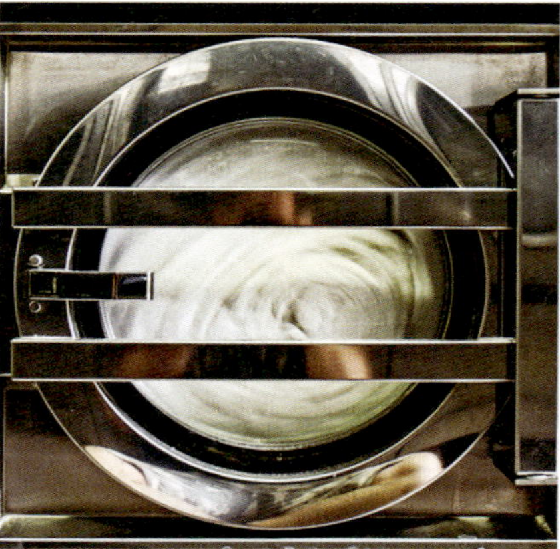

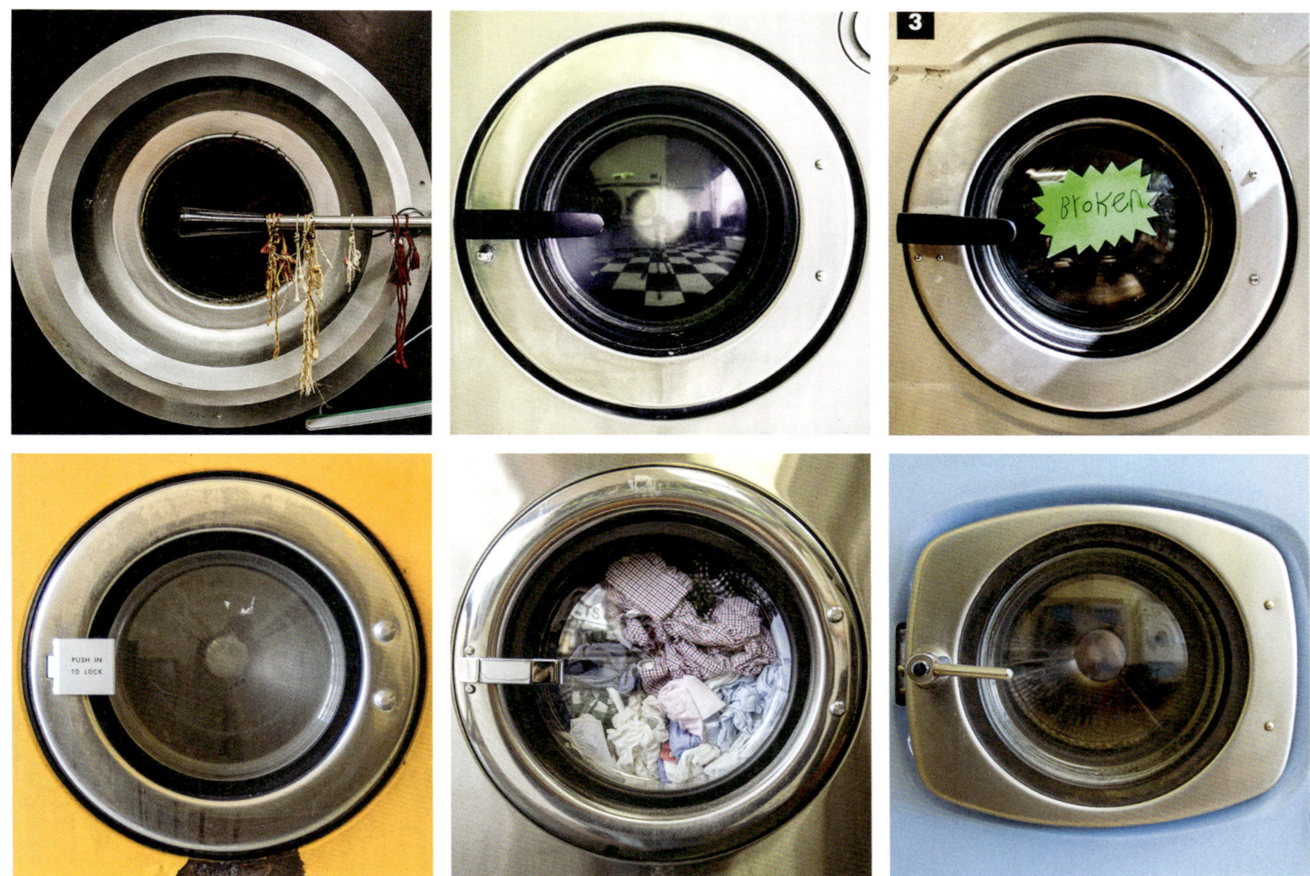
3
Broken
PUSH IN
TO LOCK

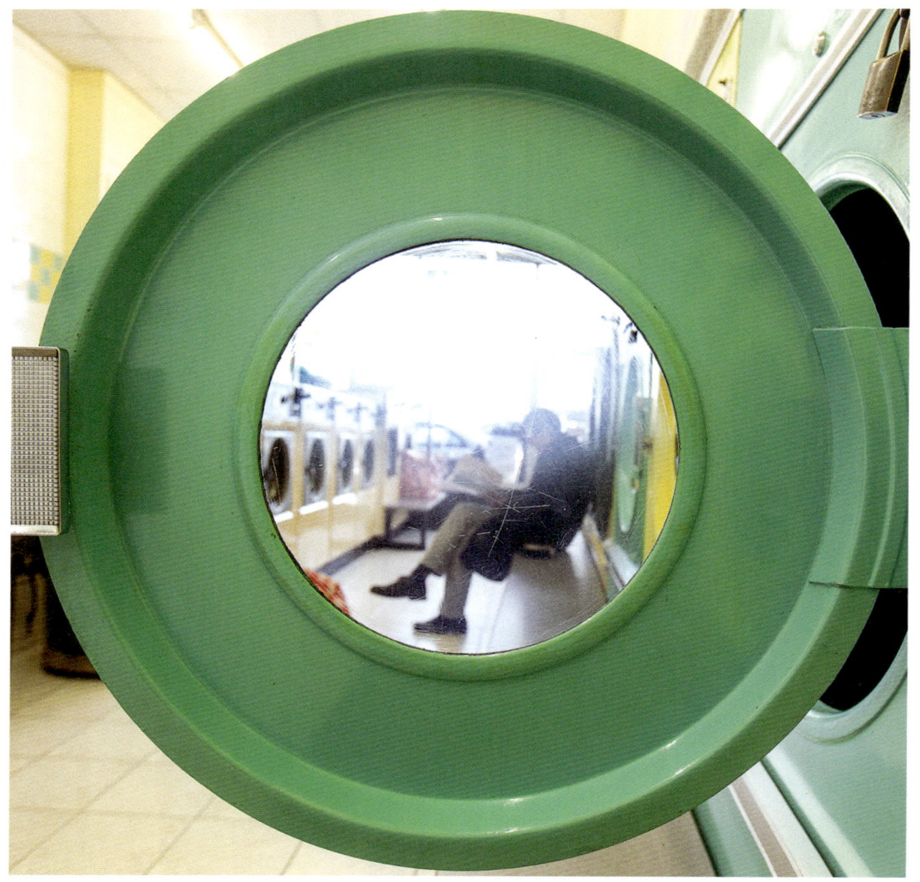

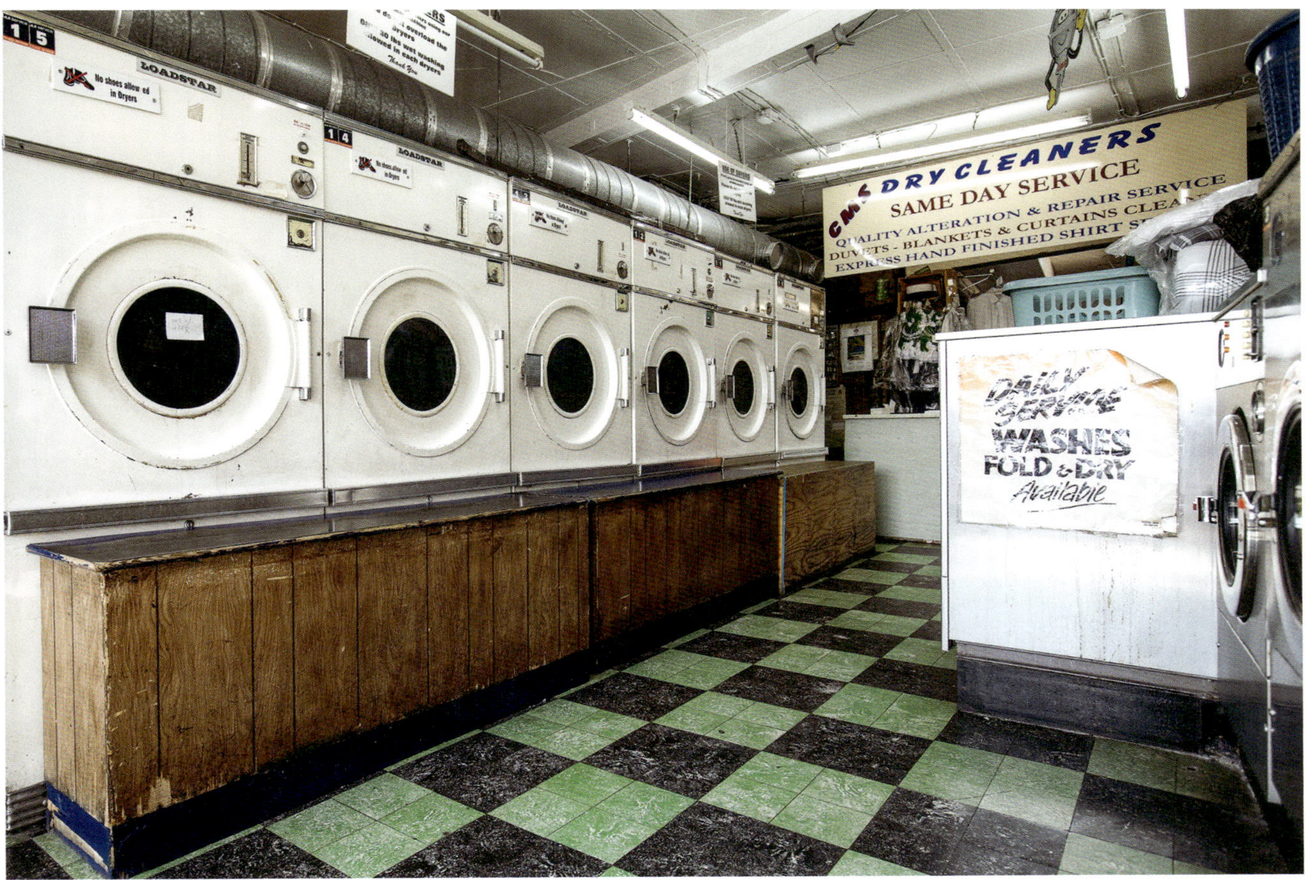
LOADSTAR
No shoes allowed in Dryers
1 5
1 4
CMS DRY CLEANERS
SAME DAY SERVICE
QUALITY ALTERATION & REPAIR SERVICE
DUVETS - BLANKETS & CURTAINS CLEANE
EXPRESS HAND FINISHED SHIRT S
WASHES
FOLD & DRY
Available

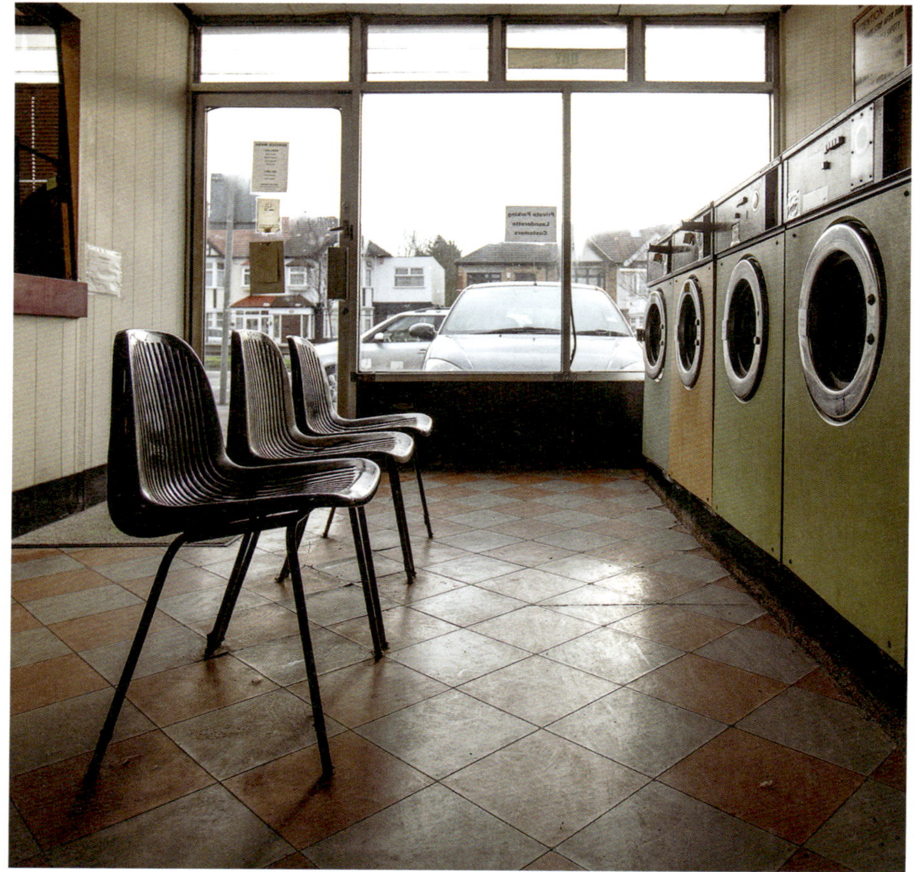

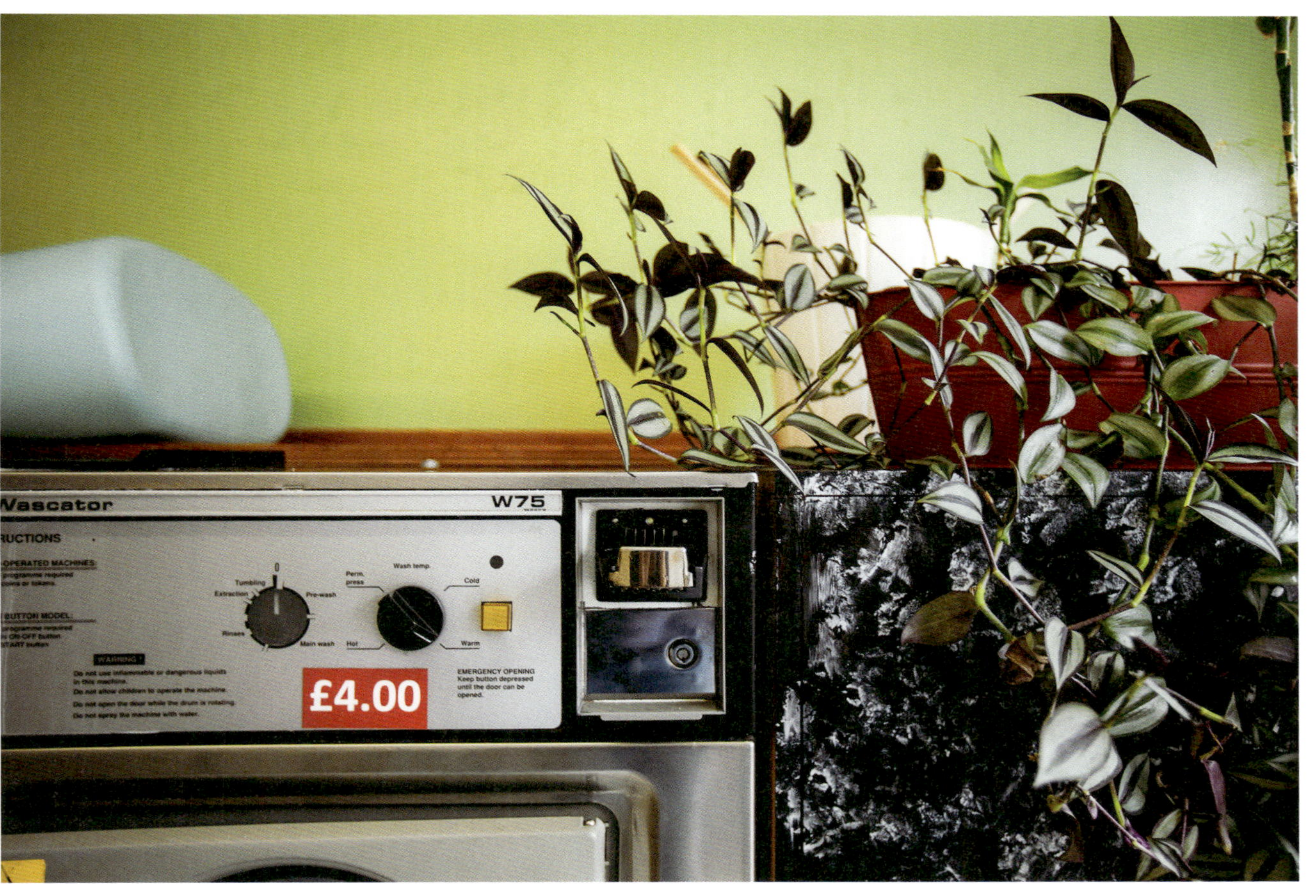
Wascator
W75
RUCTIONS
OPERATED MACHINES:
Tumbling
0
Wash temp.
Perm.
press
Extraction
Pre-wash
Cold
Rinses
Main wash
Hot
Warm
WARNING
Do not use inflammable or dangerous liquids
in this machine.
Do not allow children to operate the machine.
Do not open the door while the drum is rotating.
Do not spray the machine with water.
£4.00
EMERGENCY OPENING
Keep button depressed
until the door can be
opened.

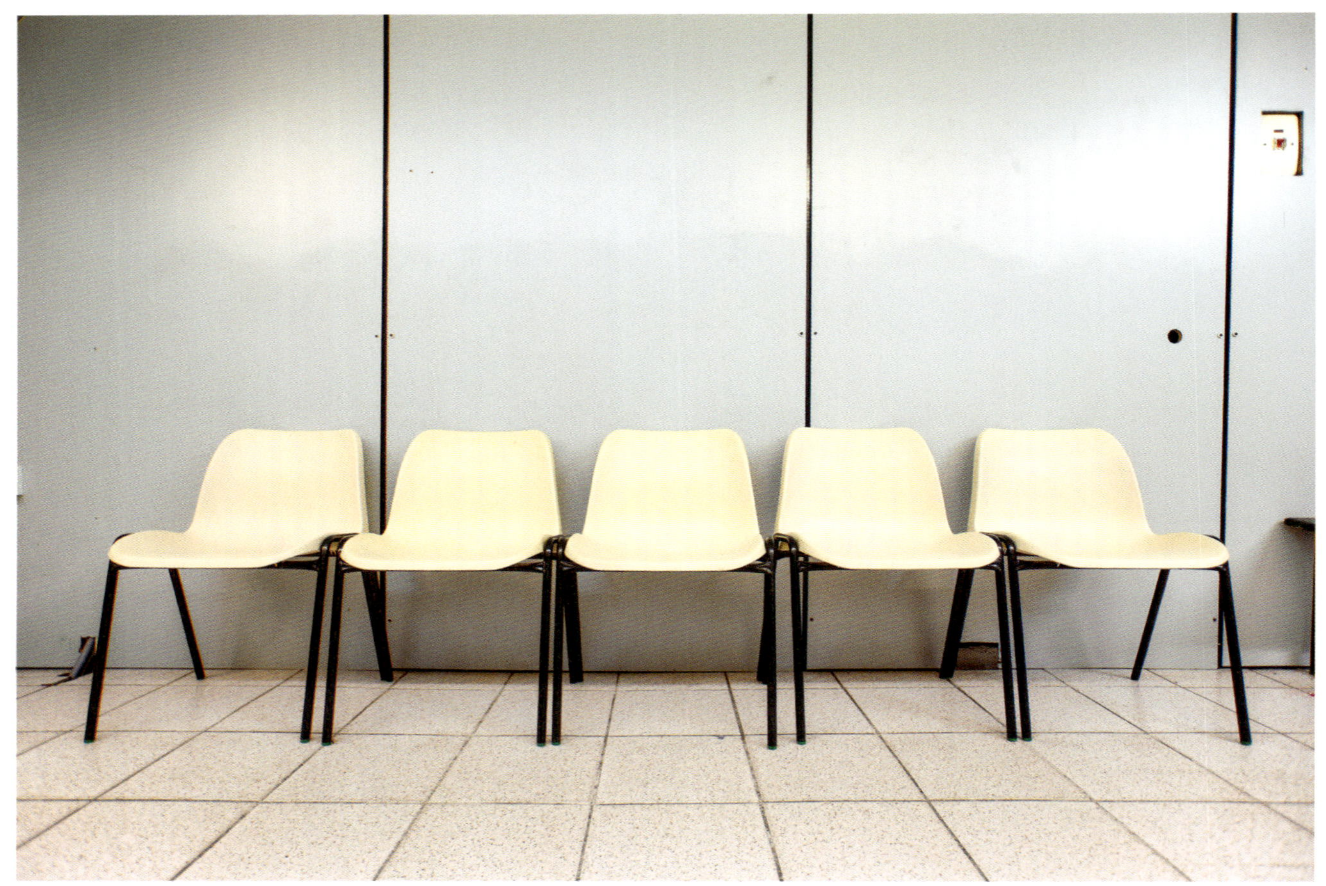

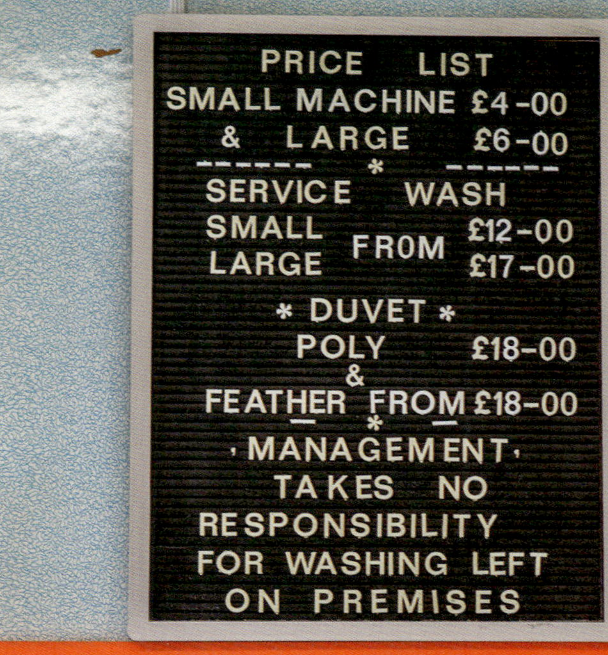

PRICE   LIST
SMALL MACHINE £4-00
& LARGE   £6-00
------ * ------
SERVICE   WASH
SMALL
LARGE   FROM   £12-00
£17-00
* DUVET *
POLY   £18-00
&
FEATHER FROM £18-00
- - * -
, MANAGEMENT,
TAKES   NO
RESPONSIBILITY
FOR WASHING LEFT
ON PREMISES
WASHER INSTRUCTIONS

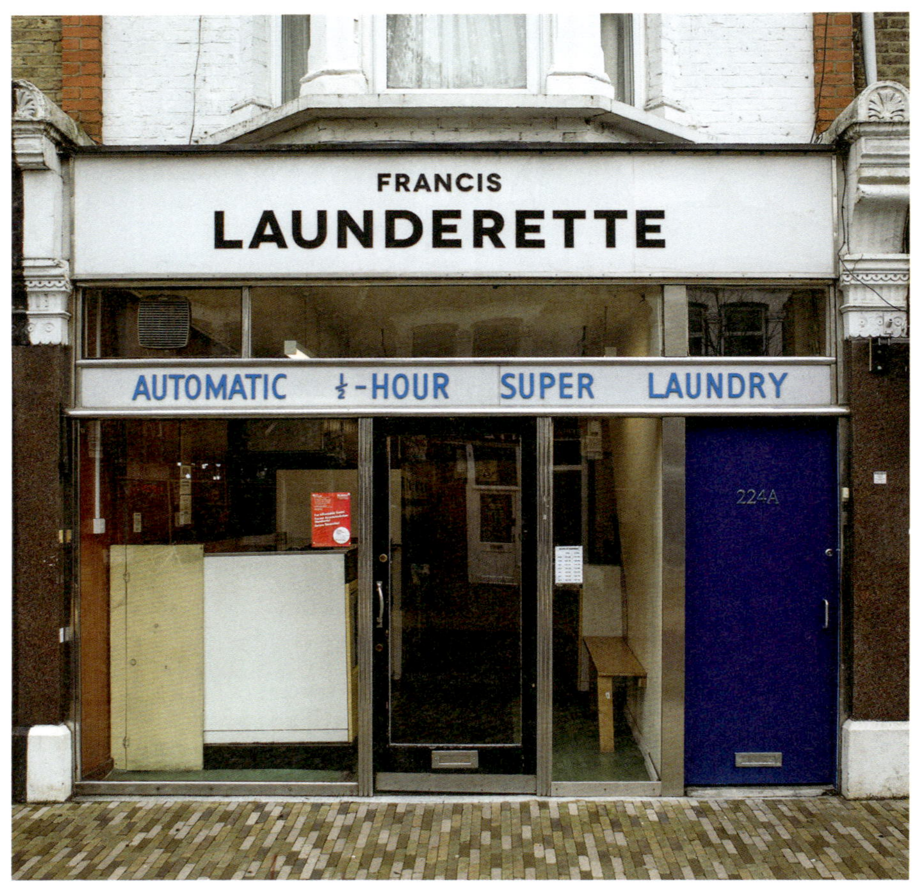
FRANCIS
LAUNDERETTE
AUTOMATIC ½-HOUR SUPER LAUNDRY
224A

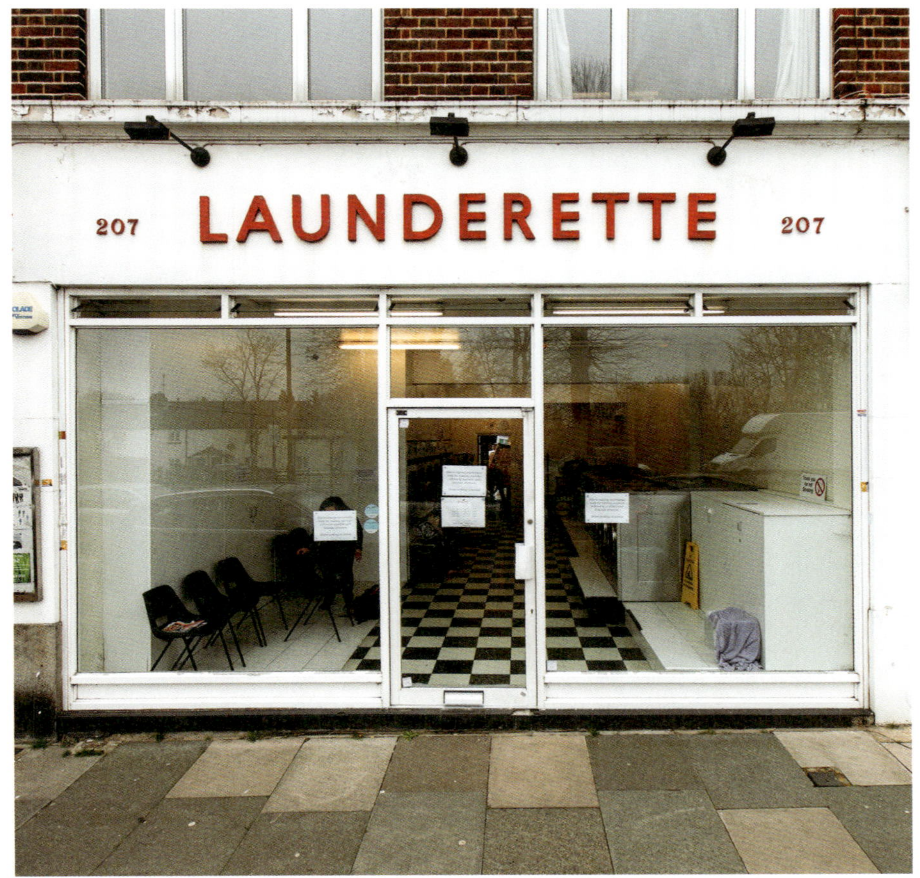

LAUNDERETTE
207
207

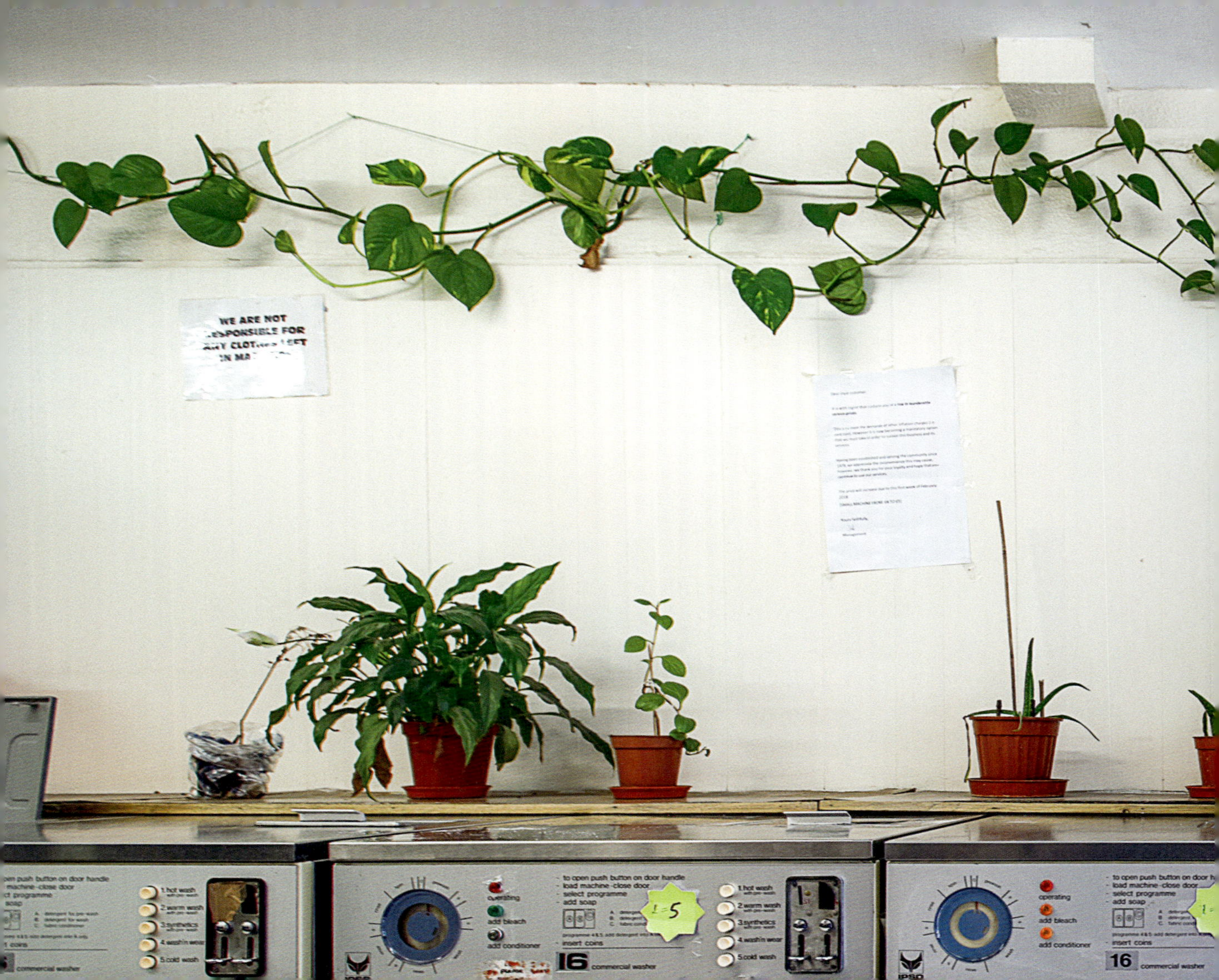

WE ARE NOT
RESPONSIBLE FOR
ANY CLOTHES LEFT
IN MA

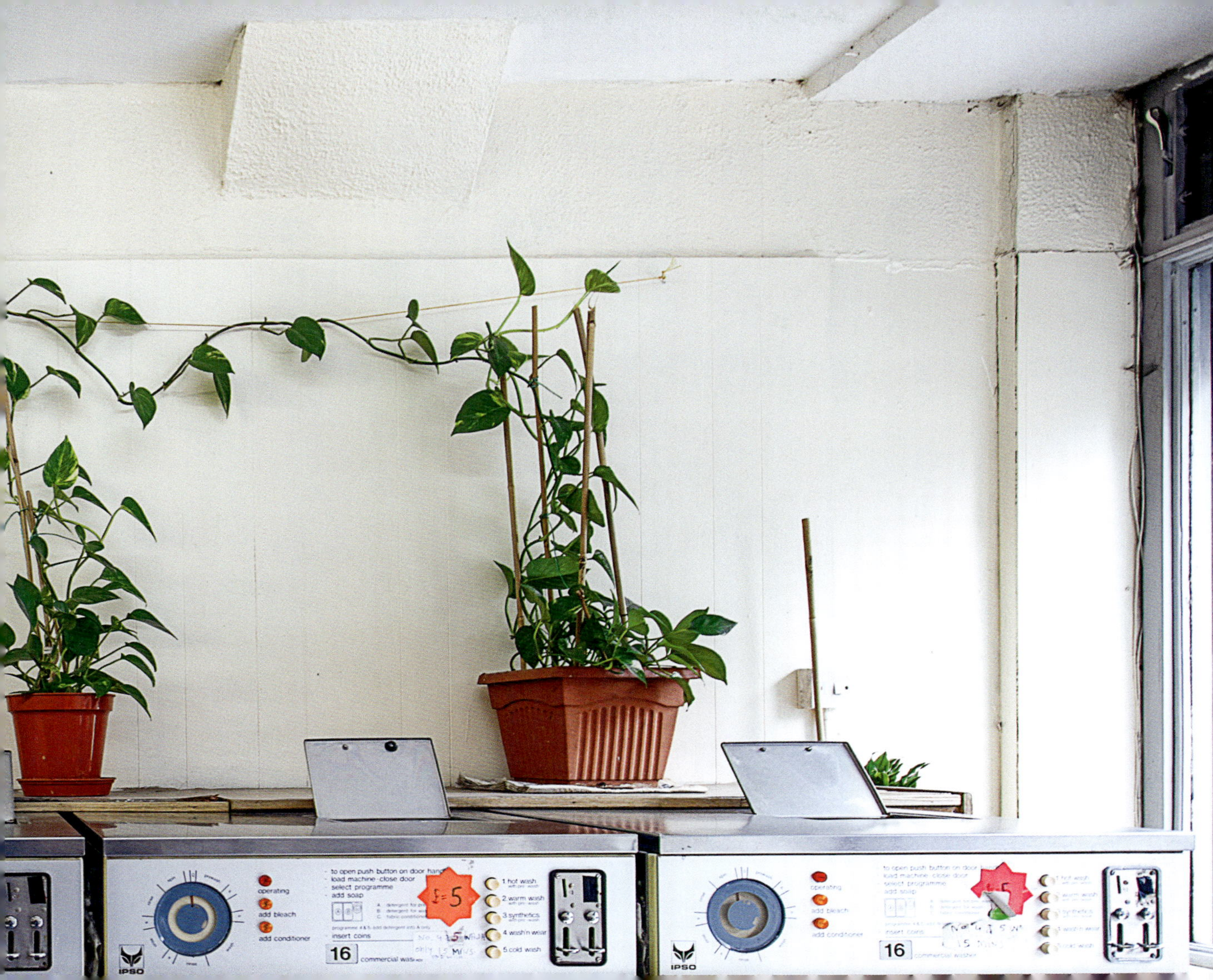
to open push button on door handle
load machine - close door
select programme
add soap
operating
add bleach
add conditioner
insert coins
16 commercial washer
£5
1 hot wash
2 warm wash
3 synthetics
4 wash'n wear
5 cold wash

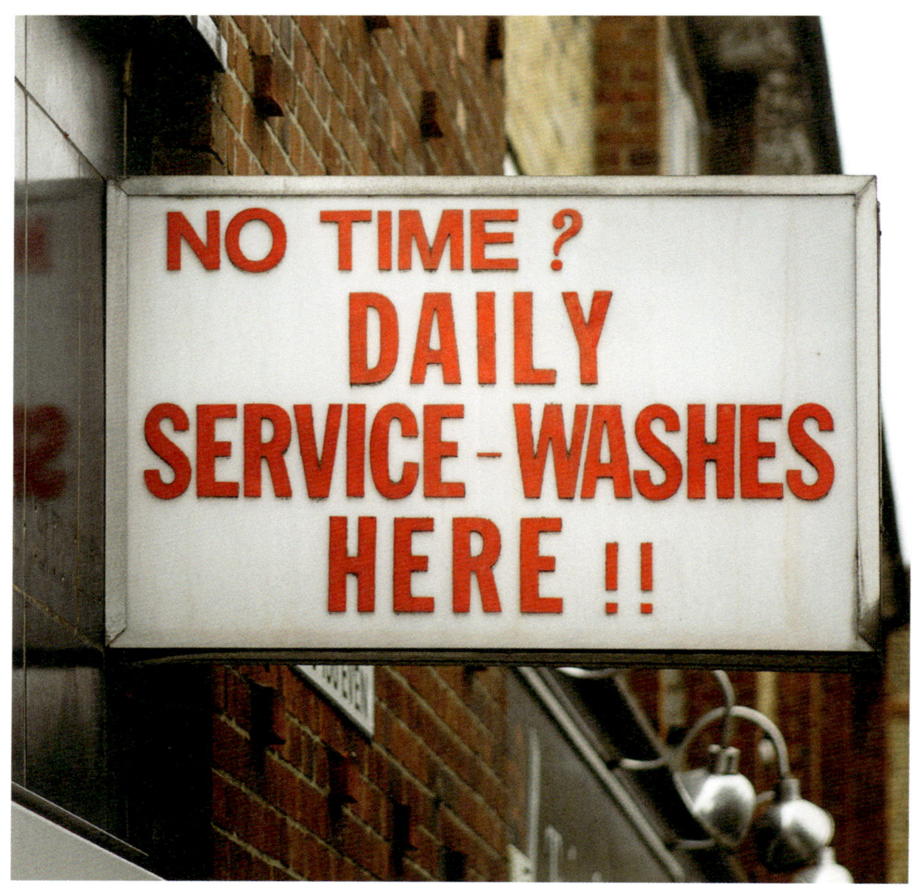

NO TIME ?
DAILY
SERVICE - WASHES
HERE !!

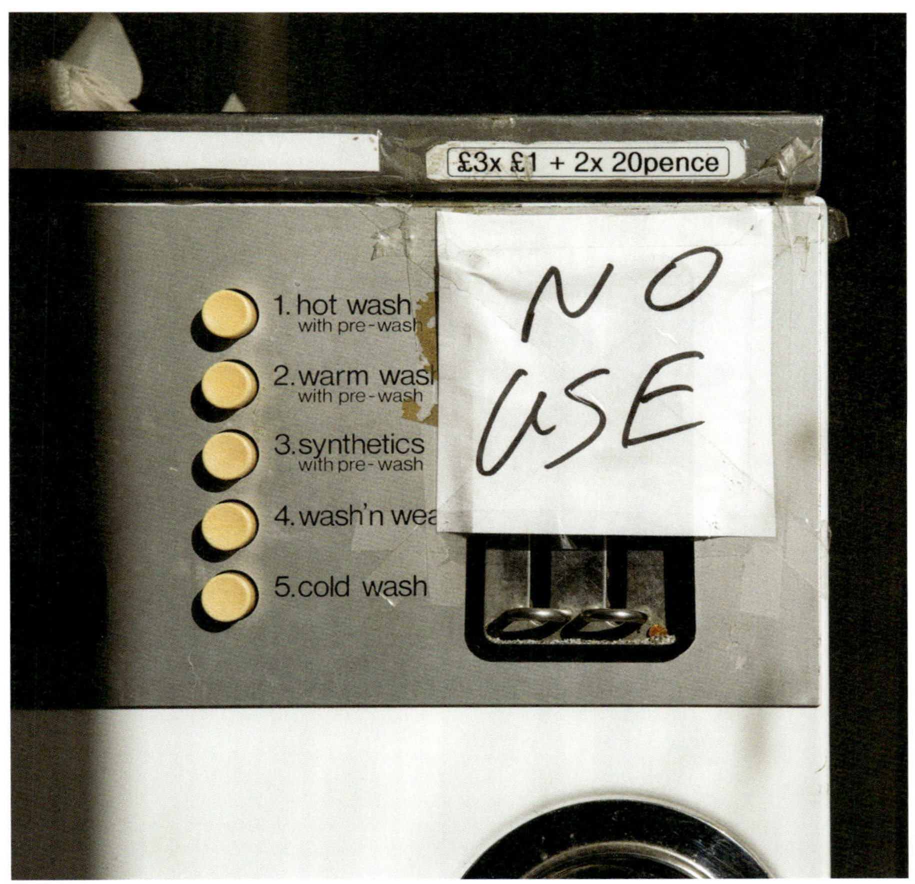
£3x £1 + 2x 20pence
NO USE
1. hot wash
with pre-wash
2. warm wash
with pre-wash
3. synthetics
with pre-wash
4. wash'n wear
5. cold wash

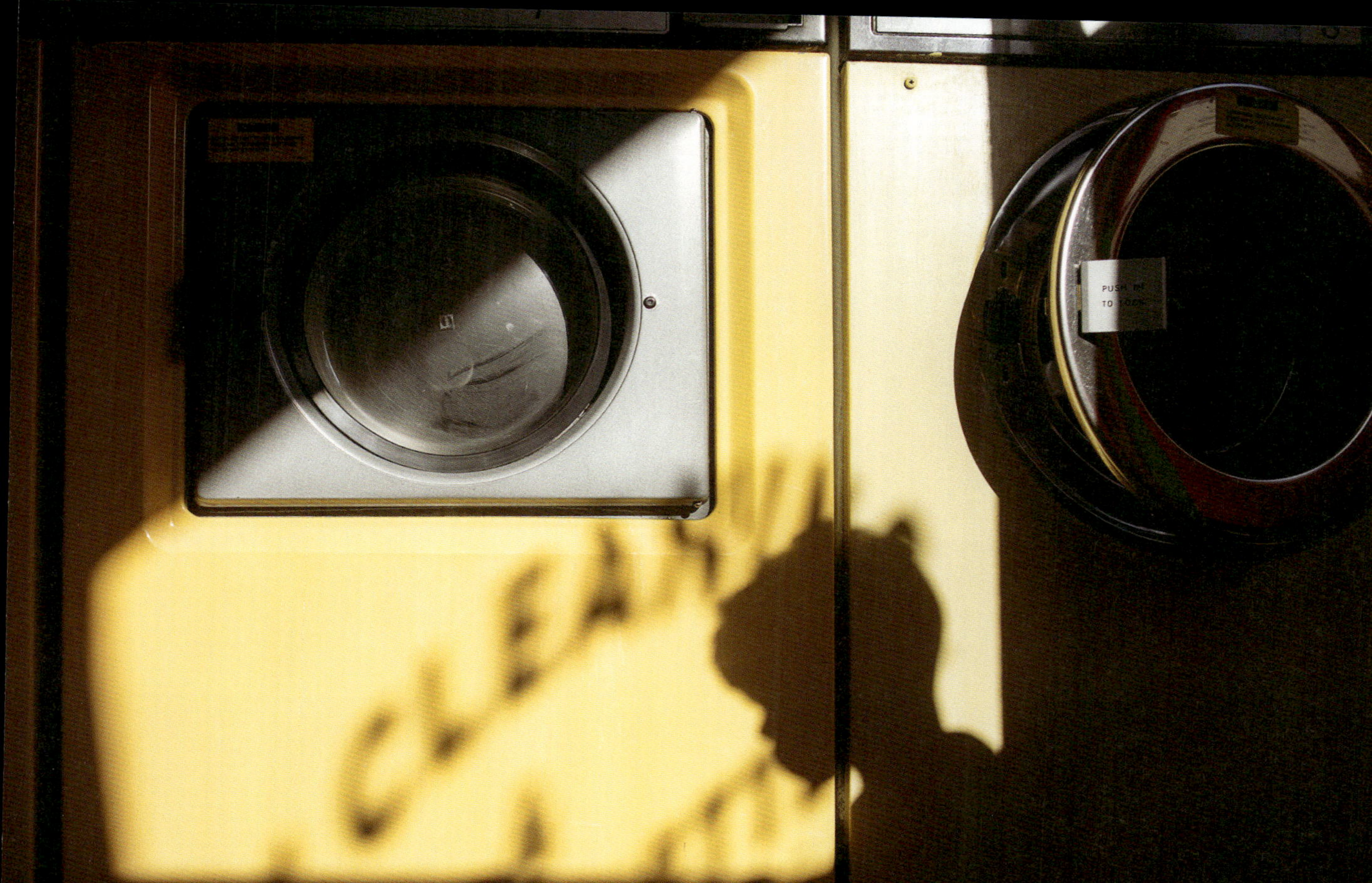
PUSH IN
TO LOCK

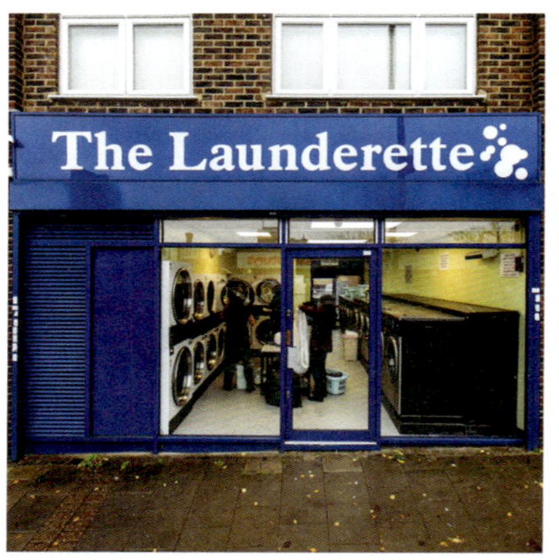
The Launderette
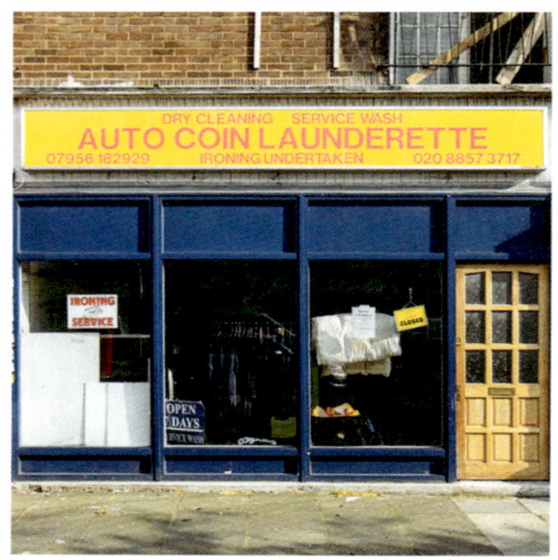
DRY CLEANING   SERVICE WASH
AUTO COIN LAUNDERETTE
07956 182929   IRONING UNDERTAKEN   020 8857 3717
IRONING SERVICE
CLOSED
OPEN 7 DAYS
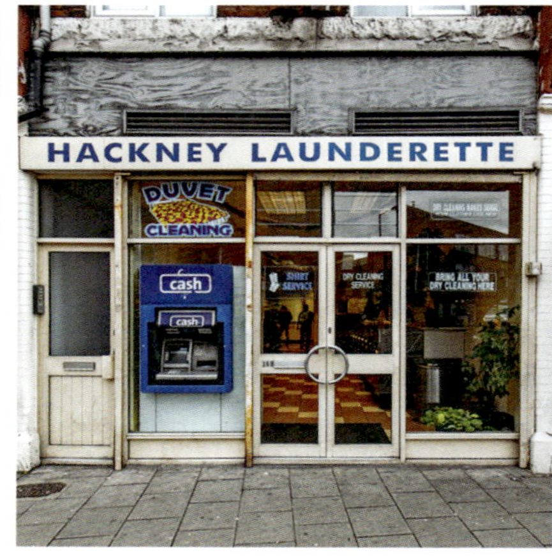
HACKNEY LAUNDERETTE
DUVET CLEANING
cash
cash
SHIRT SERVICE
DRY CLEANING SERVICE
BRING ALL YOUR DRY CLEANING HERE
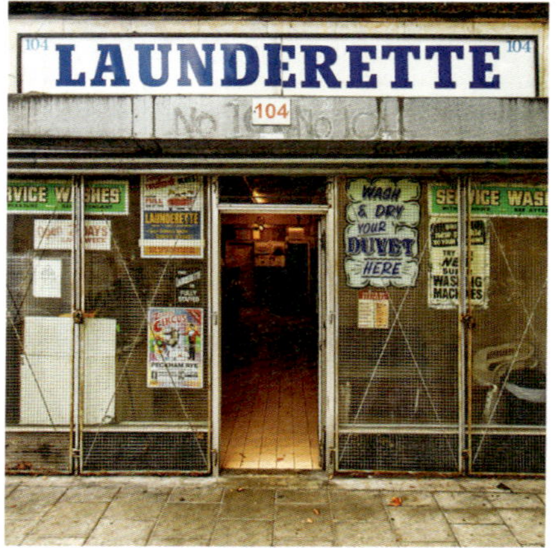
104
LAUNDERETTE
104
104
SERVICE WASHES
WASH & DRY YOUR DUVET HERE
SERVICE WASH
LAUNDERETTE
NEW WASHING MACHINES
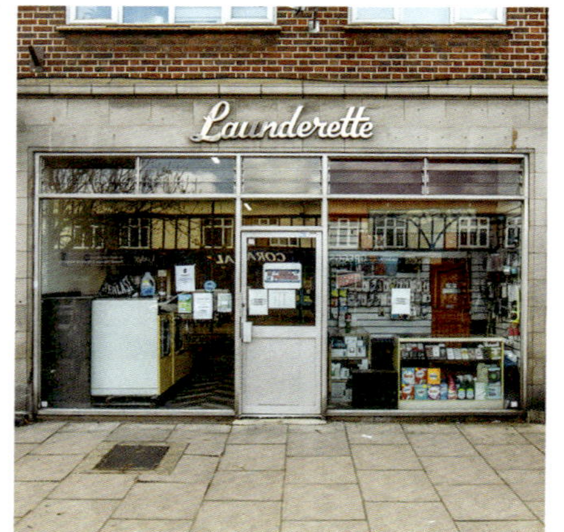
Launderette
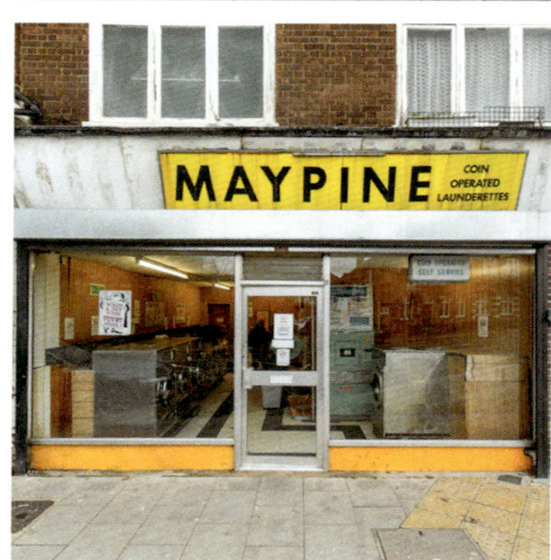
MAYPINE   COIN OPERATED LAUNDERETTES
SELF SERVICE

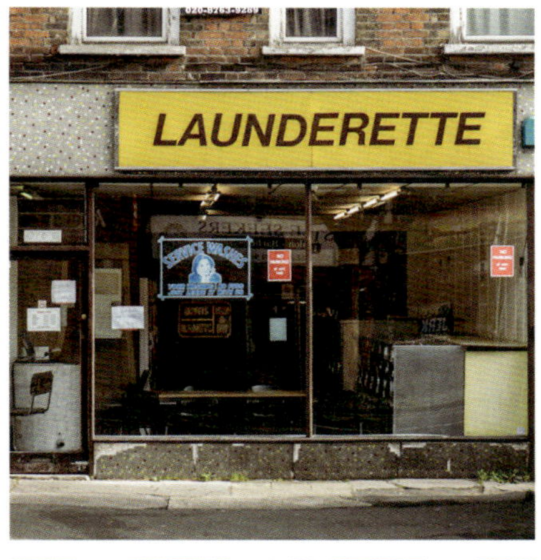
LAUNDERETTE

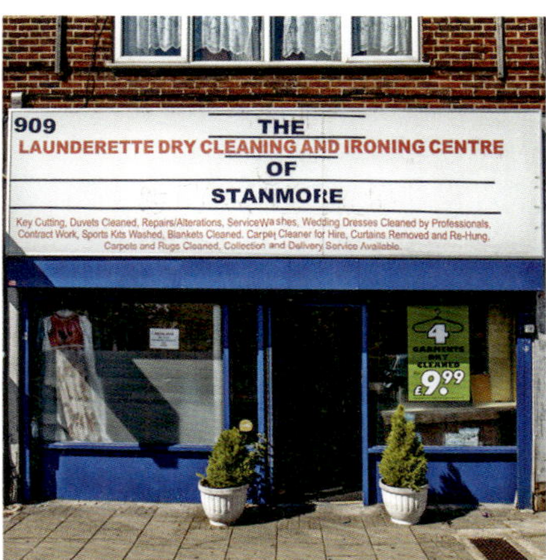
909
THE
LAUNDERETTE DRY CLEANING AND IRONING CENTRE
OF
STANMORE
Key Cutting, Duvets Cleaned, Repairs/Alterations, ServiceWashes, Wedding Dresses Cleaned by Professionals,
Contract Work, Sports Kits Washed, Blankets Cleaned. Carpet Cleaner for Hire, Curtains Removed and Re-Hung,
Carpets and Rugs Cleaned, Collection and Delivery Service Available.
4
GARMENTS
DRY
CLEANED
£9.99

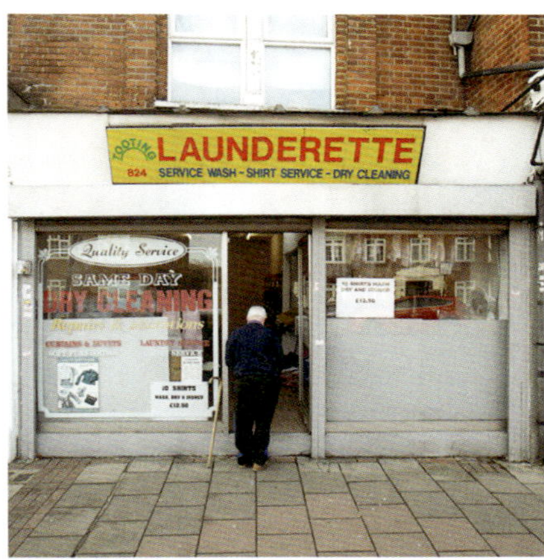
Tooting LAUNDERETTE
824   SERVICE WASH ~ SHIRT SERVICE ~ DRY CLEANING
Quality Service
SAME DAY
DRY CLEANING
CURTAINS & DUVETS

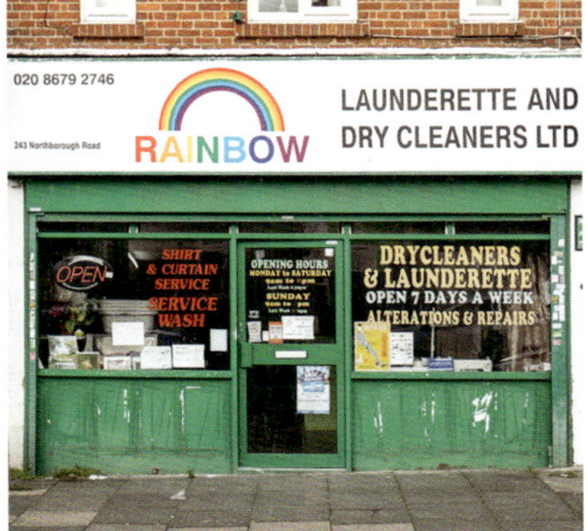
020 8679 2746
243 Northborough Road
RAINBOW
LAUNDERETTE AND
DRY CLEANERS LTD
OPEN
SHIRT
& CURTAIN
SERVICE
SERVICE
WASH
OPENING HOURS
MONDAY to SATURDAY
SUNDAY
DRYCLEANERS
& LAUNDERETTE
OPEN 7 DAYS A WEEK
ALTERATIONS & REPAIRS

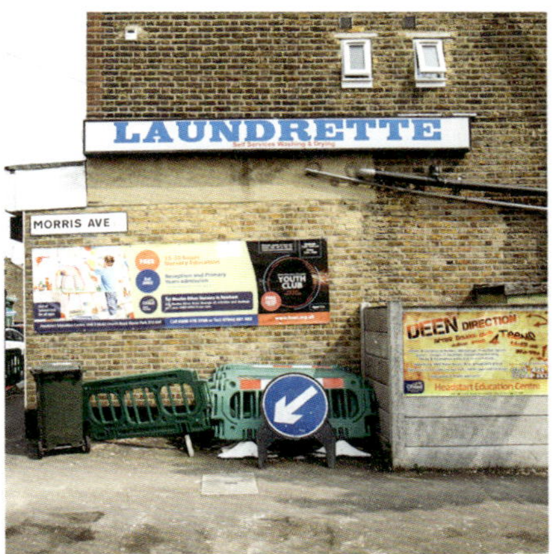
LAUNDRETTE
Self Service Washing & Drying
MORRIS AVE
DEEN DIRECTION
Headstart Education Centre

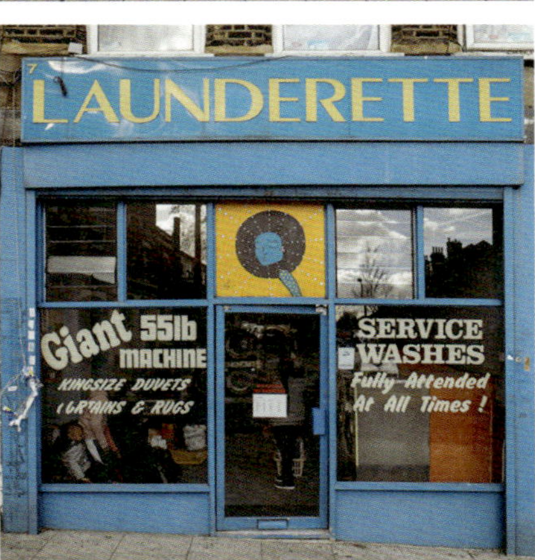
LAUNDERETTE
Giant 55lb
MACHINE
KINGSIZE DUVETS
CURTAINS & RUGS
SERVICE
WASHES
Fully-Attended
At All Times !

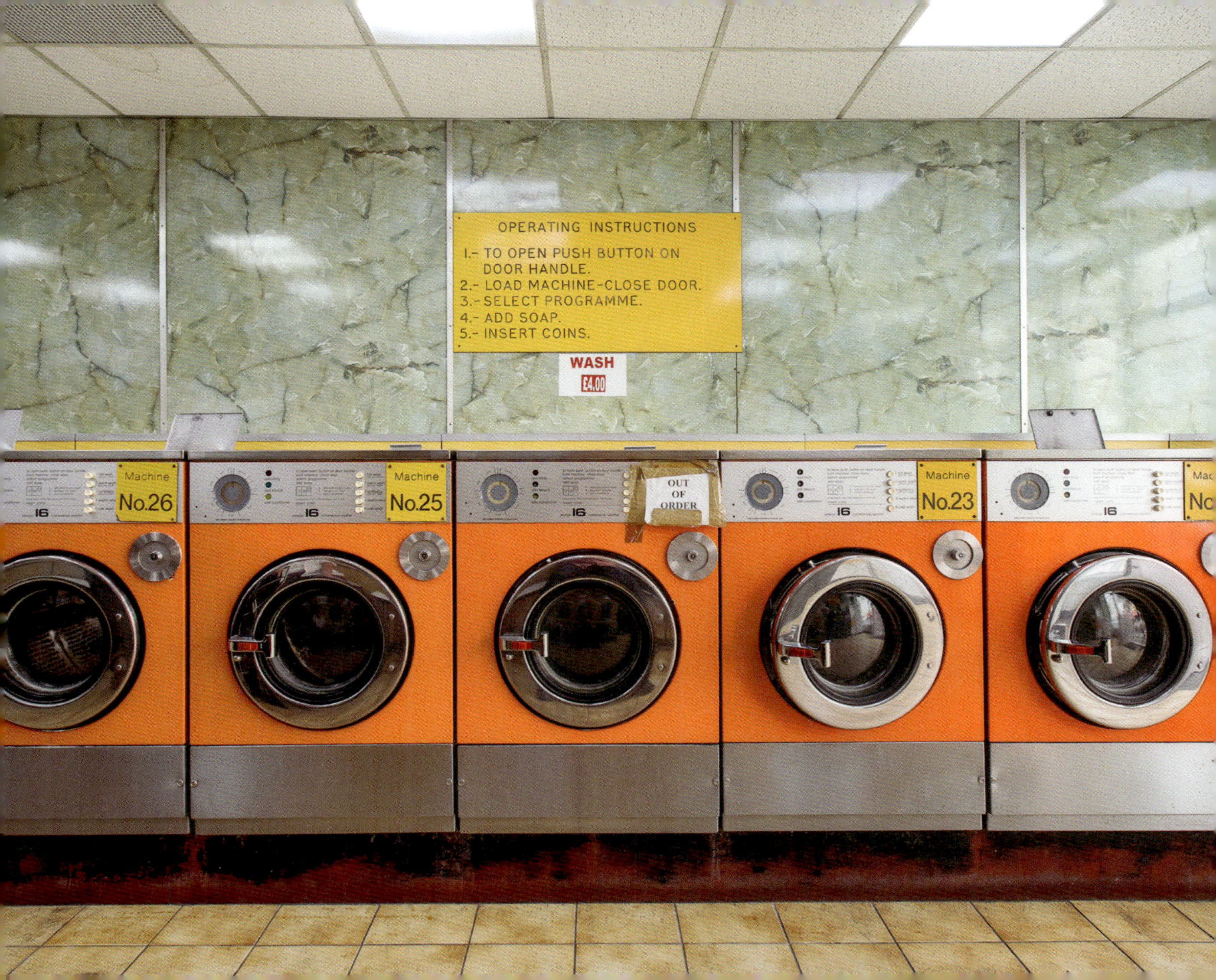
OPERATING INSTRUCTIONS
1.- TO OPEN PUSH BUTTON ON
   DOOR HANDLE.
2.- LOAD MACHINE-CLOSE DOOR.
3.- SELECT PROGRAMME.
4.- ADD SOAP.
5.- INSERT COINS.
WASH
£4.00
Machine
No.26
Machine
No.25
OUT
OF
ORDER
Machine
No.23
16

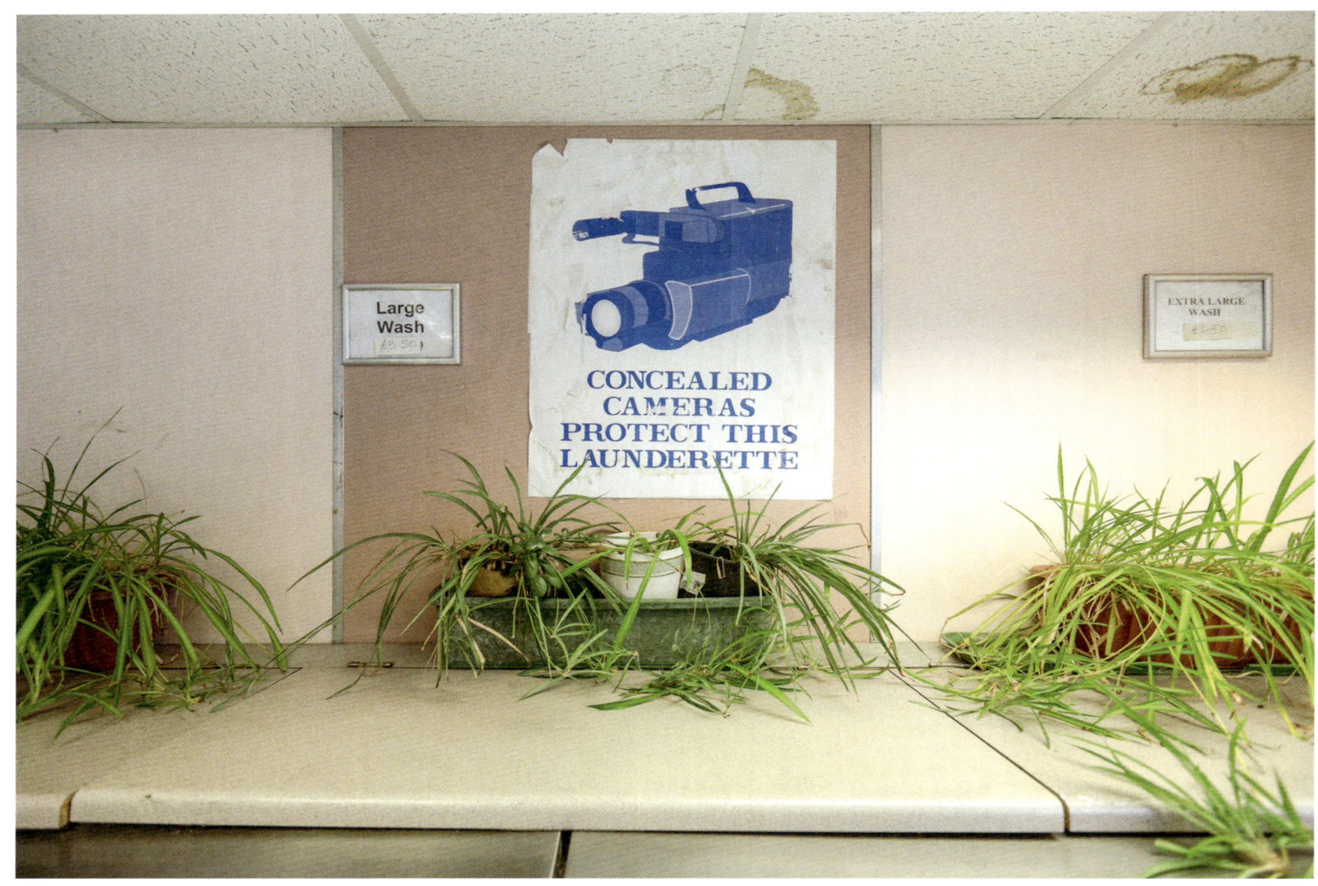

Large
Wash

EXTRA LARGE
WASH

CONCEALED
CAMERAS
PROTECT THIS
LAUNDERETTE

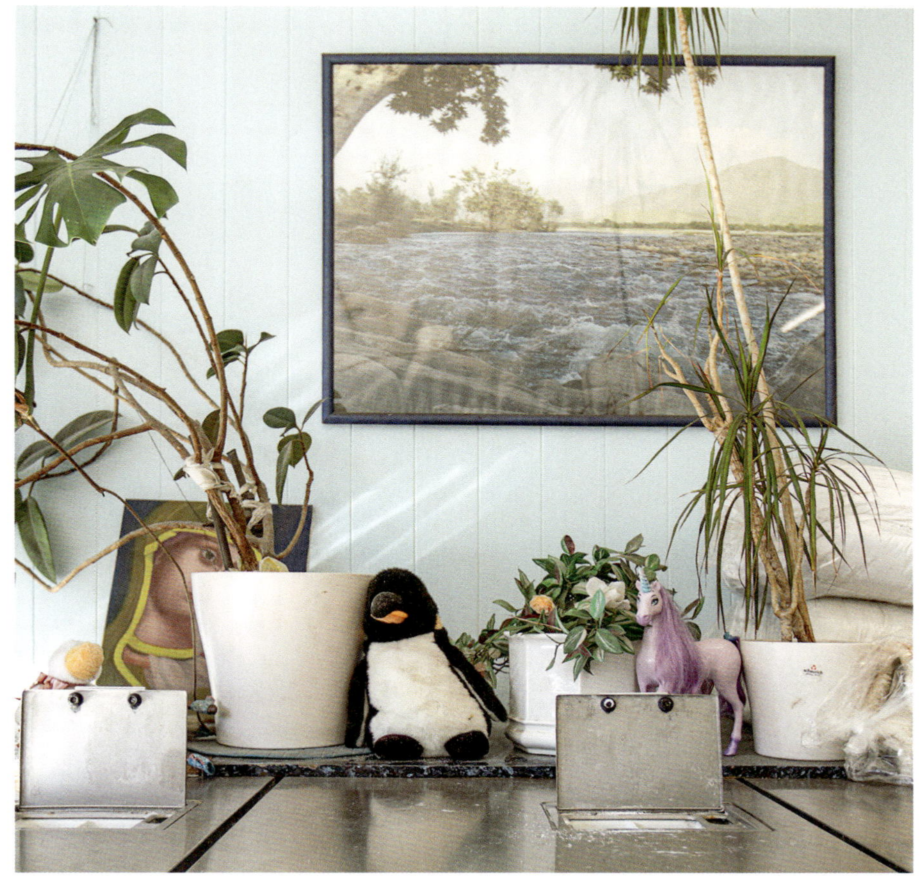

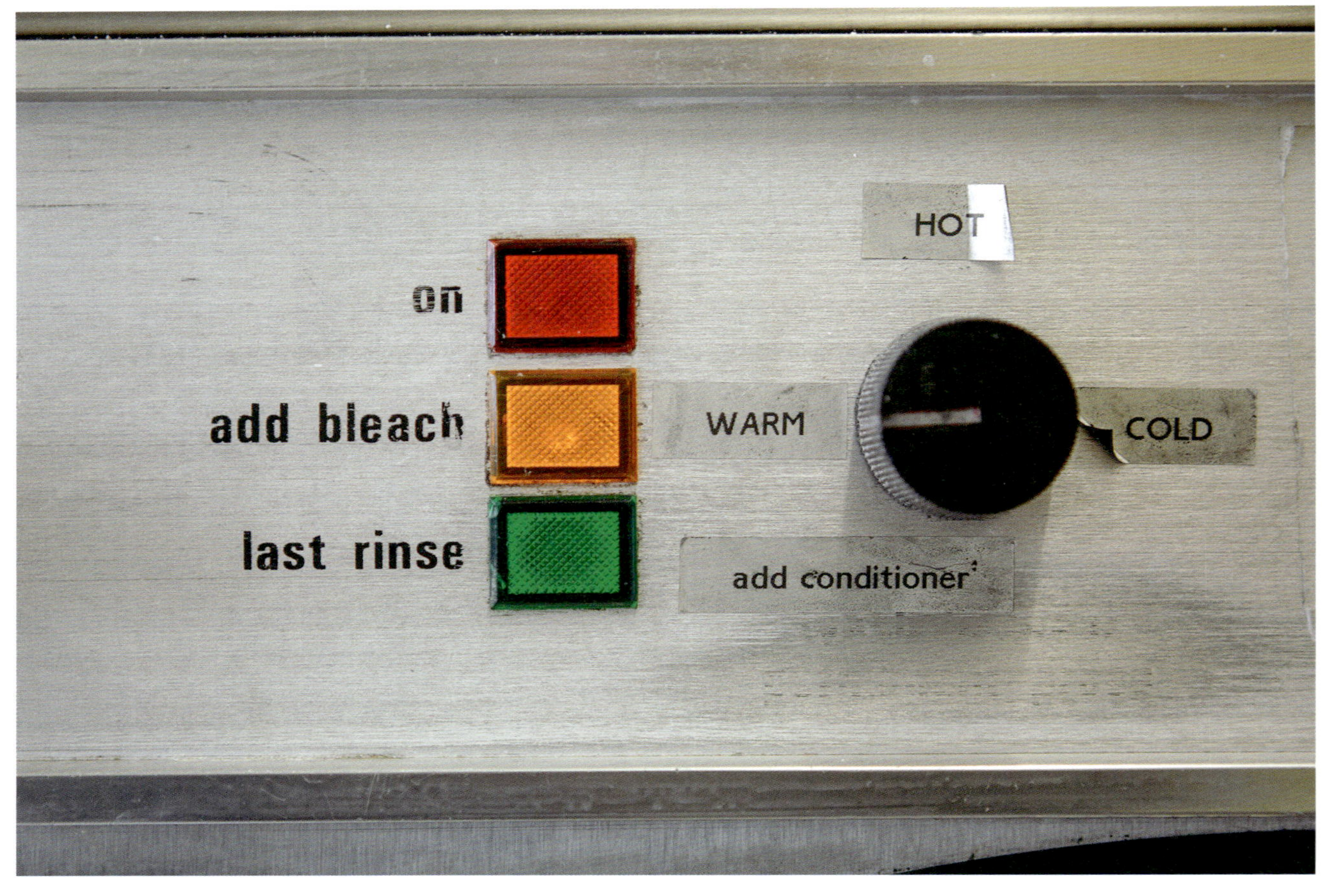

on
add bleach
last rinse
WARM
add conditioner
HOT
COLD

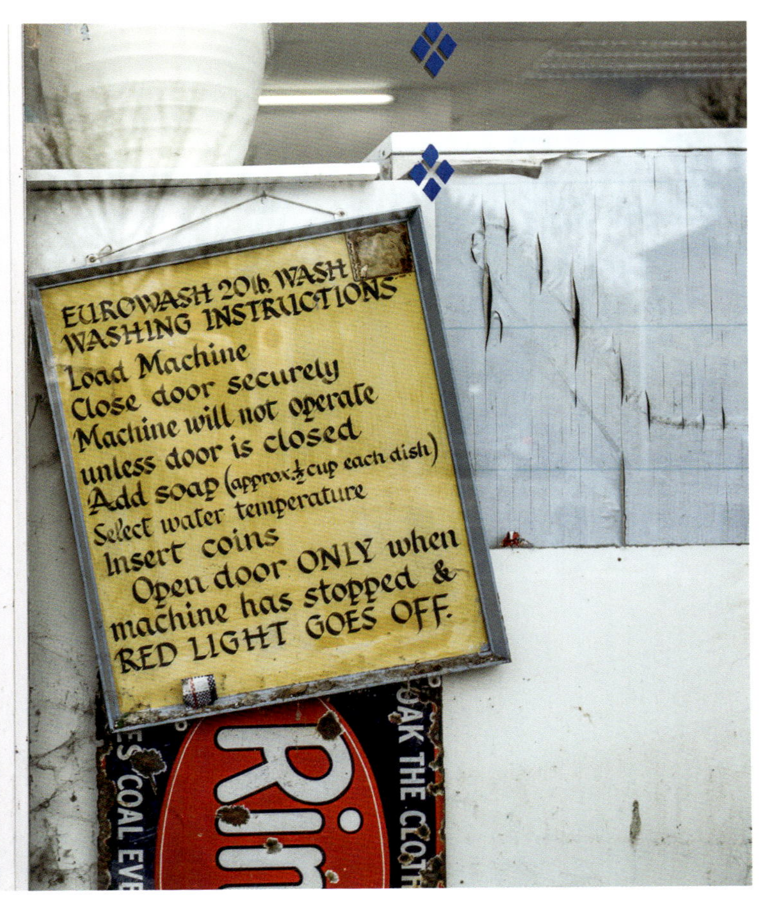

EUROWASH 20lb WASH
WASHING INSTRUCTIONS
Load Machine
Close door securely
Machine will not operate
unless door is closed
Add soap (approx.½ cup each dish)
Select water temperature
Insert coins
Open door ONLY when
machine has stopped &
RED LIGHT GOES OFF.

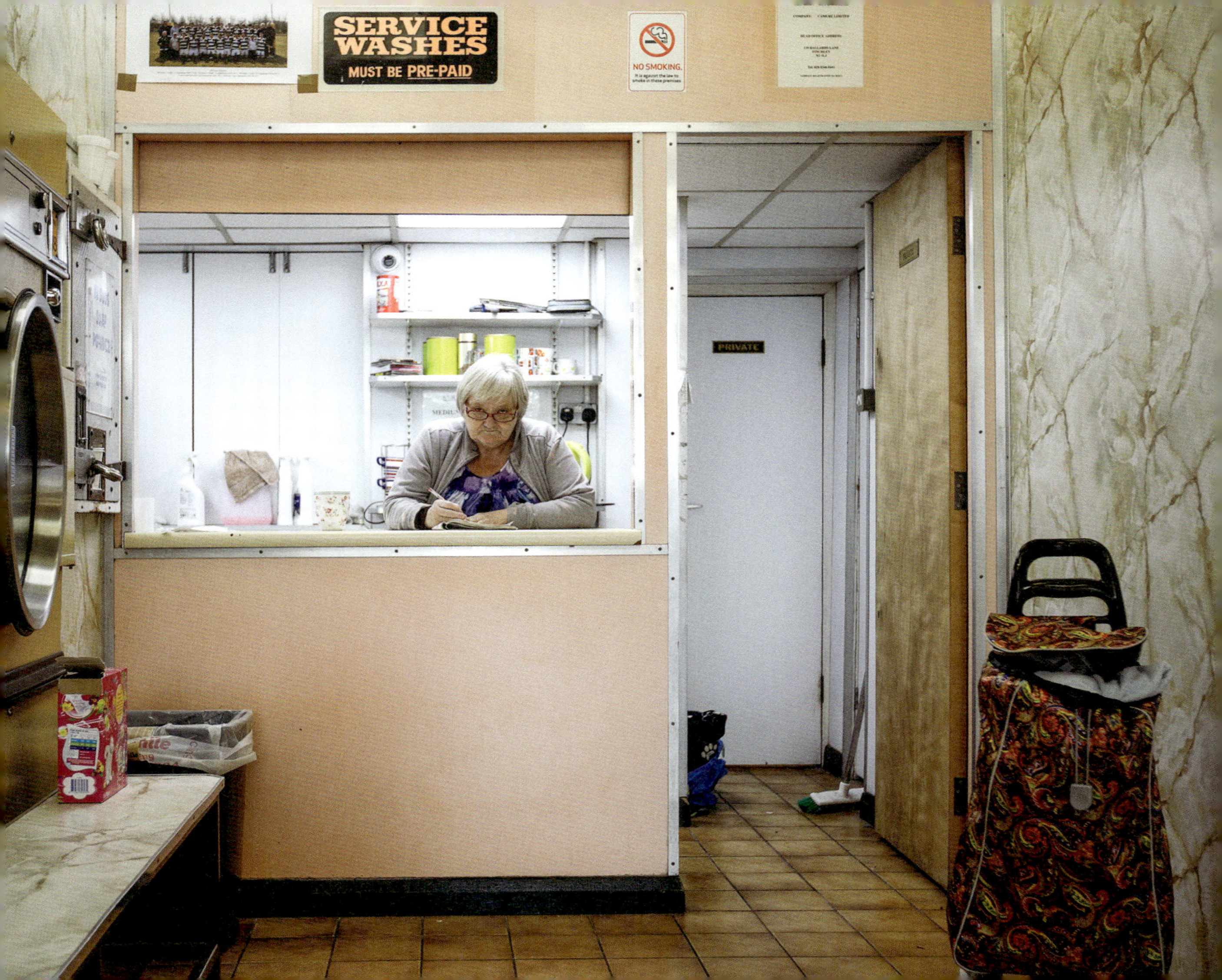

SERVICE
WASHES
MUST BE PRE-PAID
NO SMOKING.
PRIVATE

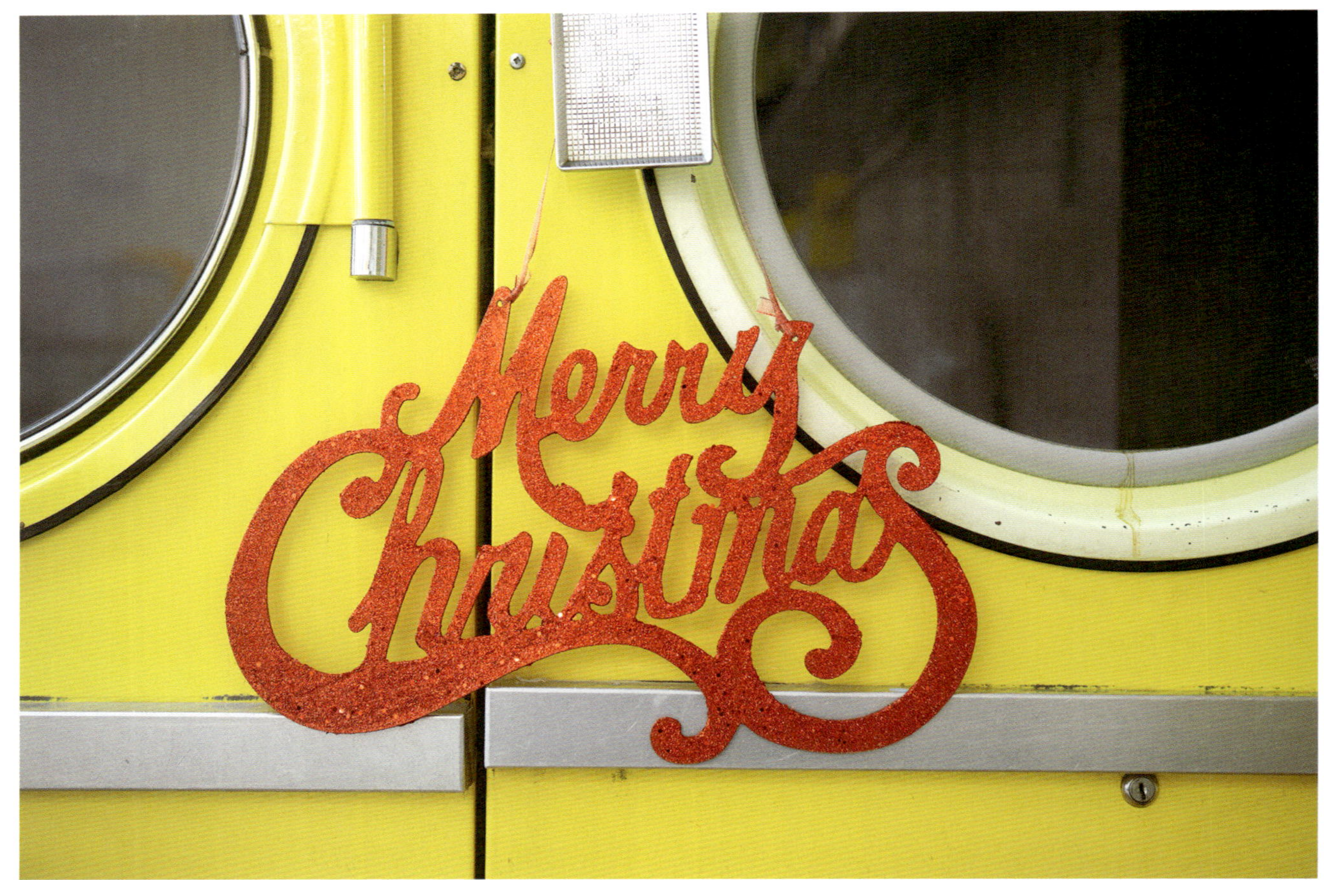
Merry Christmas

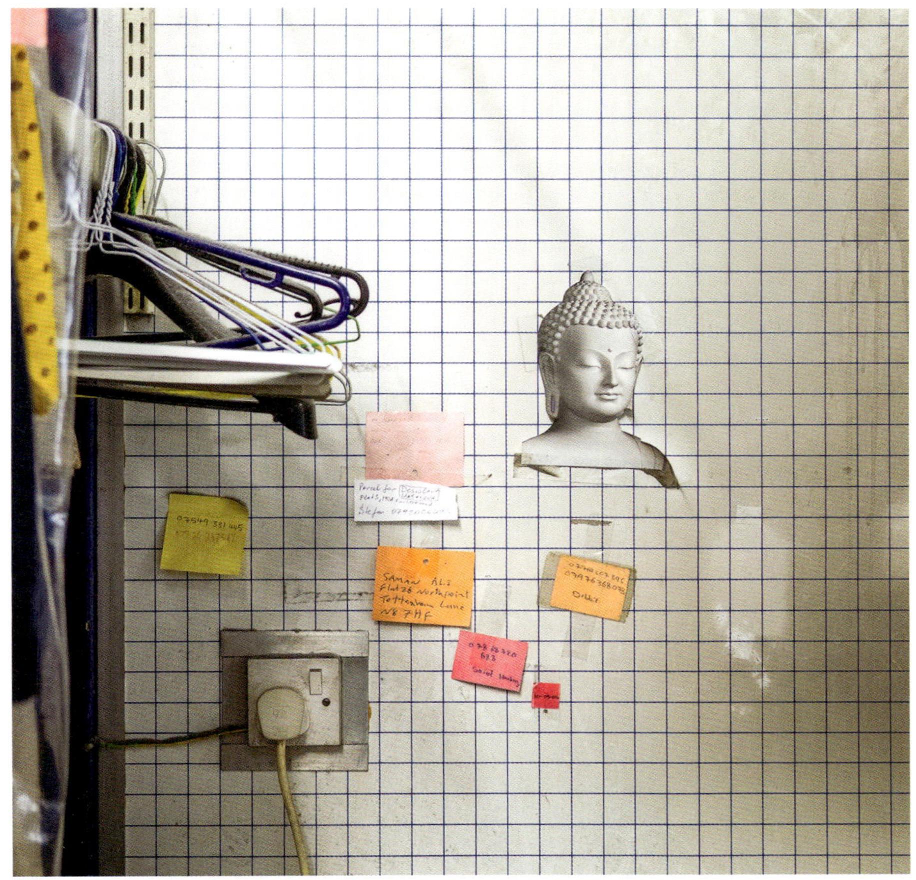

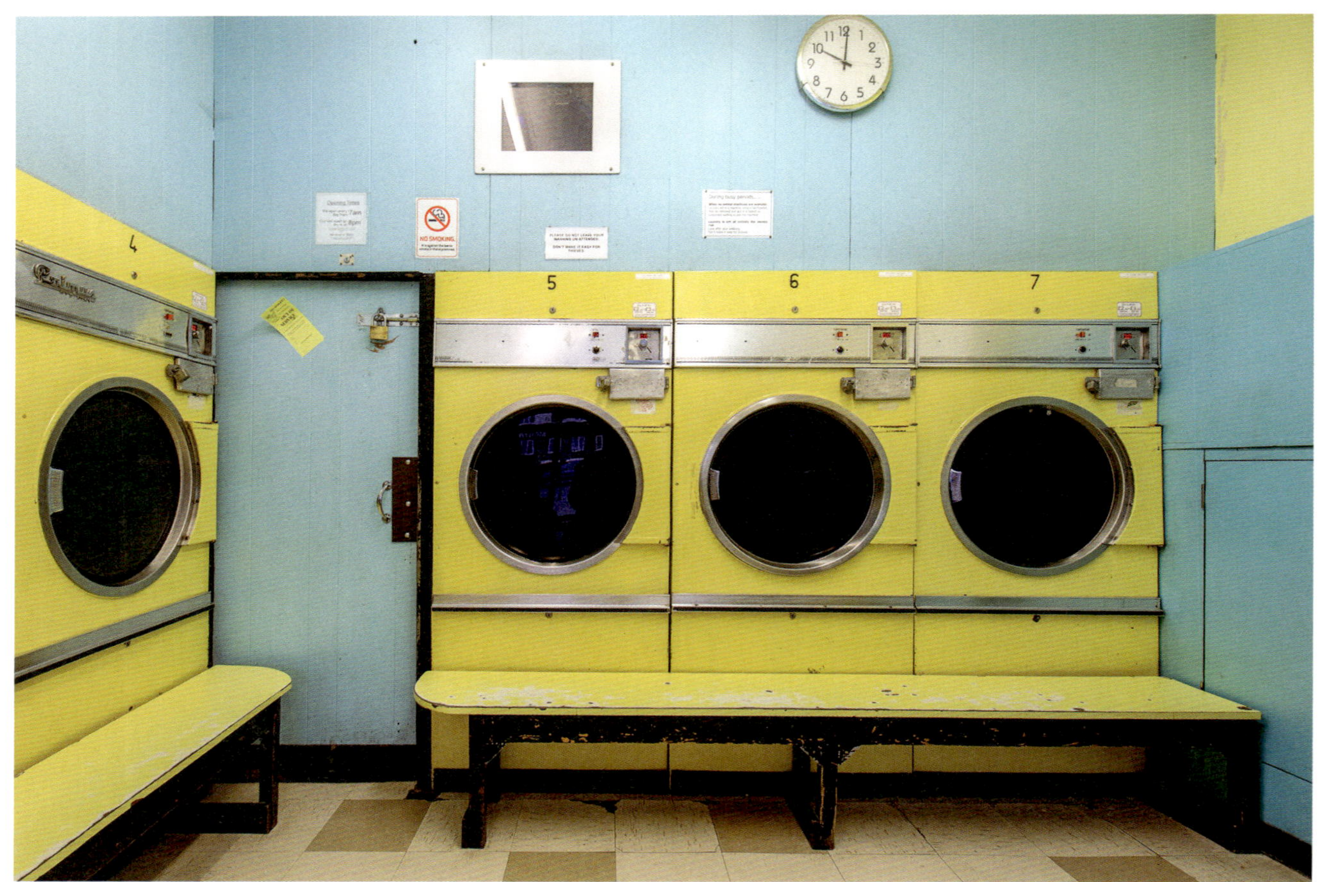

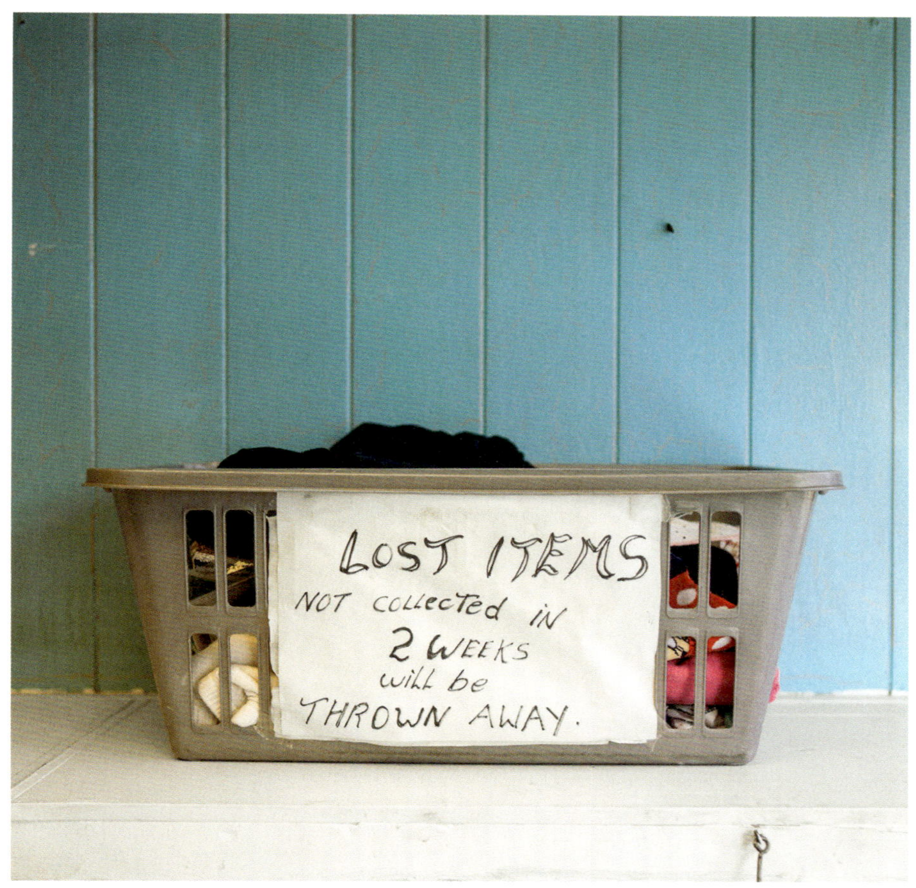

LOST ITEMS
NOT collected iN
2 WEEKS
will be
THROWN AWAY.

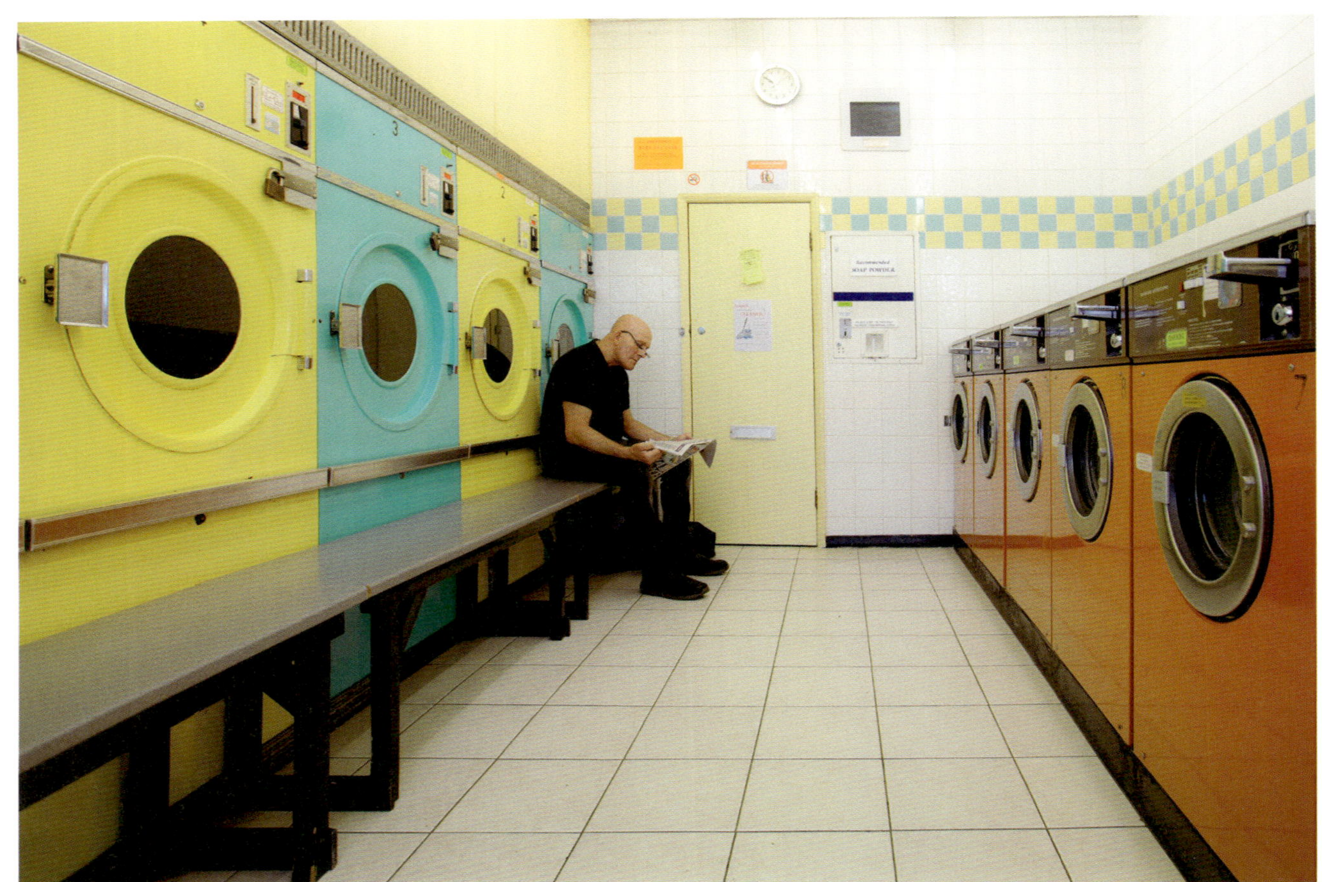

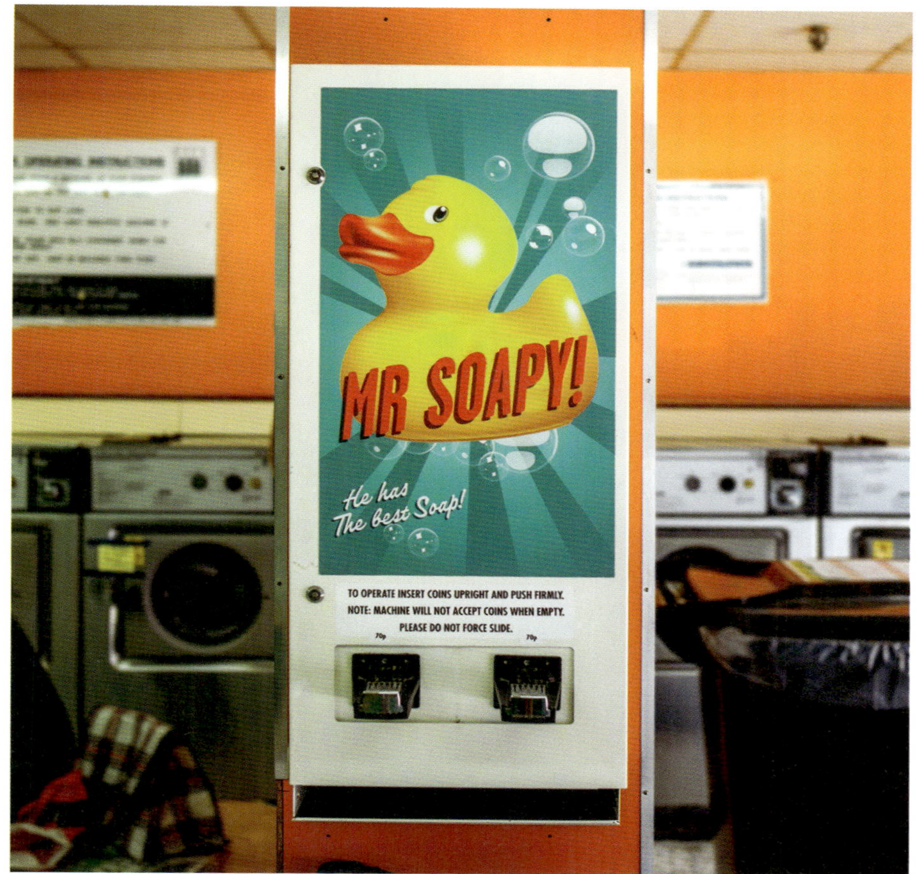

MR SOAPY!
He has
The best Soap!
TO OPERATE INSERT COINS UPRIGHT AND PUSH FIRMLY.
NOTE: MACHINE WILL NOT ACCEPT COINS WHEN EMPTY.
PLEASE DO NOT FORCE SLIDE.
70p
70p

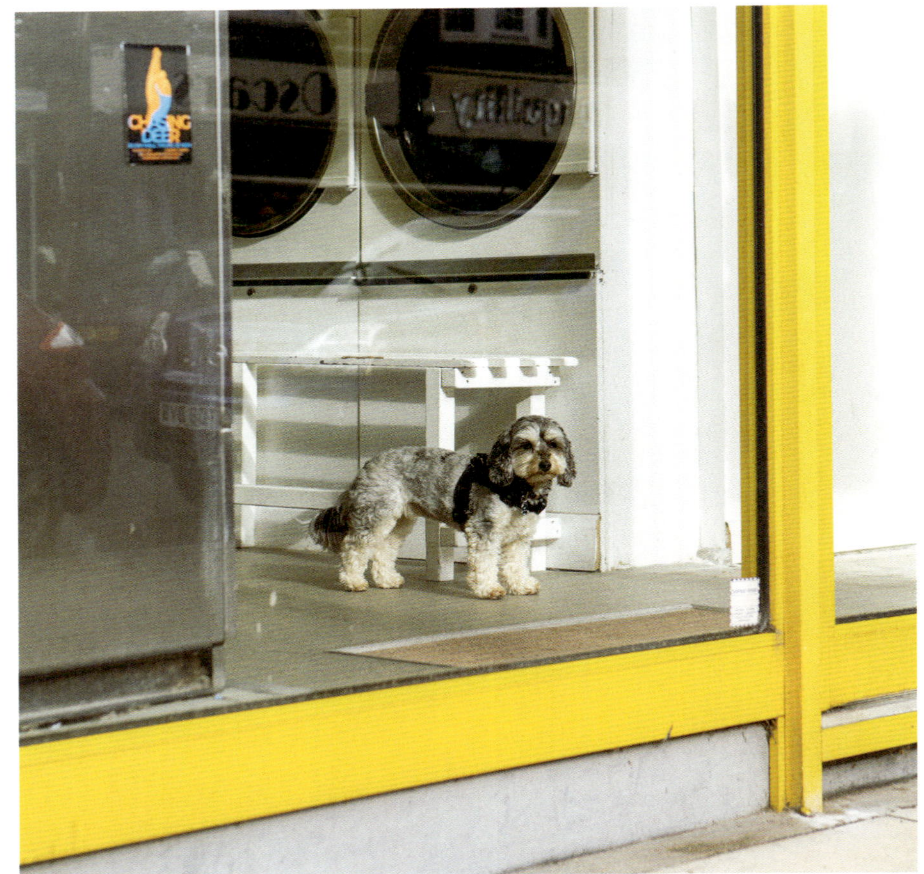

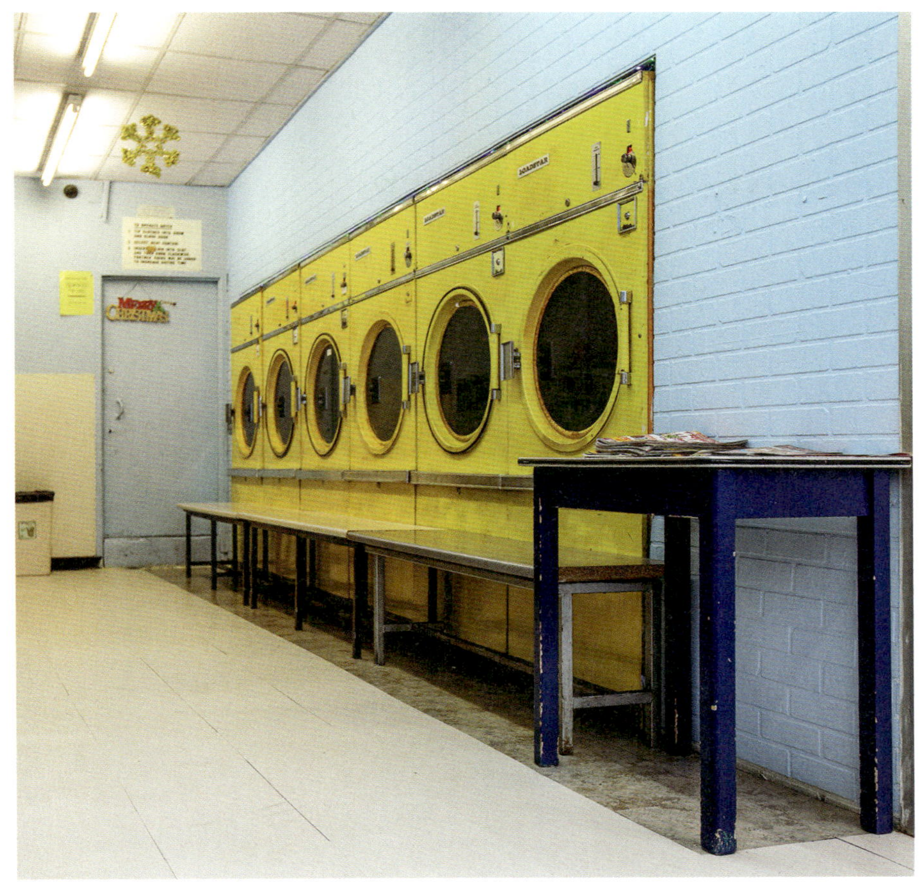

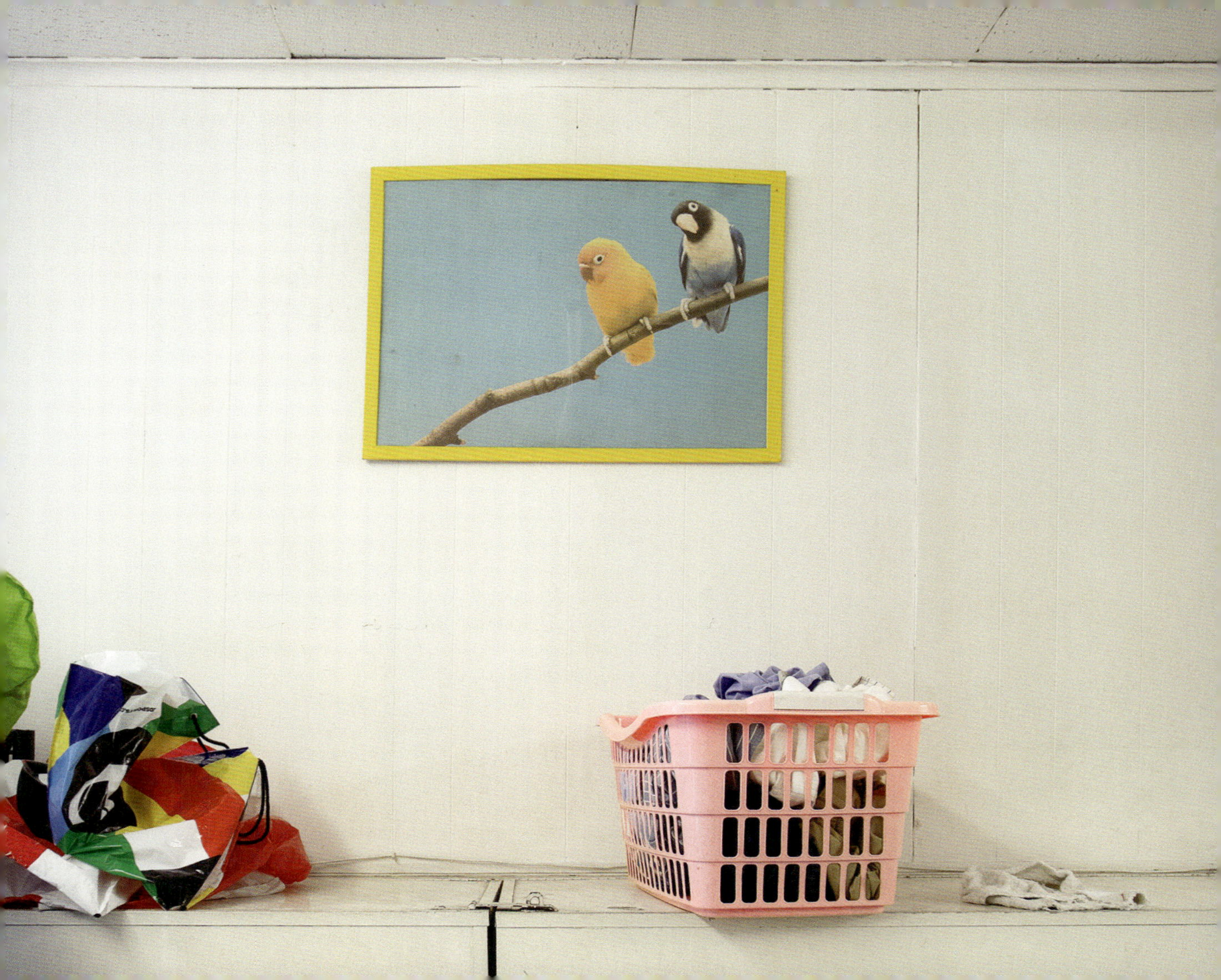

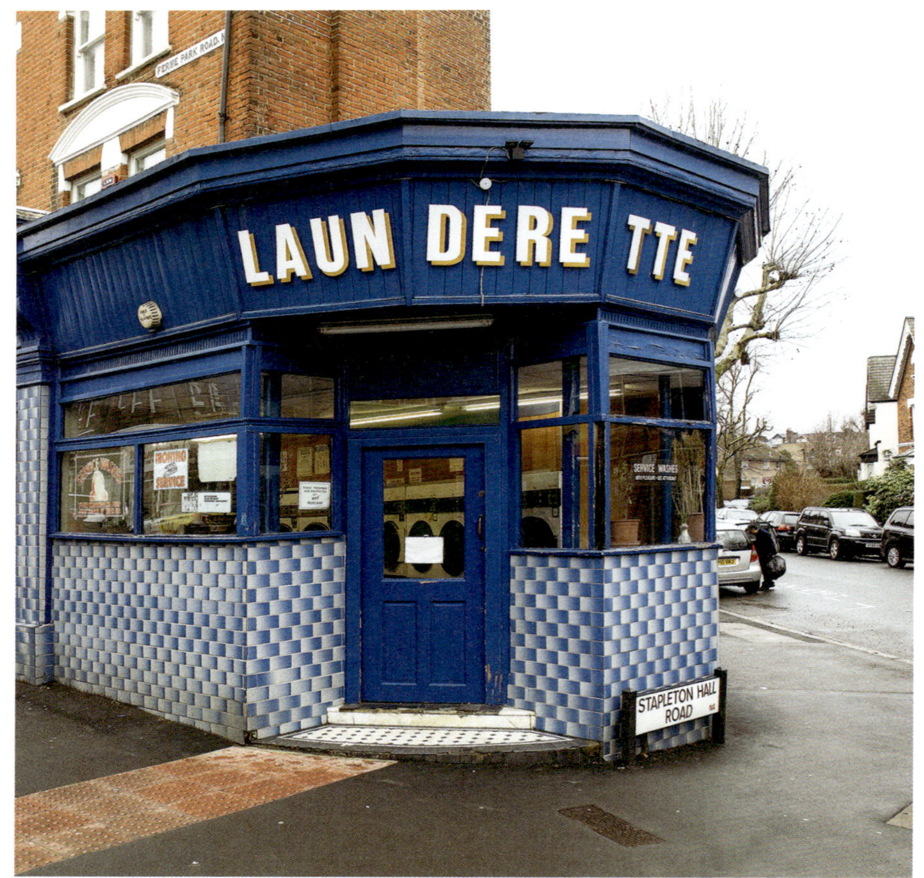

LAUN DERE TTE
STAPLETON HALL
ROAD

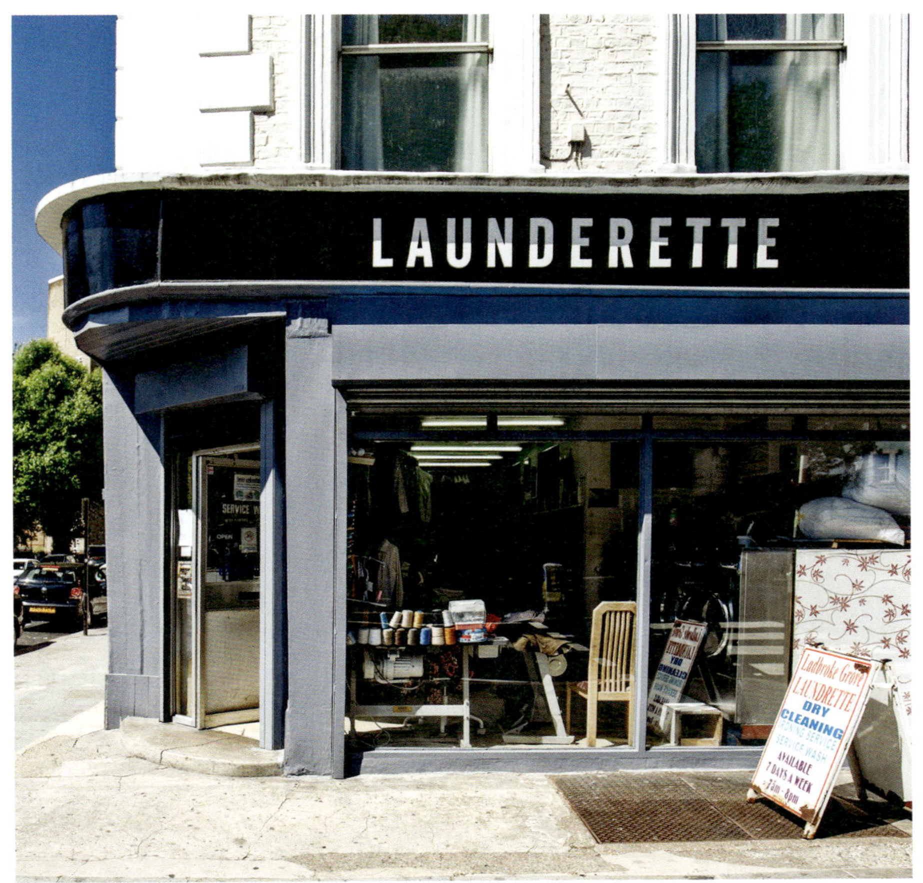
LAUNDERETTE
SERVICE WASH
OPEN
Ladbroke Grove
LAUNDERETTE
DRY CLEANING
AVAILABLE
7 DAYS A WEEK
7am - 8pm

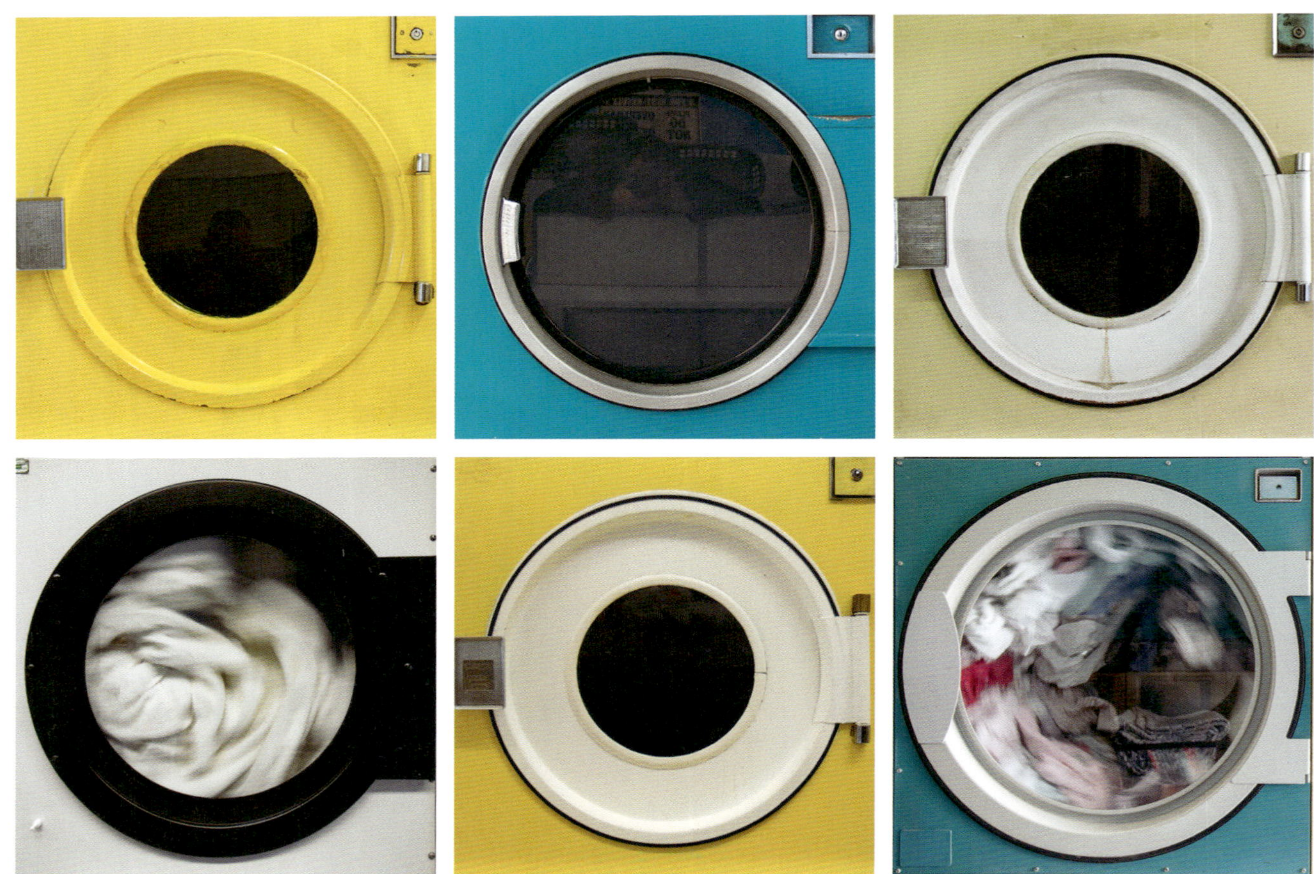

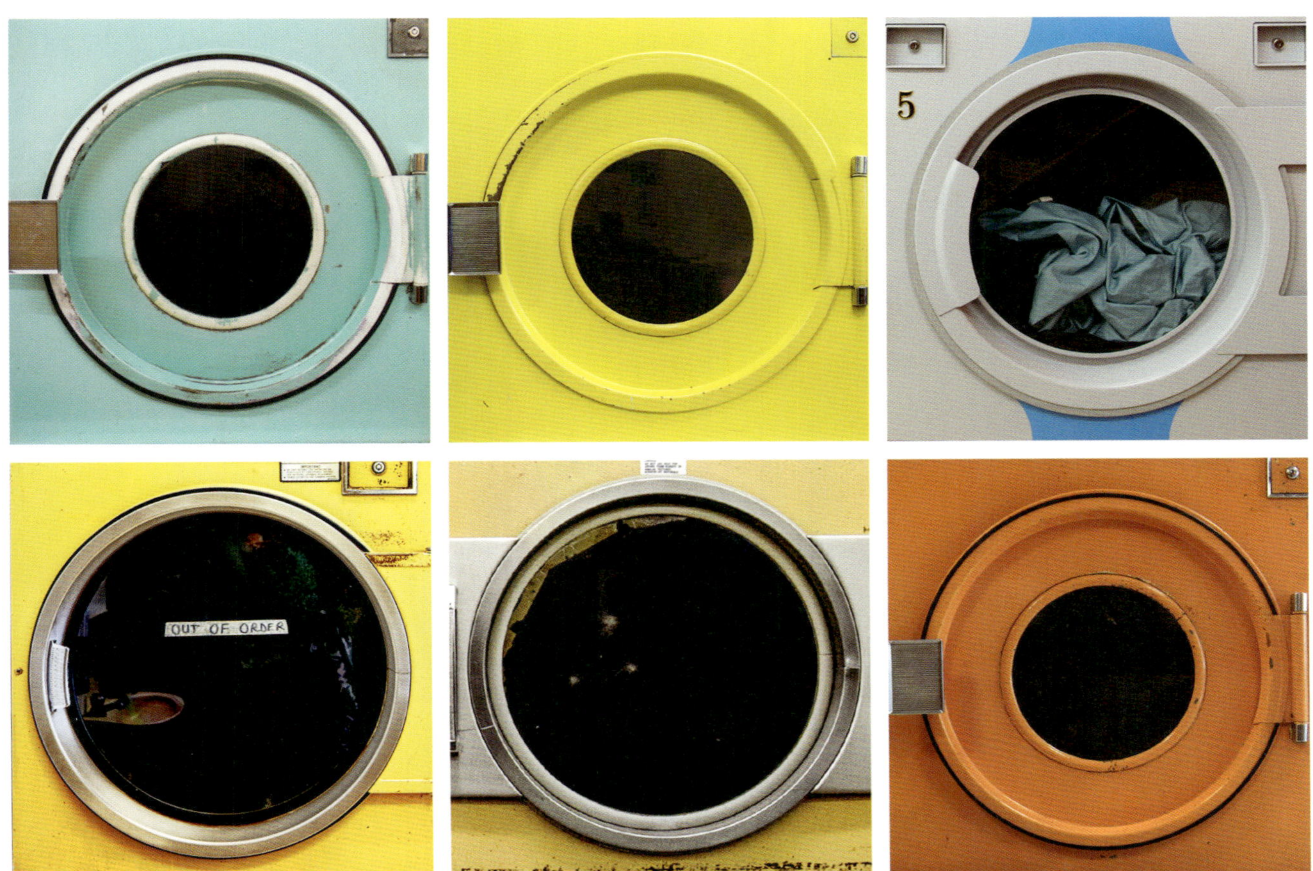
5
OUT OF ORDER

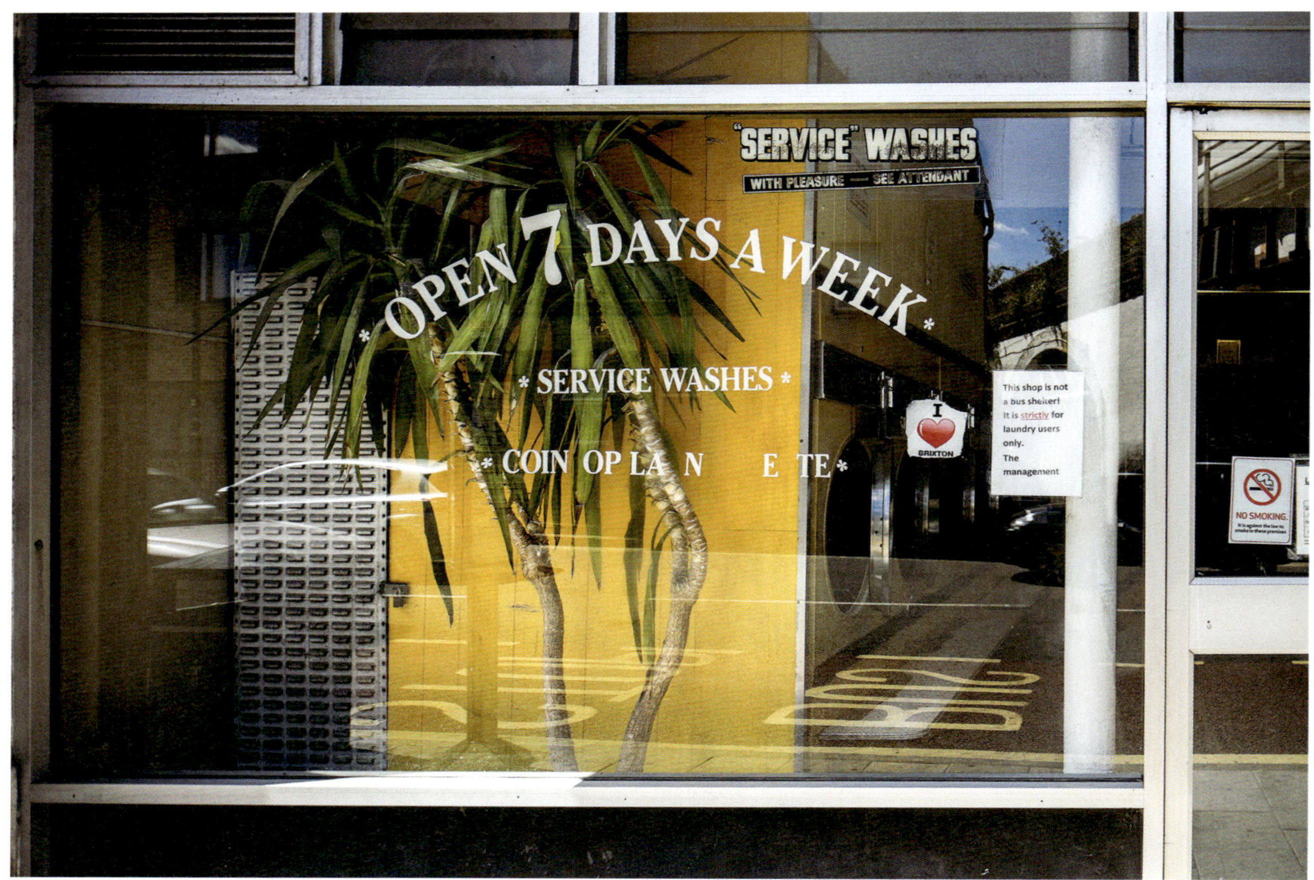

"SERVICE" WASHES
WITH PLEASURE — SEE ATTENDANT
* OPEN 7 DAYS A WEEK *
* SERVICE WASHES *
* COIN OP LA N   E TE *
I ♥ BRIXTON
This shop is not
a bus shelter!
It is strictly for
laundry users
only.
The
management
NO SMOKING.
It is against the law to
smoke in these premises

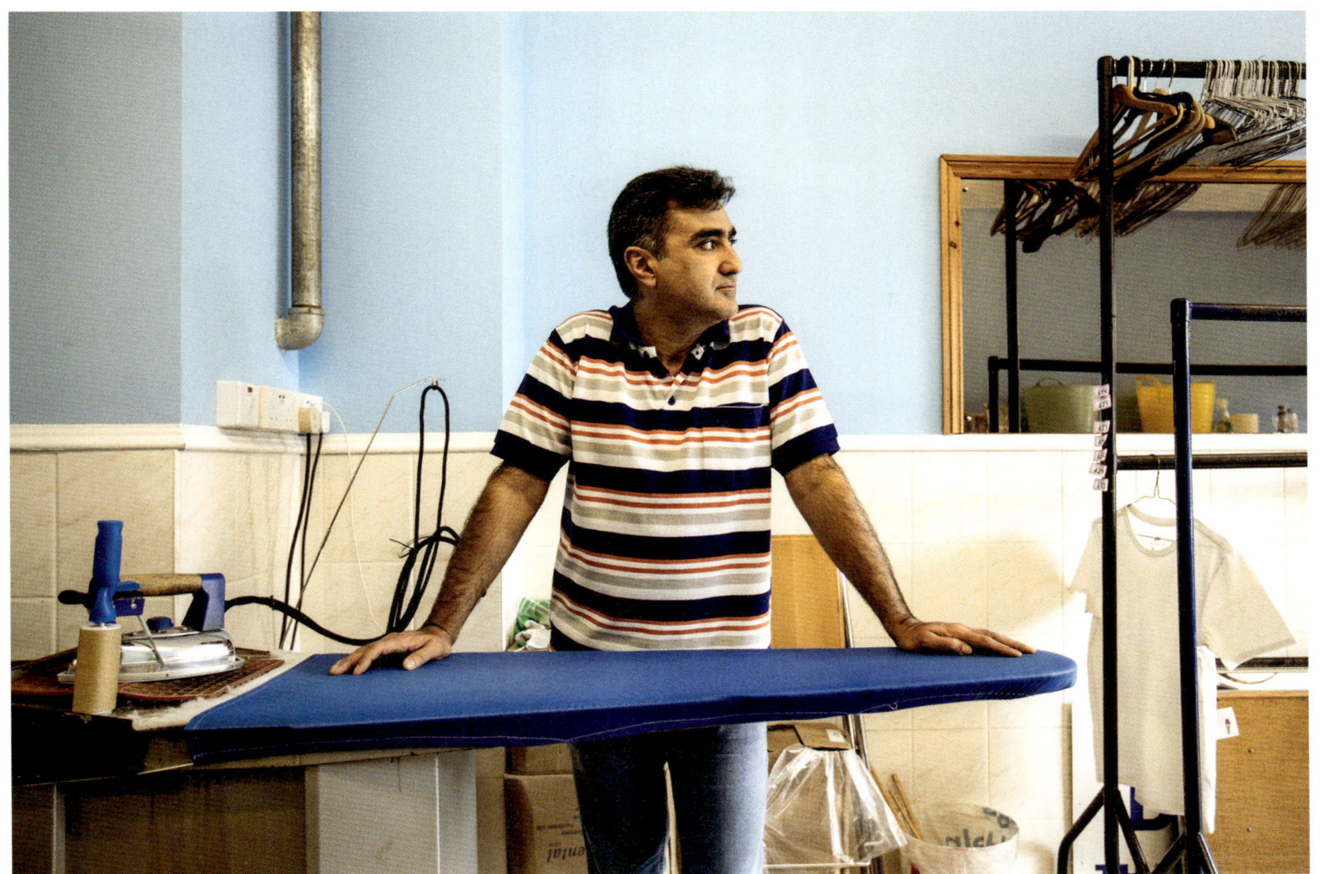

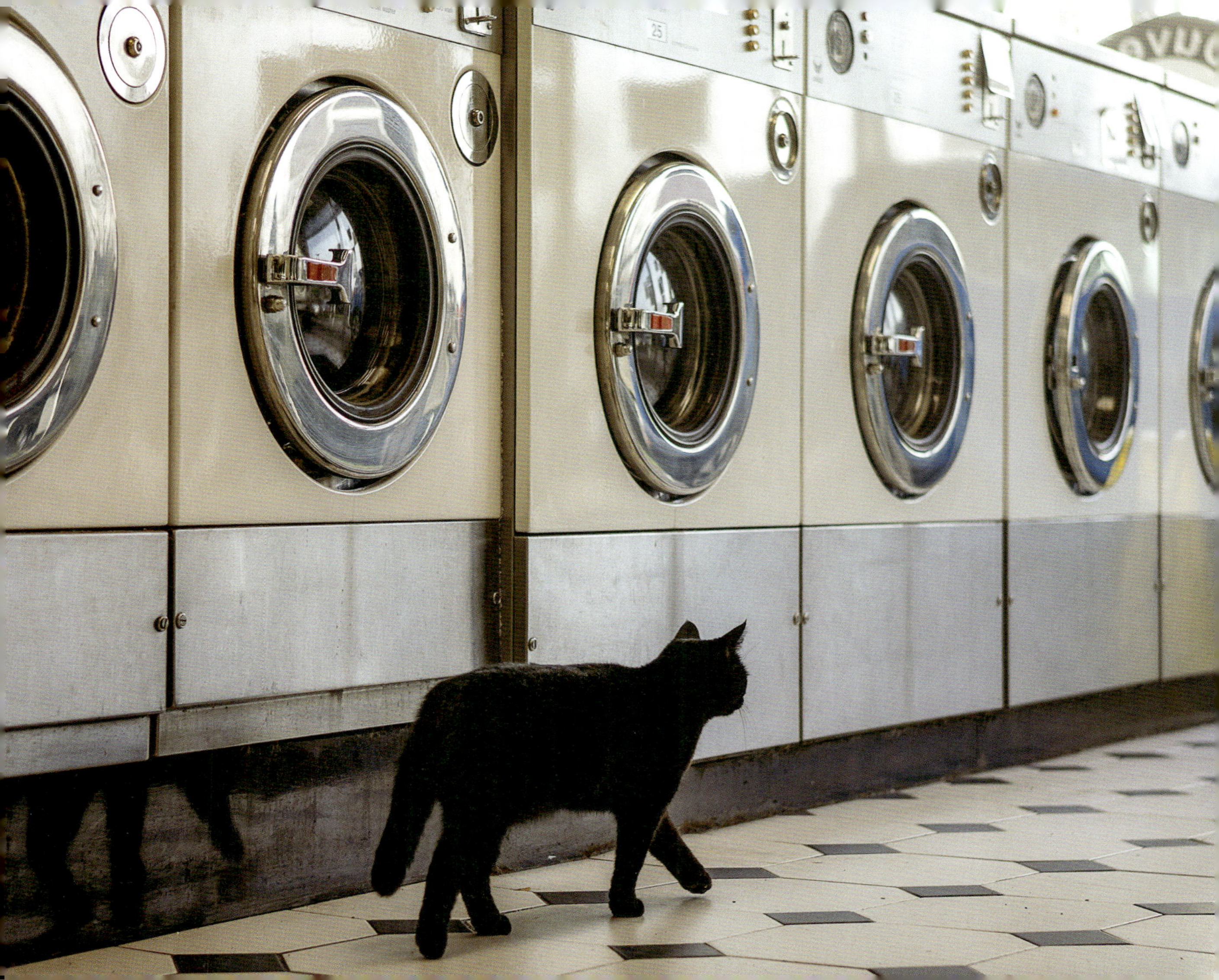

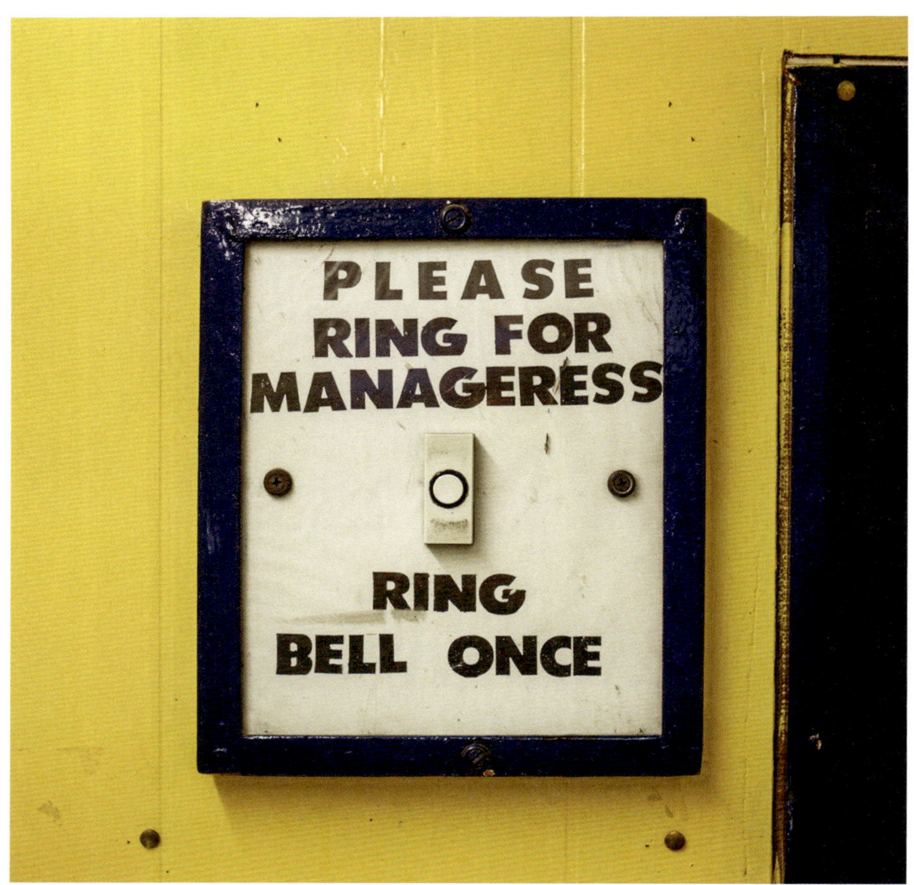
PLEASE
RING FOR
MANAGERESS
RING
BELL ONCE

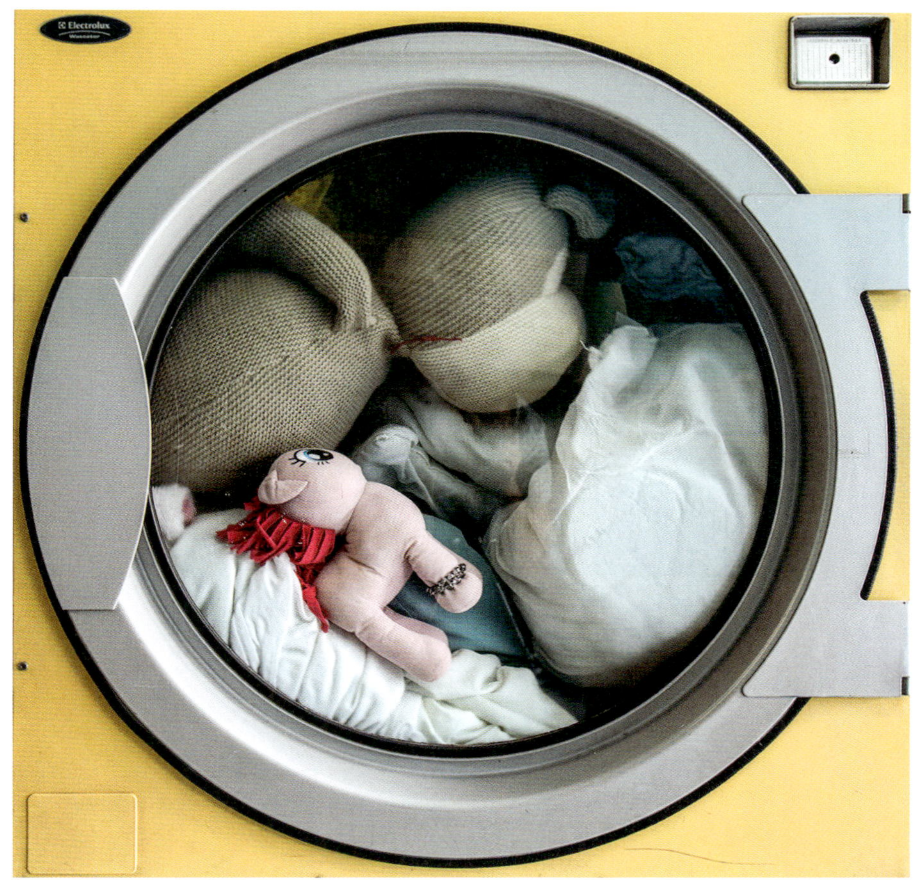

Electrolux
Wascator

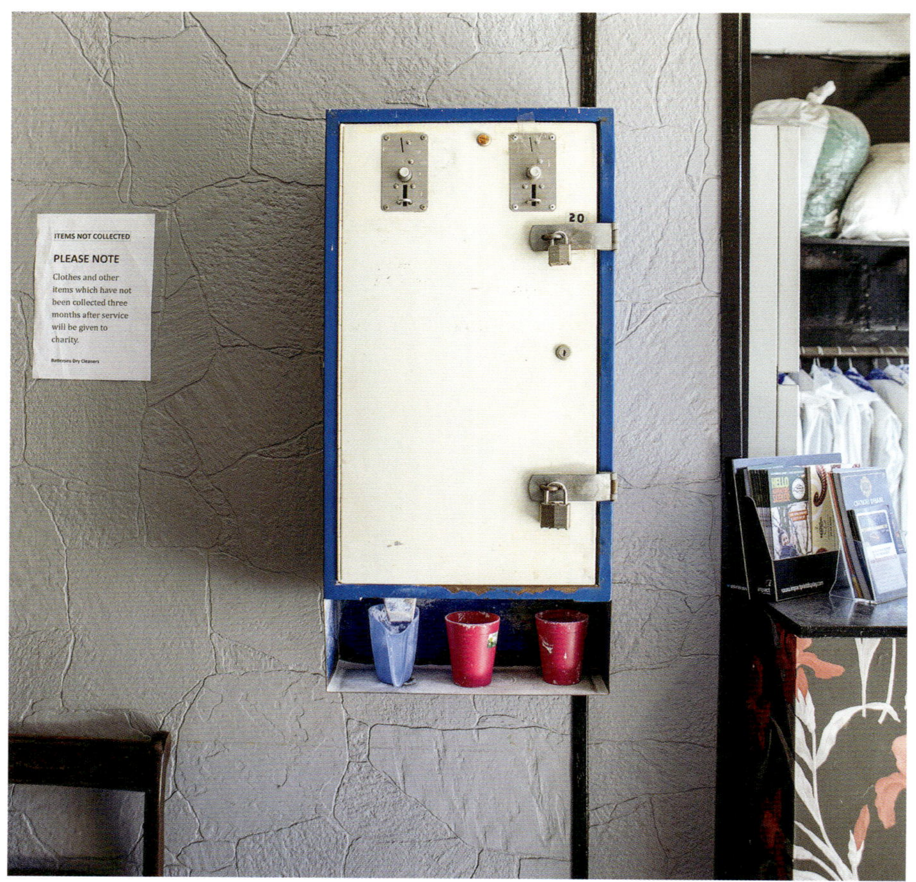

ITEMS NOT COLLECTED

PLEASE NOTE

Clothes and other
items which have not
been collected three
months after service
will be given to
charity.

Battersea Dry Cleaners

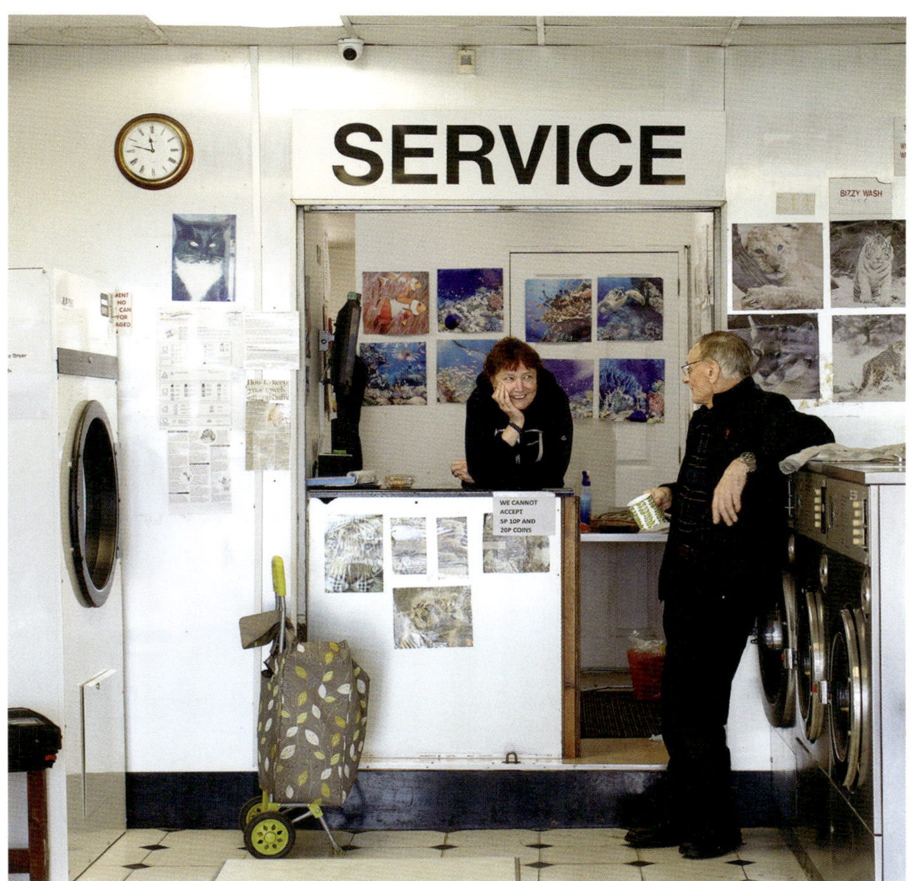

SERVICE
BIZZY WASH
WE CANNOT
ACCEPT
5P 10P AND
20P COINS

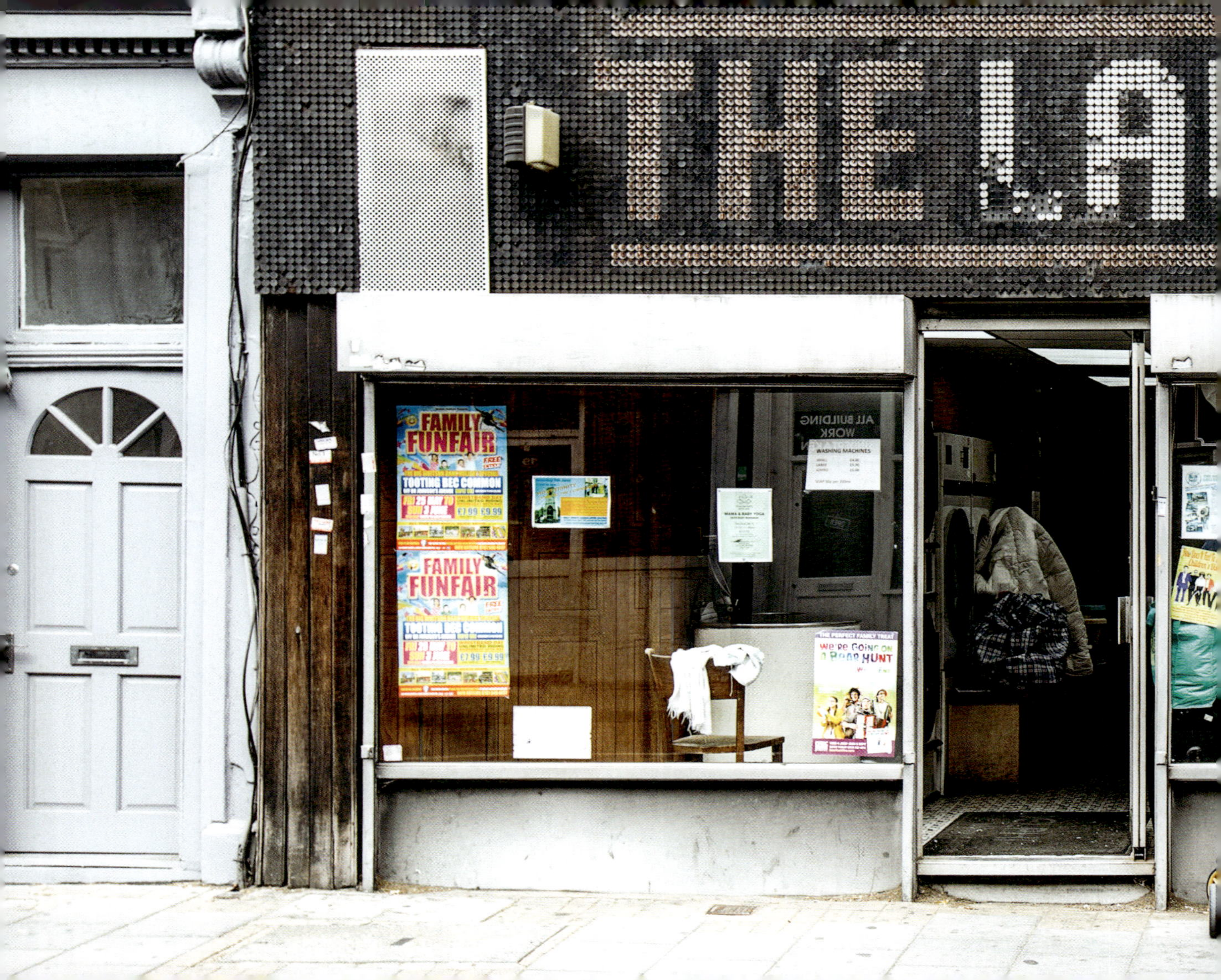
THE LA
FAMILY FUNFAIR
TOOTING BEC COMMON
FAMILY FUNFAIR
TOOTING BEC COMMON
ALL BUILDING WORK
WASHING MACHINES
WE'RE GOING ON A BEAR HUNT
THE PERFECT FAMILY TREAT

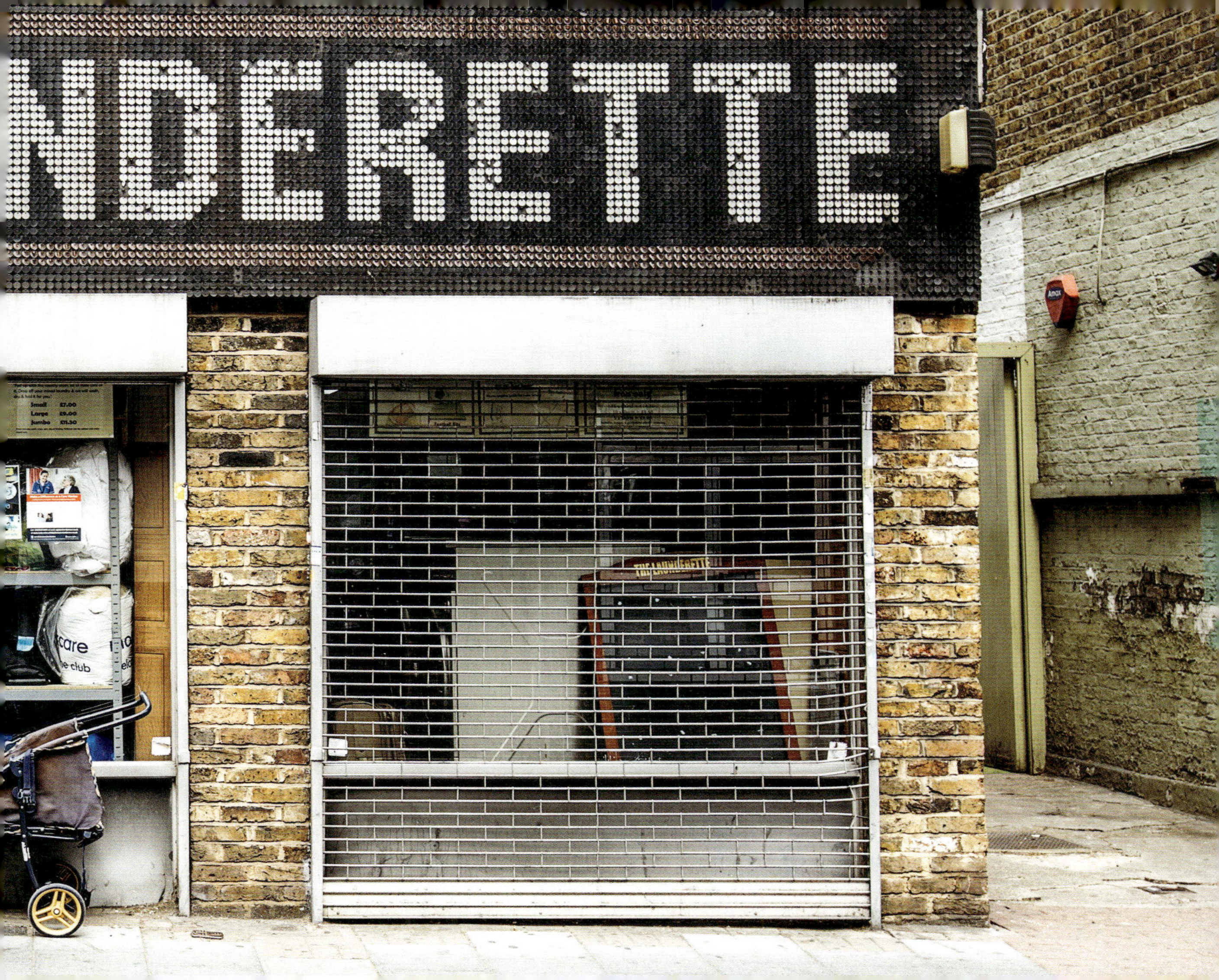
NDERETTE

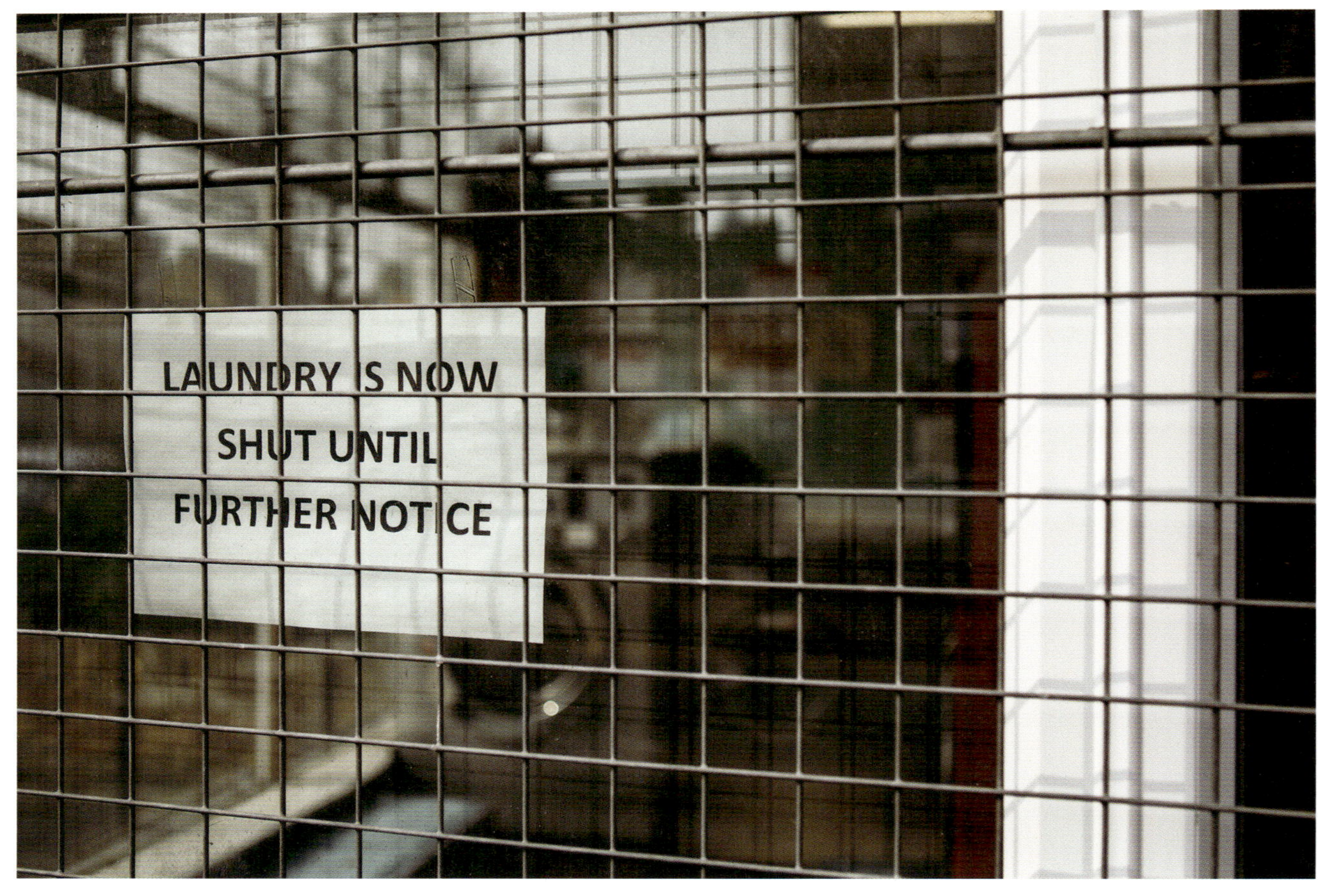

LAUNDRY IS NOW
SHUT UNTIL
FURTHER NOTICE

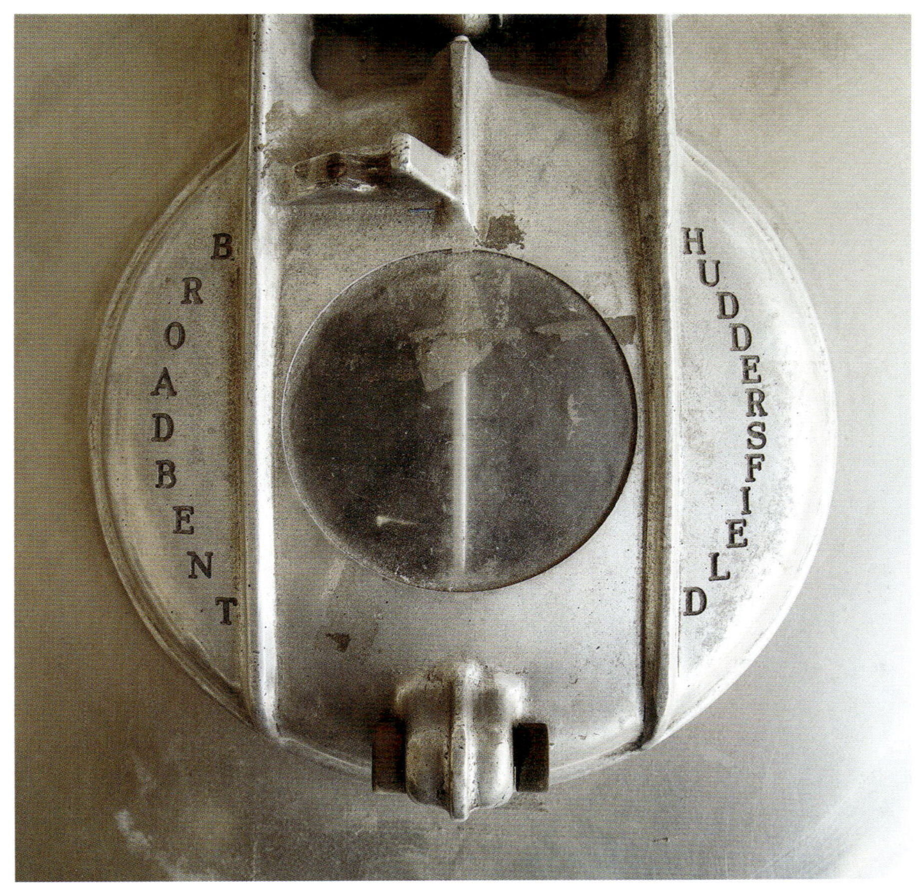

BROADBENT
HUDDERSFIELD

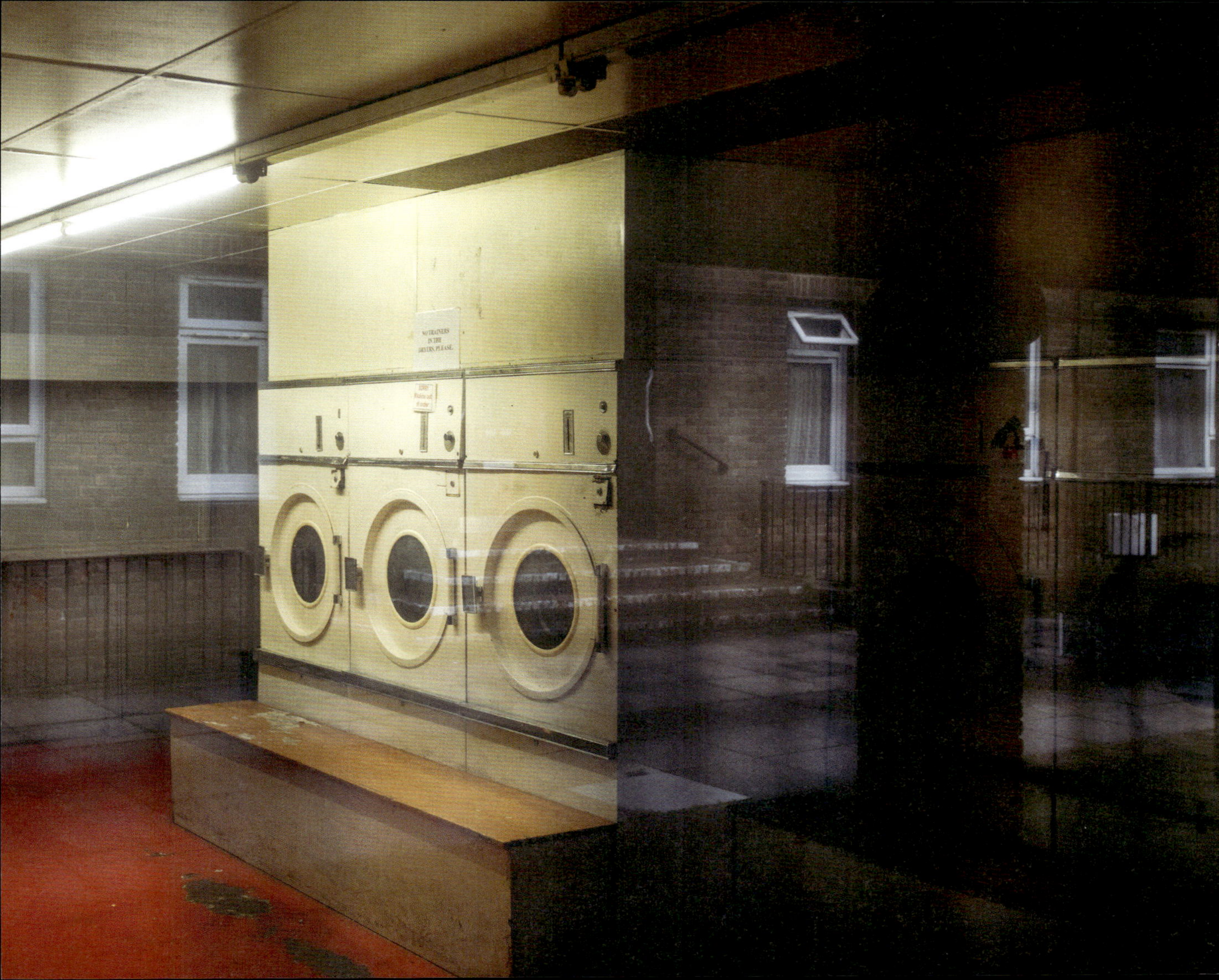

NO TRAINERS
IN THE
DRYERS PLEASE

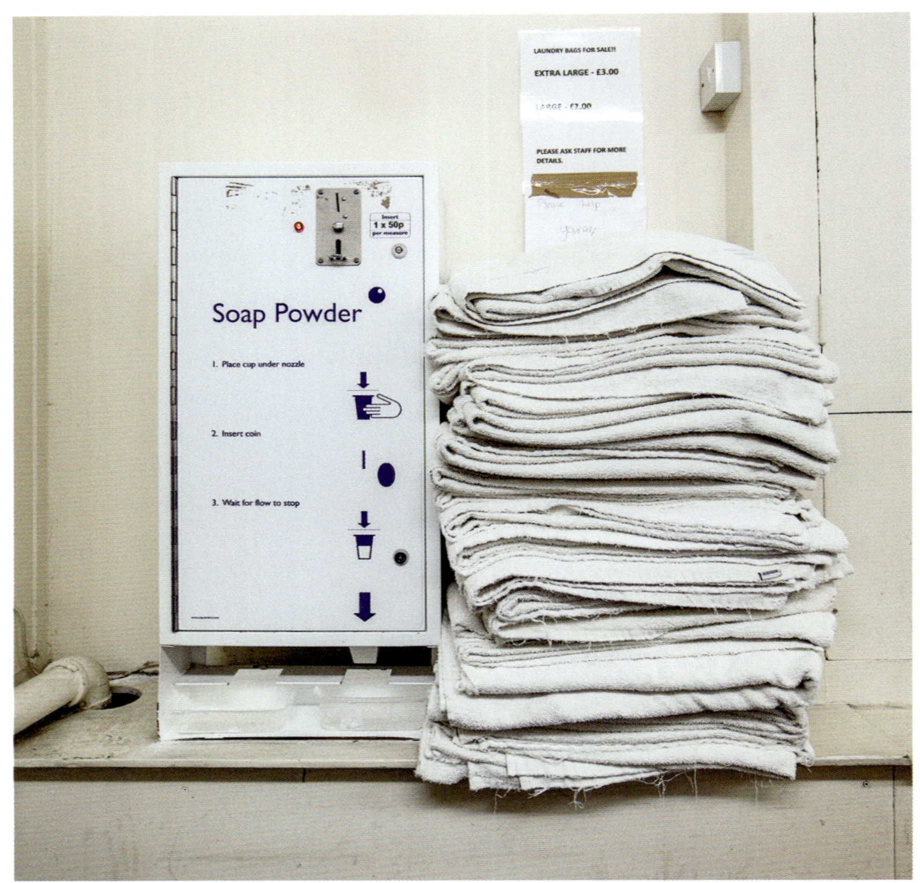
LAUNDRY BAGS FOR SALE!!
EXTRA LARGE - £3.00
LARGE - £2.00
PLEASE ASK STAFF FOR MORE DETAILS.
Please help
yourself
Insert
1 x 50p
per measure
Soap Powder
1. Place cup under nozzle
2. Insert coin
3. Wait for flow to stop

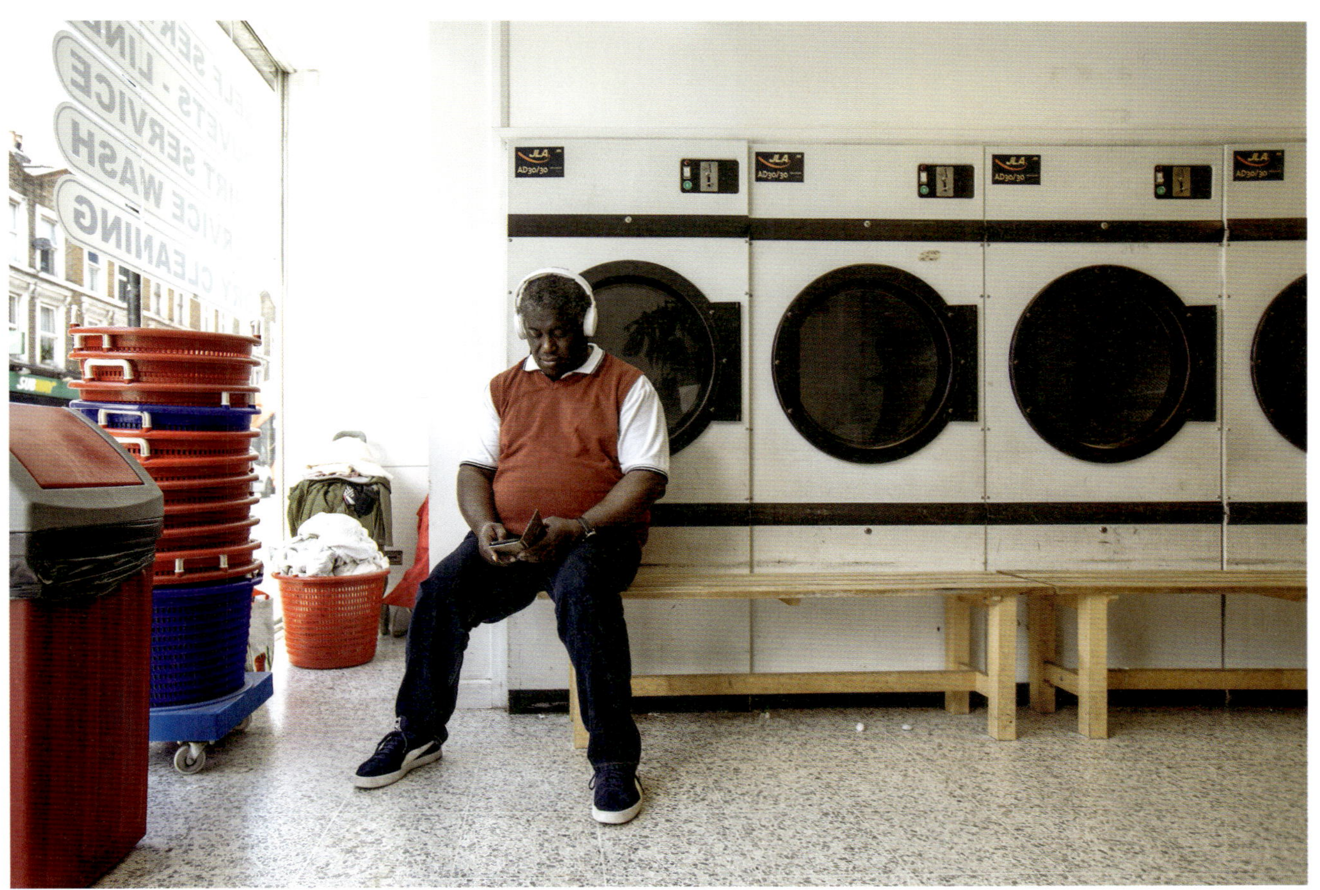

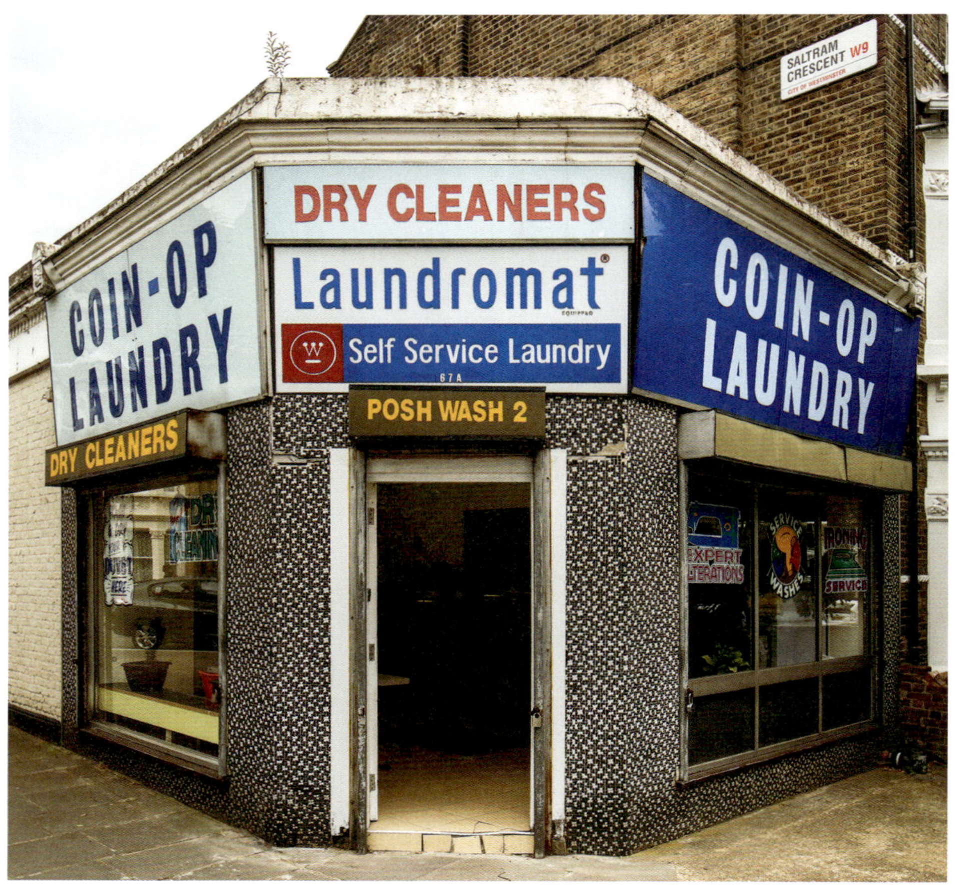

SALTRAM CRESCENT W9
CITY OF WESTMINSTER
DRY CLEANERS
COIN-OP LAUNDRY
Laundromat
Self Service Laundry
67A
DRY CLEANERS
POSH WASH 2
COIN-OP LAUNDRY
EXPERT ALTERATIONS
SERVICE WASHES
IRONING SERVICE

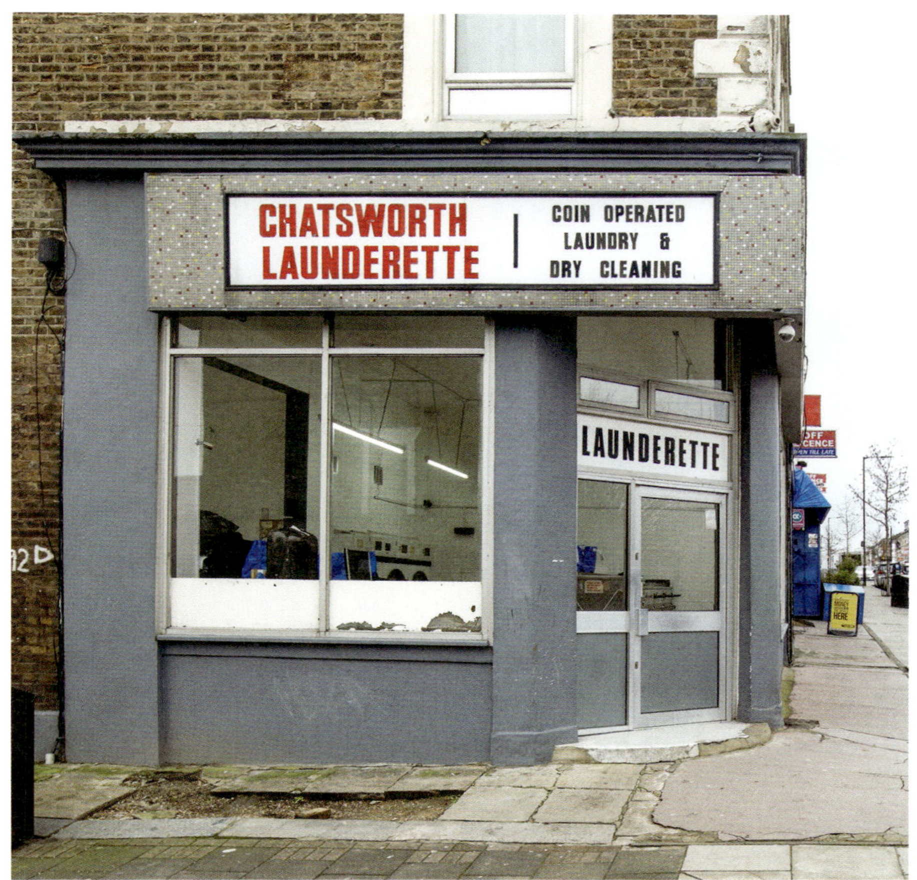
CHATSWORTH LAUNDERETTE
COIN OPERATED
LAUNDRY &
DRY CLEANING
LAUNDERETTE

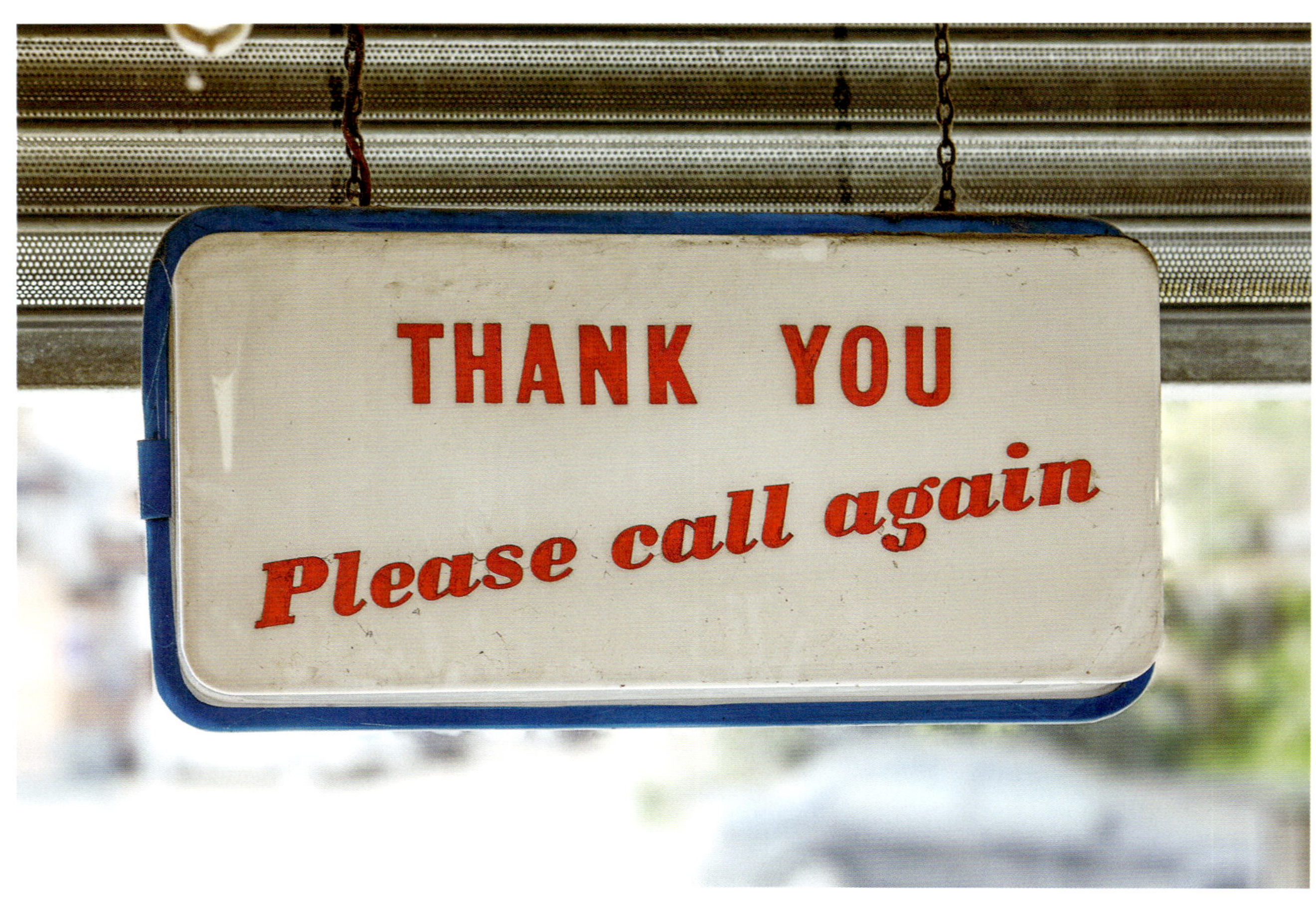
THANK YOU
Please call again

Joshua Blackburn

Joshua is a photographer, print maker and co-founder of The Artful Project gallery. In his previous life, he ran a graphic design agency for fourteen years. Before being consumed by London's launderettes, Joshua obsessed over Vegas wedding chapels, giant jawbreakers and America's roadside signs. He lives in London with his wife, two children and a pet hamster, alive at time of writing. Joshua's local launderette is five minutes away.

Acknowledgements:
I owe a debt of gratitude to all the owners and managers of London's wonderful launderettes, without whom this book would not have been possible. Thank you also to everyone at Hoxton Mini Press, who have been an absolute pleasure to work with. Finally, to Rachel, Sonny and Jude, my unfathomably patient family, to whom this book is dedicated.

Hoxton Mini Press

Hoxton Mini Press is a small, award-winning publisher based in East London. We started out by making photography books just about Hackney, working with local artists and writers, but now we make books about topics much further afield, like, er, launderettes in Peckham. Basically, we are inspired by local, urban stories of neighbourhood life told through rich photography. As the world goes online and we live in the cloud we believe that books, and the stories within them, should be cherished and stored on neat wooden shelves and then passed down through generations.

Locations

Launderama: London's Launderettes

First edition

Copyright © Hoxton Mini Press 2019. All rights reserved.
All photographs and introduction text © Joshua Blackburn
Design and sequence by Friederike Huber, Daniele Roa and Joshua Blackburn
Text editing by Faith McAllister
Production by Anna De Pascale
Repro by Touch Digital

The right of the author to be identified as the creator of this Work has been
asserted under the Copyright, Designs and Patents Act 1988.

First published in the United Kingdom in 2019 by Hoxton Mini Press.
A CIP catalogue record for this book is available from the British Library.
No part of this publication may be reproduced, stored in a retrieval system,
or transmitted in any form or by any means, electronic, mechanical, photocopying,
recording or otherwise, without the prior written permission of the copyright owner.

ISBN: 978-1-910566-60-2

Printed and bound by OZGraf, Poland

To order books, collector's editions and signed prints please go to:
www.hoxtonminipress.com